JUDGES

DAVID PANNICK

*Barrister; Fellow of All Souls College,
Oxford*

Oxford   New York

OXFORD UNIVERSITY PRESS

1987

Oxford University Press, Walton Street, Oxford OX2 6DP
Oxford New York Toronto
Delhi Bombay Calcutta Madras Karachi
Petaling Jaya Singapore Hong Kong Tokyo
Nairobi Dar es Salaam Cape Town
Melbourne Auckland
and associated companies in
Beirut Berlin Ibadan Nicosia

Oxford is a trade mark of Oxford University Press

British Library Cataloguing in Publication Data
Pannick, David
Judges.
1. Judges—England
I. Title
344.207'14   KD7285
ISBN 0–19–215956–9

Library of Congress Cataloging in Publication Data
Pannick, David.
Judges.
Bibliography: p.   Includes index.
1. Judges—Great Britain.   2. Judges—United States.
I. Title.
KD7285.P36   1987   347.42'014   87–7827   344.20714
ISBN 0–19–215956–9

Set by Latimer Trend & Co. Ltd.
Printed in Great Britain by Richard Clay Ltd.
Bungay, Suffolk

PREFACE

I N *The Trial*, a basic introduction to jurisprudence, Kafka observed that 'it never occurred to the Advocates that they should suggest or insist on any improvements in the system, while—and this was very characteristic—almost every accused man, even quite ordinary people among them, discovered from the earliest stages a passion for suggesting reforms . . .'.[1] This book consists of an advocate's reflections on the judicial system. That is a subject about which most laymen, and many lawyers, have very pronounced views in private but which the mysticism surrounding the law often inhibits them from expressing in public. The reluctance to discuss so important an area of our government is regrettable, not least because the high quality of the English judiciary ensures that our legal system has nothing to fear from debate on this subject.

I am grateful to many of my friends and colleagues at the Bar (in particular Anthony Lester QC and Michael Beloff QC) and to a number of judges who have—consciously or unconsciously—provided me with relevant material or ideas. Researching the legal problems of various clients fortuitously (though they may describe it differently) diverted me to many of the examples which follow. I am indebted to Judith Luna of Oxford University Press and Tony Honoré at All Souls for encouraging me to write this book. All Souls provided a stimulating academic environment in which to discuss some of the issues.

Parts of this book first appeared as articles in the *Guardian* from 1979 to 1987. I much appreciate the encouragement I have received from Richard Gott (Features Editor) and Tim Radford (Deputy Features Editor). The book also draws on material previously published in the *Listener* (I am grateful to Russell Twisk, the Editor, and Derwent May, formerly the Literary Editor, for their encouragement) and in *The Times Literary Supplement* (my thanks to Jeremy Treglown, the Editor). Joshua Rozenberg, Legal Affairs Correspondent of the BBC and presenter of BBC Radio 4's *Law in Action* (on which small parts of what follows have been broadcast), has been of considerable assistance. Portions of chapter 6 first appeared in *Fair of Speech: The Uses of Euphemism* (edited by D. J. Enright and published in 1985).

Most of all, I thank my wife, Denise, for allowing me to benefit from her many qualities, including judiciousness.

DAVID PANNICK

The Temple, London EC4
27 April 1987

CONTENTS

To my wife
DENISE
and to my sons
SAMUEL AND JOEL

CHAPTER 1

Introduction

I

JUDGES do not have an easy job. They repeatedly do what the rest of us seek to avoid: make decisions. They carry out this function in public. Rabelais's Judge Bridlegoose decided cases by throwing dice.[1] Most judges obey the job requirement that they 'must not spin a coin or consult an astrologer'[2] but must give reasons for their decisions. A Manhattan criminal court judge who decided the length of a jail sentence on the toss of a coin and asked courtroom spectators to vote on which of two conflicting witnesses to believe was, in 1983, barred from office by the New York State Commission on Judicial Conduct.[3]

The reasons which judges must give to justify their decisions can be gnawed over at their leisure by the teams of lawyers trained (and generously paid) to extract for the purpose of an appeal every morsel of error. The judicial decision will also provide sustenance for the armies of academic lawyers ruthlessly seeking material for the footnotes of a law review article that will conclusively show that the judge made a mistake. The judge has 'the burden of resolving, day after day and week after week, a long succession of issues, each one of which occupies the professor-critic for months and even years of specialised study'.[4]

1

The English judge has no clerks or assistants to research or write his judgments. The barristers who argue the case before him will 'vary much in their ability'.[5] Sometimes they help but often they may be a hindrance to the just determination of the issues. In a 1962 case Lord Justice Harman rejected an application for leave to appeal from the Court of Appeal on the ground that 'these pleadings ought to go, not to the House of Lords, but to the waste-paper basket'.[6]

Judges often make mistakes. Sometimes these errors are publicly identified and overruled by appeal courts with the power to substitute mistakes of their own. Even the Law Lords ('the voices of infallibility, by a narrow majority')[7] occasionally acknowledge their own, or each other's, errors.[8] Many of the judge's decisions will be made without the opportunity for adequate reflection. All of these judgments will be subject to reassessment by an audience which enjoys the benefit of hindsight. This is rarely seen in so dramatic a manner as the experience of a judge at the Knightsbridge Crown Court in 1981. He allowed a prisoner (who was being tried for alleged robbery) out on bail during the lunch break, telling him that he should return to court by 2 p.m., otherwise 'you will make me look a proper Charlie'. That evening the police were still looking for the defendant.[9] For some judges, more distressing than public humiliation and the recording of a judicial mistake in the law reports is the error on which the judge privately and obsessively broods. The will of Sir Soulden Lawrence (a judge from 1794 to 1812) directed that his estate should pay the legal costs incurred by an unsuccessful litigant whose case the judge considered that he had badly tried some years earlier.[10]

The judge has burdensome responsibilities to discharge. He has power over the lives and livelihood of all those litigants who enter his court. Is this man to go to prison; is this woman to lose her house; who is to have custody of these children; are these people to be deported? His decisions may well affect the interests of individuals and groups who are not present or represented in court. If he is not careful, the judge may precipitate a civil war, the charge made against an 1857 decision of the US Supreme court.[11] Or he may accelerate a revolution, as did Chief Justice Wright in 1688.[12] He may accidentally cause a peaceful but fundamental change in the political complexion of the country.[13]

The judge may decide matters of great importance to man ('there are many things which a girl under 16 needs to practise but sex is not one of them')[14] or to beast ('I must say, for my part, I find great difficulty ... in accepting the concept that bees may be invitees, licensees or trespassers. ... Further, in my opinion the common law concepts of bailment do not hold in considering the legal position as to bees').[15] With increasing regularity as he advances up the legal hierarchy, the judge will need to decide hard cases in which alternative solutions to the dispute may be (and often are in majority and dissenting judgments) respectably justified by reference to existing law. In such cases, the judge makes law. For centuries, English judges deceived each other into thinking that they merely applied the law made by Parliament, that their job was only 'to interpret law, and not to make law, or give law'.[16] This has changed. In considering how judges decide hard cases, 'we do not believe in fairy tales any more'.[17]

The judge is obliged to enforce laws laid down by Parliament or created by more senior judges which he may, with justification, think unfair, absurd, or downright dangerous. No doubt some judges share the view of A. P. Herbert's Lord Chancellor that 'the pity is that there is not more judge-made law. For most of His Majesty's judges are much better fitted for the making of laws than the queer and cowardly rabble who are elected to Parliament for that purpose by the fantastic machinery of universal suffrage'.[18] Eager or not, qualified or not, the judge cannot avoid acting as legislator in exceptional cases at the appellate level.

In the more typical case, the judge will be faced by issues difficult to decide because they involve competing versions of the truth told by equally implausible witnesses on matters of importance only to the litigants, and sometimes not even to them. Lord Campbell (Lord Chief Justice 1850–9 and Lord Chancellor 1859–61) felt that his 'spirit almost dies away when I think I am to pass the remainder of my days in hearing witnesses swear that the house was all secure when they went to bed, and next morning they discovered that the window had been broken and their bacon was gone'.[19] The judge will frequently be confronted by a person who is bringing a case 'which, by brooding over it, he can no longer see in an objective light ...'. Common symptoms of such cases are that 'they are brought forward years after the event and that the strength of the complaint increases as the years roll by ... [and the] plaintiff seeks to give additional momentum to his complaints by throwing in charges of "fraud" and "conspiracy"'.[20]

Occasionally, the judge will find it difficult to take seriously the issues brought before him. In 1935 the US Supreme Court rejected an application from someone 'who wanted the Court to help him wage a war against Turkey'.[21] The US judge, more than his English counterpart (who does not have the duty of interpreting a written Constitution), must be ready to decide all manner of unusual issues, from whether Bible-reading by astronaunts in space breaches the US Constitution (it does not)[22] to whether an employee dismissed for abusive language on learning that his

4

employer had used for commercial purposes a photograph of his feet in shackles has a claim under Title VII of the Civil Rights Act 1964 (he does not).[23] In 1986 the US Supreme Court refused to hear a lawyer's appeal against a ticket for speeding issued in 1982. Chief Justice Burger expressed his anger at such an 'utterly frivolous' claim and criticized the lawyer for treating the legal system as 'a laboratory where small boys can play'.[24]

Sitting all day listening to vexatious litigants and verbose lawyers, the judge's work can be 'very dull'.[25] Lord Devlin retired as a Law Lord in 1964 at the youthful—in judicial terms[26]—age of 59 because his work 'had become tedious instead of exhilarating'.[27]

When the judge is dealing with people at their most unattractive or their most unreasonable, or when they are most completely revealed as cheats, liars, or murderers, he cannot easily comply with his judicial oath to 'do right to all manner of people after the laws and usages of this realm, without fear or favour, affection or illwill'.[28] It can be a strain acting as 'the living oracle'.[29] This is particularly so when, as occasionally may happen, the judge has other matters on his mind. In Tolstoy's *Resurrection*, the President of the court was 'anxious to begin the sitting and get through with it as early as possible, in time to call before six o'clock on the red-haired [woman] with whom he had begun a romance in the country last summer'. The second judge was feeling gloomy, having just been told that his wife would not be making him any dinner that evening. The third member of the court was suffering from gastric catarrh.

Now, as he ascended the steps to the platform, his face wore an expression of deep concentration, resulting from a habit he had of using various curious means to decide the answers to questions which he put to himself. Just now he was counting the number of steps from the door of his study to his chair: if they would divide by three the new treatment would cure his catarrh. If not, the treatment would be a failure. There were twenty-six steps, but he managed to get in an extra short one and reached his chair exactly at the twenty-seventh.[30]

Occasionally the job of the judge is extremely danger-ous. In 1664 an aggrieved litigant was convicted of offering someone £100 to kill the judge, Sir Harbottle Grimston, Master of the Rolls.[31] In 1981 a man was found guilty of the murder of the judge who had given him a sentence of eighteen months' borstal training thirteen years earlier. The judge was stabbed to death. On being sentenced to life imprisonment with a recommendation that he serve not less than twenty-five years in prison, the defendant was taken from the dock at Leeds Crown Court shouting at the judge, 'I won't forget you . . . I'll cut your throat when I get out.'[32] This is not what Lord Chancellor Hatherley meant when he said in the 1860s that he rarely delivered a written judgment because he found it 'injurious to his health'.[33]

Judges today face tribulations, as well as trials, not contemplated by their predecessors. Lord Chancellor Hail-sham suggested in 1984 that one High Court judge had, a few years earlier, 'been hounded, as I think, to his death as a result of criticisms of a single sentence imposed by him' in a much publicized criminal trial.[34] Parliament has recognized the pressures of the job by providing that before the Lord Chancellor recommends anyone to the Queen for appoint-ment to the Circuit Bench, the Lord Chancellor 'shall take steps to satisfy himself that the person's health is satisfac-tory'.[35] There is no such statutory requirement in relation to High Court and more senior judges. But, in practice, all those appointed to full-time judicial posts 'must satisfy the

Lord Chancellor that their health is satisfactory'.[36] This seems essential in the light of the reminiscences of Lord Roskill as to the mental strain which the job can impose. Soon after his elevation from the Court of Appeal to the House of Lords, he observed that 'some years ago a newly appointed Lord Justice gloomily remarked that until he had become a member of the Court of Appeal he had wrongly thought that slavery had been abolished'. Lord Roskill added that, in his experience, 'the work load is intolerable: seven days a week, 14 hours a day . . .'.[37] In 1985 Lord Justice Purchas spoke of 'the stress and anxiety I have felt in dealing with this appeal as a member of a two-judge appellate court'. He thought that the case, which concerned the Consumer Credit Act 1974, was sufficiently important to merit a three-judge Court of Appeal.[38]

It is, no doubt, a comfort to the ailing or exhausted judge, who is endangering his physical and mental health in the service of his country, that should his death or incapacity while hearing a case result in a litigant incurring additional costs—for example by needing to start the case again before a comparatively fresh judge—the Lord Chancellor has power to reimburse those expenses to the unfortunate party.[39]

Far less reassuring to the judge is the knowledge that he will be strongly criticized if he becomes disillusioned with the job and resigns to take up another less dangerous and less demanding occupation. In 1970 Mr Justice Fisher retired from the High Court bench after serving for less than three years. His decision to work in the City resulted in 'attitudes of outrage that might be appropriate in the headmistress of a finishing school who hears that one of the most promising of her pupils [has] gone off to be a bunny girl'.[40] By tradition, a judge who resigns or retires cannot go back to the Bar.[41] According to Lord Hailsham, the prospective High Court judge 'should approach the Bench with the enthusiasm of a bridegroom approaching marriage, or of a priest approaching priesthood'.[42] Lord Denning even denied the High Court judge the luxury of personal ambition: 'Once a man becomes a judge, he has nothing to gain from further promotion'—though it may not escape his attention that High Court judges are paid less than Court of Appeal judges who are paid less than Law Lords and that more attention is given to the pronounce-ments of more senior judges—'and does not seek it.'[43]

Not every judge needs to impose upon himself the agony which Learned Hand (a US Court of Appeals judge) attributed to the conscientious Benjamin Cardozo, a Justice of the US Supreme Court from 1932 to 1938: 'At times to those of us who knew him, the anguish which had preceded decision was apparent, for again and again, like Jacob, he had to wrestle with the angel all through the night; and he wrote his opinion with his very blood.'[44] Infrequently will the judge have the considerable advantage claimed by Judge Alan King-Hamilton in an important criminal trial at the Old Bailey in 1977 of feeling 'half-conscious of being guided by some superhuman inspiration' with regard to his summing-up to the jury 'throughout its preparation, and also when delivering it'.[45]

The specific qualifications we require of our judges may change in some respects. The appointment of Sir Lloyd Kenyon as Chief Justice in 1788 was opposed by his predecessor, Lord Mansfield, because Kenyon 'did not know the characters of the Greek language, and of Latin knew only some scraps to be misquoted'.[46] The more fundamental qualities sought for in the judge remain con-stant. Allowing for the development of a secular society, the advice given to Moses by his father-in-law, Jethro, remains valid: we should look for 'capable, God-fearing men

8

among all the people, honest and incorruptible men [to] sit as a permanent court for the people'.[47]

Not surprisingly, only a limited number of people measure up to these demanding criteria. One of the framers of the American Constitution, Alexander Hamilton, was well aware that 'there can be but few men in the society who will have sufficient skill in the laws to qualify them for the stations of judges. And making the proper deductions for the ordinary depravity of human nature, the number must be still smaller of those who unite the requisite integrity with the requisite knowledge.'[48] Some of those otherwise qualified may be deterred by the adverse job conditions, described above. Others will be inhibited by natural humility ('Who am I to sit in judgment on any-body?', Mr Justice Birkett asked his diary in 1944),[49] or by feelings of revulsion at having to send people to prison ('Who in hell wanted to judge people. I mean what would I say to them?', thought Rumpole the barrister).[50]

New York City has found it so difficult to recruit judges that it started to advertise the posts.[51] By contrast, there still remain large numbers of lawyers eager to do the job in England. 'It is rare indeed for a High Court judgeship to be declined; and not many refuse the Circuit bench.'[52] In some cases it may simply be that, as a judge's wife once told a barrister, 'he likes being prayed for in Cathedrals'. Some people relish the pomp and ceremony—the 'knighthoods, invitations to dine with the Lord Mayor of London and the highest possible priority at functions like agricultural shows in the country'—which go with the job.[53] For the occasional judge it may even be true, as was said of John Bayley (a judge in the early decades of the nineteenth century) by an observer from France, 'il s'amuse à juger'.[54]

Despite its frustrations and difficulties, judicial work is, according to Lord Hailsham, 'a privilege, a pleasure and a duty'.[55] The pleasures of being a judge can be immense. As Judge Learned Hand explained:

A judge's life, like every other, has in it much of drudgery, senseless bickerings, stupid obstinacies, captious pettifogging. . . . These take an inordinate part of his time; they harass and befog the unhappy wretch, and at times almost drive him from that bench where like any other workman he must do his work. If that were all, his life would be mere misery, and he a distracted arbiter between irreconcilable extremes. But there is something else that makes it—anyway to those curious creatures who persist in it—a delectable calling. For when the case is all in, and the turmoil stops, and after he is left alone, things begin to take form. From his pen or in his head, slowly or swiftly as his capacities admit, out of the murk the pattern emerges, his pattern, the expression of what he has seen and what he has therefore made. . . . That is a pleasure which nobody who has felt it will be likely to underrate.[56]

II

Only in England could the vocation of the judge be described as 'something like a priesthood' or 'analogous to the Royal Family', requiring practitioners to 'seclude themselves' in various ways.[57]

English judges rarely give press interviews or appear on television. Only occasionally do they write about the job they perform. They do not allow cameras into their courts. They discourage sociological studies of their activities, such as sentencing. Like members of the Magic Circle who face expulsion if they explain how the trick is done, judges are eager to protect the mysteries of their craft. They do not respond to public criticism (on those rare occasions when they are subjected to it). Political scientists respect this desire for privacy by ignoring the judiciary when debating the nature of government.

In England we expect the judge to adopt a respectable lifestyle, free from any hint of the unusual, let alone the deviant. It was said of a leading post-war Queen's Counsel that he was not appointed to the bench simply because his 'was not the conduct expected of one of His Majesty's future judges'. His offences included climbing a pillar to touch the ceiling at his birthday party at the Savoy Hotel, and owning greyhounds.[58] In 1954 Sir Winston Churchill told the House of Commons that judges are required to conform to standards of 'life and conduct far more severe and restricted than that of ordinary people'. 'What', the Prime Minister asked rhetorically, 'would be thought of a Lord Chief Justice if he won the Derby?'[59] It may well be that this enforced isolation from the pleasures and pains of ordinary life is directly responsible for the traditional inability of some judges to understand the concerns of those who appear in their court. 'What', Mr Justice Wool (one of A. P. Herbert's judges) asks counsel, 'is the Derby?'[60]

In 1950 a Member of Parliament, Mr Marlowe, recommended an even greater degree of judicial isolation. It is impossible, he argued, 'for a High Court judge to discharge his functions properly if he knows that during the day he will sit on the Bench with a prisoner in the dock before him, and later in the evening may be sitting side by side with the prisoner in the bus'.[61] So effective is the isolation of our judiciary that the personalities and characteristics of our judges are unknown to laymen. Only a very small proportion of the population could name a single judge of the Court of Appeal or Appellate Committee of the House of Lords. The biographer of Lord Atkin (who served as a Law Lord from 1928 to 1944) rightly observed that this judge, although responsible for some of the major developments in the common law this century, remained 'virtually unknown' outside legal circles.[62] Such ignorance has deprived judges of deserved praise and necessary criticism. The illnesses that have afflicted various judges in their last years on the bench, impairing their ability adequately to discharge their functions, have not been publicized until long after their deaths. Some years after his death in 1933, it was revealed that Mr Justice McCardie had committed suicide by shooting himself. He had substantial gambling debts, and 'had been keeping a mistress in the country, while a titled lady in London claimed to be pregnant by him'.[63]

The English judge is a unique phenomenon. He would not, like some French judges, belong to a radical trade union which calls for a one-day strike to protest about the treatment of a magistrate by the Government.[64] Unlike an Iranian Islamic judge, Ayatollah Sadeq Khalkhali, the English judge would not lead a group of specially trained commandos determined to kill opponents of the ruling party of the State.[65] Judges in England do not act as undercover agents to assist police investigations into allegations of bribery and corruption. The Illinois judge who sat in Cook County Traffic Court while secretly wired for sound and taping conversations for the purposes of an FBI investigation into judges, lawyers, court officials, policemen, and defendants would find no parallel in England.[66] Nor would the English judiciary adopt another idea favourably considered by some members of the Illinois judiciary: attending a 'charm school' of lectures and seminars on how to act in a judicial manner. English judges already know the secrets imparted at the school: 'Be a judge. Call the shots. . . . Don't let the public know, even if you agree, that all muggers should be sent to the gas chamber. . . . You are what you wear.'[67]

The English judge ensures in a quiet but effective manner

that his pay accords with his status. He avoids the public display of militancy that sometimes affects judges from other nations who lack such influence. In 1981 the President of Sudan accepted the resignation of 290 judges aggrieved about low pay.[68] Judge Frank Coffin of the US Court of Appeals complained in 1985 about the inadequacy of 'compensation' for judges. In the previous few years, he lamented, judicial salaries had become so insufficient that only the mediocre or the wealthy would henceforth be willing to take judicial appointments.[69] Perhaps disappointing pay levels help to explain why a clinical psychologist was helping judges in Massachusetts to cope with stress. He organized a one-day study course to discuss basic texts such as Albert Camus's *The Outsider* and Joseph Conrad's *Heart of Darkness* to help the judges to 'expand their perspective on stress'. He also provided counselling to enable the retired judge 'to maintain self-esteem'.[70] In the 1970s a Californian judge underwent psychoanalysis 'to get at the root of his inability to pass judgment'.[71]

In the unlikely event of the English judiciary seeking help from psychologists or psychoanalysts, they would not publicize the fact. And any judicial stress would not be caused by worries about low pay. When, occasionally, English judges have been concerned about their pay, their grievances have been listened to in private and acted upon. In the 1930s, the judges successfully resisted a general economy measure of a cut of 20 per cent in all official salaries. As Lord Chancellor Sankey recorded in a memorandum, the judges were 'rather bent upon giving trouble unless their demands are satisfied'. They had no need to carry out the threat.[72] In 1979 'many of the judges were aggrieved. The younger judges were disappointed. They could not provide properly for the education of their children, their holidays and the like.' A salary increase made

them 'reasonably satisfied'.[73] Even when the judges did not
'feel that they are underpaid' in 1985,[74] the Government
decided to implement a recommendation of the salary
review board and award them a pay increase of 15 per cent.

When Lord Hailsham compared the judiciary to the
priesthood[75] he did so in a sense different to that meant by
Jeremy Bentham who had condemned 'the artifices of
priestcraft' practised by lawyers to the detriment of laymen.[76] Because judges are like priests, they have the virtues
of a monastic order. They are incorruptible and conscientious. It is many decades since a serious scandal stained the
reputation of the English judiciary. Even allowing for the
different demands of the legal systems, it is difficult to
imagine the Law Lords tolerating, as did the Supreme Court
of India in 1986, a waiting list of over 10,000 constitutional
cases.[77]

Yet, as Bentham was well aware, English judges also have
the vices of priestcraft. They have their own language and
dress, which isolates them from laymen who find it difficult
to understand the workings of the legal system. They carry
out their important duties in the absence of the camera and
the microphone, their existence known to the public primarily through the often misleading and sensational newspaper
reports of the idiosyncrasies of judicial mavericks. Consequently, English judges are the recipients of unmerited
abuse and unjustified compliments. They are treated as
symbols of an all-powerful but incomprehensible force
which is not susceptible to the standards of rational analysis
applied to all other public institutions. James Morris wrote
of a hill tribe in India who were in dispute with their
Government about local land rights. The case came on
appeal to a court sitting in London. The elders of the tribe
were discovered 'sacrificing a kid to propitiate a distant but
omnipotent deity: "We know nothing of him, but that he is

a good god, and that his name is the Judicial Committee of the Privy Council".'[78] In England we remain, in some respects, as immature in our understanding of the workings of the judiciary and as eager to believe that the judiciary is a mysterious entity which is entitled to our reverence and unquestioning obedience.

The low profile adopted by the English judge erroneously leads people still to expect to find in court what George Orwell described as 'that typically English figure, the hanging judge, some gouty old bully with his mind rooted in the nineteenth century, handing out savage sentences'. The judge survives in literature and in popular belief, if not often in the courts, as 'that evil old man in scarlet robe and horse-hair wig, whom nothing short of dynamite will ever teach what century he is living in but who will at any rate interpret the law according to the books and will in no circumstances take a money bribe'. For Orwell the judge was 'one of the symbolic figures of England. He is a symbol of that strange mixture of reality and illusion, democracy and privilege, humbug and decency, the subtle network of compromises, by which the nation keeps itself in its familiar shape.'[79]

The judge retains this symbolic importance. What has changed markedly is the general standard of judicial performance. Today it is high, most probably higher than ever before in terms of ability, conduct, and understanding of the needs of society. One rarely comes across contemporary judges who, like the subject of one of Abraham Lincoln's anecdotes, 'would hang a man for blowing his nose in the street, but ... would quash the indictment if it failed to specify what hand he blew it with'.[80] Judges no longer resign in protest against reforms of civil procedure that rid the law of obscure technicalities, as did Baron Parke in 1855.[81] Unlike Sir Orlando Bridgeman, Chief Justice in the

1660s, they would not resist a change in the physical location of their court on the ground that it contravened the Magna Carta.[82] Nor do they display the stubbornness of the eighteenth-century Welsh judge, Samuel Lovell, who refused 'when overtaken by the tide . . . to mount the coach-box to escape drowning, unless a precedent could be quoted for a judge's doing so'.[83]

With a few exceptions, judges today know the law and are willing to apply it in a tolerant and civilized manner. Most of our judges are conscientious. Of a small minority could it now be said, as it was of John Copley, a senior judge in the early nineteenth century, that they 'sat as seldom as possible and rose as early as possible and did as little as possible'.[84]

There will always be judges who, like Mr Justice Archer in the seventeenth century, make themselves 'the laughing stock of the profession'[85] or on whom, like Sir Julius Caesar (Master of the Rolls 1614–36), counsel are able occasionally to play 'a slye jeste'.[86] Mr Justice J. C. Lawrance, 'a stupid man, a very ill-equipped lawyer and a bad judge', so ineffectively tried a commercial case in 1892 (he 'knew as much about the principles of general average as a Hindoo about figure-skating') that there was born the idea of a Commercial Court to try such issues, presided over by judges who understood something of commercial law.[87] It has been suggested that one of the most important cases in Canadian constitutional law, decided by the Judicial Committee of the Privy Council, 'was determined by the [casting] vote of Sir Sidney Rowlatt, a "taxation judge", who . . . sat throughout the 1937 hearings in his overcoat making neither note nor comment'.[88] Canada understandably abolished the appeal to the Judicial Committee in 1949.

Judicial mavericks will always exist. But the high standards displayed by most judges ensure that the judiciary has little to fear from greater openness and accountability. Indeed, it has everything to gain in terms of a more widespread understanding and appreciation of its distinction. The unique virtues of the English judiciary would not be threatened if its members were brought out of their self-imposed seclusion and into the sunlight where their performance could be more effectively assessed. In addition, the greater publicity might even reveal some room for improvement in one or two judges. The case for reform of judicial administration does not depend on the merit or demerit of the individual holders of the office. Judicial administration is important because judges perform a vital and difficult function of government under the rule of law. Because judges are part of government, acting on our behalf, we are entitled to require them to abandon their priesthood and to present their activities for assessment by laymen. Any aspects of judicial administration which create barriers between the legal system and the community it serves need justification in a democratic society. In considering these issues, it is important to remember, above all else, that judges are fallible human beings.

III

Judges are mere mortals but they are asked to perform a function that is truly divine. 'Judge not that ye be not judged.'[89] The 7-year-old son of Robert Louis Stevenson's fictional judge, Lord Hermiston, could not understand, 'If judging were sinful and forbidden, how came papa to be a judge? to have that sin for a trade? to bear the name of it for a distinction?'[90]

Judges are subject to the same ambitions, passions, prejudices, and fears as their contemporaries. If you prick them, they bleed. However high the general standard of judicial competence, there will always be human weak-nesses which affect judgment. This may be endearing: at the Old Bailey in 1981, a judge told a defendant that she would be put on probation for her criminal offence, rather than be sent to prison, because 'you have caught me on a good day ... I became a grandfather this morning again'.[91] Or it can be disturbing: when a lawyer of Japanese extraction requested additional time to prepare for a trial in the 1970s, a US judge responded, 'How much time did you give us at Pearl Harbor?'[92] A Michigan judge agreed to reduce the bail bond required of a defendant from $10,000 to $500 on condition that the defendant had 'his hair cut in a fashion similar' to that of the judge.[93] In 1985 a New York judge was formally admonished for commenting, as a female advocate entered his courtroom, 'What a set of knockers!'[94] The ability to give a dissenting judgment may not always suffice to enable the judge adequately to release the tension he feels by reason of the conflicting approach taken by his fellow judges. At the US–Iran claims tribunal in The Hague in 1984, a Swedish judge was physically assaulted by two Iranian judges. They claimed he was pro-American. 'If [Judge] Mangard tries to enter this tribunal again', threa-tened one of the Iranian judges, 'either his body or mine will roll down the steps of the court.'[95]

Because judges are men, not machines, we must expect judicial frailties and not judge them too harshly. But we can, and should, take necessary precautions to limit the damage such imperfections might otherwise do to the interests of justice. Only by careful scrutiny of all aspects of the judiciary can we hope to detect, deter, and defeat potential injustices.

The extent to which the dignity and majesty of the Bench is not necessarily incompatible with the baser pre-occupations of the human mind is well illustrated by the

expressions of petty irritation and anger, vanity and jea-
lousy which have afflicted judges in their mutual relations.
American judges regularly attack the sensitivities of their
colleagues, though rarely with the force or the style
adopted in a 1979 judgment of the California Court of
Appeal. The Court had to decide whether the appellants
were properly convicted of possessing obscene films with
an intent to distribute them. The majority of the judges
reversed the conviction of the appellants. Associate Justice
Hanson dissented. In response to his dissent, Associate
Justice Thompson, with whom Judge Lillie agreed, said that
they felt 'compelled by the nature of the attack in the
dissenting opinion to spell out a response'. They did so, in
seven numbered propositions: '1. Some answer is required
to the dissent's charge. 2. Certainly we do not endorse
"victimless crime". 3. How that question is involved
escapes us. 4. Moreover, the constitutional issue is significant. 5. Ultimately it must be addressed in light of precedent. 6. Certainly the course of precedent is clear. 7. Knowing that, our result is compelled.' The initial letters of the
seven propositions spelt 'Schmuck' and left the reader of the
law report in no doubt as to their view of their dissenting
colleague. The judgment added a reference to a German
dictionary, in case anyone had missed the point.[96]

American judges are frequently harsh in their descrip-
tions of judgments with which they disagree. They angrily
shout that 'by a *tour de force* reminiscent not of jurists such
as Hale, Holmes and Hughes, but of escape artists such as
Houdini, the Court eludes clear statutory language, . . .
legislative history and uniform precedent . . .'.[97] By contrast,
judicial recrimination is rarely found in the decisions of
English judges. The tradition is that 'personal attacks are
politely concealed'.[98] Appeal courts overturn the decisions
of judges in lower courts in the nicest possible way. 'With

the utmost respect' they announce that they have 'reached a different conclusion' from the judge in the court below.[99] If the appeal court concludes that the trial judge has gone badly wrong, then it will explain that 'with the greatest respect to the judge and his commendable desire to ensure that no injustice was done to a party in the position of [the applicant], we cannot see what material he had on which to base his conclusion . . .'.[100] In this context, the critical comments of the House of Lords in 1984 in allowing an appeal from a Divisional Court judgment which Lord Diplock described as 'astonishing', 'inexplicable', and containing 'reasons that I have not found easy to follow',[101] amounted to a major outburst which caused much surprise.

Dissenting judges apologize that they 'have the misfortune to disagree with' their colleagues.[102] They are 'naturally diffident in disagreeing with [their] noble and learned brethren'.[103] Typical of the English judicial style is Theo Mathew's fictional Divisional Court judge who 'was so bothered by trying to decide, whilst the other judgments were being delivered, whether he should say that he agreed with them or that he concurred with them, that he had a nervous breakdown from which he never recovered'.[104]

Judicial language in England is often rigorous and forceful but rarely abusive. For this reason, on the rare occasions when personal criticism occurs, or is thought to occur, it causes deep resentment. The prime example of this was in 1941. Lord Atkin dissented from the interpretation of the Defence (General) Regulations 1939 adopted by the majority of the Appellate Committee of the House of Lords. He described the conclusion reached by the other judges as 'fantastic' and said that he had 'listened to arguments which might have been addressed acceptably to the Court of King's Bench in the time of Charles I'. He knew of 'only one authority which might justify the suggested method of construction', and he cited Humpty Dumpty in Lewis Carroll's *Alice Through the Looking Glass*: 'When I use a word ... it means just what I choose it to mean, neither more nor less.' He added that he viewed 'with apprehension the attitude of judges who on a mere question of construction when face to face with claims involving the liberty of the subject show themselves more executive minded than the executive'.[105]

Lord Atkin's outspoken dissent is now recognized to have stated the law correctly. In 1979 Lord Diplock said he thought 'the time has come to acknowledge openly that the majority of this House in [1941] were expediently and, at that time, perhaps, excusably, wrong and the dissenting speech of Lord Atkin was right'.[106] But in 1941 Lord Atkin's judgment caused much offence. Atkin had resisted a suggestion from Lord Chancellor Simon ('I am all in favour of enlivening judgments with literary allusion but ...'), who had seen an advance copy of the speech, that he should censor his remarks.[107] After delivering judgment in the House of Lords, Atkin took his daughter to lunch. 'They sat at a table together. Nobody joined them. Lords Macmillan and Romer seemed to be preoccupied on entering the room.'[108] Atkin's daughter later recalled that Lord Wright, another Law Lord, 'passed us by without a word ... but I think perhaps my father knew he was going to be unpopular'.[109] So outraged were some of Atkin's colleagues that Lord Maugham, who had presided at the hearing, wrote a letter to *The Times* criticizing Atkin's language in the dissenting opinion. It was widely believed that Atkin 'never really recovered from this treatment before his death in 1944'.[110]

Equally sensational was the public row between Mr Justice McCardie and Lord Justice Scrutton in 1932. The case of *Place* v. *Searle* concerned a claim by a husband against another man for allegedly enticing away his wife. In the Court of Appeal Lord Justice Scrutton described it as 'a squalid and not a very interesting case which had somehow been elevated by the newspapers into a case which afforded good copy, apparently because some ingenious counsel had considered that there was some likeness between this case and the Trojan War. Anything less like the godlike Hector and Achilles and "the face that launched a thousand ships" he found it difficult to conceive but the case had apparently attained great notoriety.' The Court of Appeal allowed the appeal from the decision of Mr Justice McCardie. Lord Justice Scrutton observed that 'Mr Justice McCardie had referred to Judges with sociological knowledge. He (Lord Justice Scrutton) thought that the less sociological knowledge was brought into the discussion of these legal questions the better.'[111]

But what caused a break in diplomatic relations between the two men were the following sentences of the judgment of Lord Justice Scrutton (which were omitted from the published law report): 'If there is to be a discussion of the relationship of husbands and wives, I think it would come better from judges who have more than theoretical knowledge of husbands and wives. I am [a] little surprised that a gentleman who has never been married should, as he has done in another case, proceed to explain the proper underclothing that ladies should wear.' McCardie, a bachelor, was infuriated. He wrote to Lord Hanworth, the Master of the Rolls, requesting that no appeal from a decision of his should in future be heard by a Court of Appeal of which Scrutton was a member. McCardie then delivered in court what he described as a 'public rebuke' to Lord Justice Scrutton: 'Before I start this case I wish to say a few words. I shall take my usual note of the evidence which will be given, and it may be that an appeal will take place. If there be an appeal, I shall not supply any copy of my notes until I am satisfied that Lord Justice Scrutton will not be a member of the Court which tries the appeal.' After peace-making efforts by Lord Hanworth, McCardie eventually calmed down and announced that in 'the interest of litigants' he would supply a copy of his notes in accordance with the usual practice.[112]

More recently, the distinctive style of Lord Denning provoked unusually strong feelings in other judges. Lord Simonds was once moved to describe a dissenting opinion of Lord Justice Denning in the Court of Appeal as 'a naked usurpation of the legislative function under the thin disguise of interpretation'.[113] This did not deter Lord Denning, as Master of the Rolls twenty years later, from acting as if he were entitled 'to give gratuitous advice to judges at first instance to ignore decisions of the House of Lords'.[114]

The force of some judicial personalities, and the conflicts on the Bench to which they can give rise, are well illustrated by the excesses of Lord Hewart, Lord Chief Justice 1922–40. So arrogant a judge was he that 'he could scarcely bear to have his authority on a legal point questioned. "Why on earth did you differ from me yesterday?", he would greet members of the Court of Appeal who had reversed one of his judgments. The less strong-willed judges avoided him, so as not to be involved in a scene.'[115] Because Hewart felt that he had not been properly consulted about the appointment of Cyril Asquith (son of the Liberal Prime Minister) to the Bench, Hewart abused his power as Lord Chief Justice and assigned the unfortunate Asquith 'to try a number of notorious criminal cases at the Old Bailey', an area of the law in which Asquith had limited experience, 'where an error would have had an unfortunate effect on Asquith's reputation'.[116]

In previous centuries judges have similarly displayed

their emotions in less than creditable ways. In the late fifteenth century the common-law judges were offended by the conduct of Lord Chancellor Rotheram. He had granted an injunction on the ground that a judgment of the Court of King's Bench had been fraudulently obtained. The common-law judges were so indignant that they asked counsel to plead before them to uphold their original decision.[117] The harmony of the English Bench was disturbed during the Chief Justiceship of Lord Mansfield in the second half of the eighteenth century. The other judges were aggrieved by Lord Mansfield's failure to consult them before giving judgment and by his resentment of any opinion contrary to his own. As a result, Mr Justice Yates sought and obtained a transfer to the Court of Common Pleas[118] 'to avoid His Lordship's covert sarcasms'.[119] In eighteenth-century Scotland 'some offence' had made Lord Monboddo 'resolve never to sit on the Bench with President Dundas; and he kept this vow so steadily that he always sat at the clerk's table even after Dundas was gone'.[120]

No student of the American judiciary could believe that high judicial status immunizes men and women from childlike displays of petulance and prejudice. The anti-Semitism of Mr Justice McReynolds led to his boorish behaviour to fellow Supreme Court Justices. He refused to speak to Brandeis from 1916 to 1919 or to sit next to him (as seniority demanded) for an official Court photograph in 1924 or to sign the Court's resolution on Brandeis' retirement in 1939. He 'habitually turned his back on Justice Cardozo' and he 'refused to attend Felix Frankfurter's robing ceremony' on Frankfurter's appointment to the Supreme Court in 1939.[121]

The US Supreme Court has frequently been the scene of personal animosity. In the 1850s Chief Justice Taney angrily accused an anti-slavery Justice of leaking to the press information about a court decision.[122] In the middle years of this century the acrimony on the court reached farcical levels. Justice Roberts refused to speak to Justices Black, Douglas, or Murphy.[123] Douglas and Frankfurter were scarcely on speaking terms.[124] Justice Jackson made a public statement in 1946 'attacking Justice Black as a "stealthy assassin" whose disregard of judicial proprieties threatened to bring the Court into disrepute'.[125] There was an 'increasing display of acrimony' between Frankfurter and Chief Justice Warren.[126] It is surprising that the court was able to distract itself sufficiently from these preoccupations to get any work done.

Even the Justices of the American Supreme Court appear adult compared with senior Californian judges. In 1978 Chief Justice Rose Bird of the California Surpreme Court was accused of delaying the pronouncement of judgment in an important and controversial case so as to assist her campaign for re-election to her post. After the election, which the Chief Justice narrowly won, complaints about the court prevarication forced her to agree to an investigation by the State Judicial Performance Commission. The trial of the California Supreme Court—much of which was conducted in public and televised to a fascinated legal and lay audience—was of especial interest for the comments, mostly injudicious, of the judges about each other. The hearings revealed that the court was not the home of a happy band of brother and sister judges. The Commission was told that for two months Rose Bird had not been on speaking terms with another judge, William Clark. He had, she complained, 'insulted her with a footnote' which was later moved to the main body of one of his judgments. She had, to a certain extent, revenged herself for this slight. 'Because of her feeling of personal insult', she refused to keep a promise to give the old carpeting from her office to the unfortunate assistant of her estranged colleague.[127]

Judicial foibles are of interest and importance because they reveal the reality behind the mask of objectivity presented in court. No one who has had any dealings with the law would dispute that the personality and interests of the judge vitally affect the way in which he decides the case, as to style and as to substance. It is a dangerous 'myth that, merely by putting on a . . . robe and taking the oath of office as a judge, a man ceases to be human and strips himself of all predilections, becomes a passionless thinking machine'.[128]

The identity of the judge matters. On the death of Chief Justice Vinson (who had been an obstacle to the US Supreme Court striking down laws which segregated blacks and whites) just prior to reargument in the crucial case of *Brown* v. *Board of Education* in 1953, Mr Justice Frankfurter (a committed opponent of race discrimination) remarked that this was 'the first indication I have ever had that there is a God'.[129] In 1935 the first Lord Chancellor Hailsham was anxious to persuade Lord Sankey to sit on the Appellate Committee of the House of Lords in a significant case so that it would not be necessary to ask Lord Atkin who 'is rather apt to take the opportunity of making the law as it ought to be, instead of administering it as it is'.[130] On the US Supreme Court, individual judges have needed to learn how to encourage their brethren to concur in a judgment. Mr Justice Black would not join any opinion which included a reference to a decision written by Mr Justice McReynolds. Mr Justice Douglas would not join any opinion which referred to the American Law Institute, which he detested. Mr Justice Frankfurter used crude flattery ('Were I to retire tomorrow, one of the most gratifying memories I would carry with me of my whole judicial life would be your behaviour in *Yancy*') to encourage the third-rate Mr Justice Whittaker to support Frankfurter's views on the issues which came before the Court.[131]

Those who appoint judges can never be sure how they will turn out. President Theodore Roosevelt was frustrated by the performance of Oliver Wendell Holmes on the US Supreme Court: 'I could carve out of a banana a Judge with more backbone than that.'[132] The liberal Chief Justice Warren was a great disappointment to President Eisenhower. Once in place, judges are difficult to remove. They become convinced that their continued occupation of high office is vital to the welfare of the nation, whether to prevent the appointment of a less well qualified successor or, as Chief Justice Taft believed in the 1920s, 'in order to prevent the Bolsheviki from getting control'.[133]

Harold Laski wrote to Justice Oliver Wendell Holmes that he 'wished that people could be persuaded to realise that judges are human beings; it would be a real help to jurisprudence'.[134] Such a realization would be of especial assistance to judicial administration.

CHAPTER 2

Expertise and Bias

I

BECOMING involved in a lawsuit is like 'being ground to bits in a slow mill; it's being roasted at a slow fire; it's being stung to death by single bees; it's being drowned by drops; it's going mad by grains'.[1] Hundreds of thousands of people are exposed to such torture each year, some of them actually choosing to initiate the process. They invariably find the experience painful, protracted, and expensive. When it has run its course, they often realize that it was futile. Yet there remains a queue of victims impatient for their turn.

Occasionally it is only the existence of the lawsuit that gives meaning and purpose to the life of the litigant. Sometimes it is only the fact of litigation that gives the subject-matter of the dispute (a strip of land squabbled over by neighbours, or a rarely used household object claimed by both parties in divorce proceedings) any value or importance.

In some cases the subject-matter of the dispute may not even exist. The leading case in the law of negligence concerned an allegation that the decomposed remains of a snail were contained in a bottle of ginger-beer. In 1932 the House of Lords held, by a majority of 3 to 2, that the alleged facts gave rise to a cause of action in negligence.[2] The Law Lords did not decide what is still in dispute among lawyers (and presumably also among manufacturers and vendors of ginger-beer): whether the snail's remains were or were not present in the bottle. A judicial decision will not necessarily resolve the crucial question at the root of the litigation. In 1985 Norris McWhirter issued a summons against the Independent Broadcasting Authority for allegedly broadcasting on a television programme what he described as 'a grotesque and ridiculing image of my face superimposed on the top of the body of a naked woman'. Other viewers may not remember the alleged incident. That would not be surprising for the image, according to Mr McWhirter, was broadcast for no more than a quarter of a second. It was, he claimed, identified by his 15-year-old nephew using a freeze-frame button on his video recorder. 'Look, there's Uncle Norris', were the young man's immortal words.[3] In quashing the summons on the ground that the facts alleged did not amount to a criminal offence, the Divisional Court[4] did not decide whether the offending image of Mr McWhirter had in fact been broadcast. That question will, no doubt, give pause for thought to future readers of the law reports.

As part of the function of deciding disputes, the courts provide a public service, at almost no charge to customers (who pay for their lawyers but not for the judge and the courtroom), by offering those who are greedy, vexatious, exhibitionist, aspiring to canonization, or just plain impossible a platform on which to perform. People will sue each other about everything and nothing. In Multnomah County District Court, Portland, Oregon, a special 'dog court' was created in 1979. There was enough legal business arising out of the activities of the canine population to keep a judge occupied for one day a week.[5]

Traditional disputes are becoming less amenable to compromise out of court. Fresh causes of action are becoming justiciable where once nobody would have expected the judiciary to have an answer. The growth in legal business has caused a considerable expansion in the size of the judiciary. Until 1813 'there were only two Chancery Judges ... and until 1830 there were only twelve Common Law Judges'.[6] In 1925 Parliament provided that 'for the more convenient despatch of business in the High Court' there should be six Chancery judges, seventeen King's Bench judges (plus the Lord Chief Justice), and three Probate, Divorce and Admiralty judges (including a President). The Court of Appeal at that time consisted of five Lords Justices (plus the Master of the Rolls).[7] To cope with the growth industry of litigation, by May 1986 there were seventy-seven High Court judges and twenty-two Lords Justices of Appeal (excluding the Lord Chief Justice, the Master of the Rolls, the President of the Family Division, and the Vice-Chancellor).

There are some 25,000 part-time Justices of the Peace and over sixty Stipendiary Magistrates dispensing justice in Magistrates' Courts. There are about a thousand Recorders and Assistant Recorders sitting part-time and nearly 400 Circuit Judges sitting full-time in the Crown Court and County Court. At the apex of the judicial system sit ten Law Lords who hear the final appeal to the Appellate Committee of the House of Lords.[8]

Each of these judges is expected to resolve wisely, according to law, and so that the parties conclude that they have had a fair hearing, the wide variety of hitherto insoluble disputes that come into court. Not surprisingly, judges are unable invariably to display omniscience on the legal and non-legal matters raised in their courtrooms. Few, if any, judges are today improperly motivated by bias towards, or against, one party or his cause. But all judges are necessarily influenced in the decisions they make by their upbringing and experience.

II

Lord Chancellor Hailsham acknowledged in 1984 that 'from time to time . . . a Judge says a particularly silly thing' which is then widely publicized.[9] The more detached the judicial comment is from contemporary ideas and ideals, the more extensive the consequent publicity. Some judges have achieved a considerable degree of expertise in making such statements and in displaying an immunity from contemporary knowledge and concerns.

In 1966 Lord Justice Harman noted that in his youth 'psychiatrists had not been invented' and that 'no-one was any the worse for it'.[10] During the *Oz* obscenity trial in 1971, Judge Argyle needed to ask, 'What is *Hair*?', at a time when even Princess Anne was dancing on the stage of the famous rock musical. For good measure, the judge was further unaware that H. L. A. Hart was a distinguished Oxford Professor of Jurisprudence or that 'right on' was, as the prosecutor explained, 'a revolutionary expression'.[11]

In 1957 a libel action based on an article about three Labour politicians who were alleged to have been drunk at a conference in Venice was tried before Lord Goddard. Why, he asked, was the article entitled 'Death in Venice': who had died there?[12] In 1979 Mr Justice Cantley heard a case about the legality of a ban imposed by the Football Association on a former England football manager. The judge announced that he had 'the great qualification of not knowing any of [the relevant footballers or administrators] or anything about them'. Later in the proceedings he asked a barrister, 'Kevin Keegan, does he play for England or Scotland?'[13] In a 1985 case Mr Justice Harman displayed a lack of knowledge of popular music by asking, 'Who is Bruce Springsteen?'[14] It is almost credible that Mr Justice Snubb (elevated to the Bench by the pen of A. P. Herbert) should enquire of the barristers appearing in his court, 'What is a crossword?'[15]

Judges deserve credit when they admit to gaps in their knowledge of topics which preoccupy large parts of the population. In a 1943 libel case before the Court of Appeal, Lord Justice Scott explained that 'on behalf of the plaintiff in the court below it was said that the word "pansy", as applied to a man, has a slang sense, often used, of an opprobrious character. . . . I personally was not alive to the slang meaning of the word, nor, I think, was my brother MacKinnon, but my brother Goddard fortunately was quite alive to it, having had judicial experience as a result of which he had come to know about it.'[16] Too often judges do not own up to their need for continuing education. They frequently compound their reluctance to recognize their inexpertise with a readiness to express themselves in court on all types of subjects about which they know little or nothing, in terms derived neither from the common law nor from common sense.

In this respect, sex often brings out the worst in a judge. In 1982 a judge at Ipswich Crown Court fined a rapist, rather than sending him to prison, after finding that his teenage victim, who had innocently accepted a lift in his car, was 'guilty of a great deal of contributory negligence'.[17] Also in 1982, a judge at the Cambridge Crown Court told a jury in a rape trial to remember the expression 'stop it, I like it'. He added: 'It is not just a question of saying "no". It is a question of how she says it, how she shows and makes it clear. If she does not want it, she has only to keep her legs shut and he would not get it without force and there would be marks of force being used.'[18] In 1983 an Old Bailey judge heard the case of a man who committed a sexual offence against a friend's daughter, who was aged 7. The judge was reported in a newspaper the next day (a Saturday) as having said in court: 'It strikes me as being one of the kind of accidents that could almost happen to anyone.' On the following Monday the judge told a crowded courtroom that he was referring the newspaper report to the Attorney-General. What he had actually said on the previous Friday, he insisted, was: 'This is of course a serious offence, offending against a little child, but it strikes me, without belittling the offence, it is one of the kind of accidents which happen in life to almost anyone—although of a wholly different kind.' The judge sentenced the man to two years' imprisonment.[19]

Judicial outspokenness is not always a wise policy. As Lord Justice Scrutton observed in 1932, a judge who has never been married should not 'proceed to explain the proper underclothing that ladies should wear'.[20] The judicial difficulty is that broad expressions of principle on matters on which judges can claim no special expertise may be necessary to decide the case before the court. In 1980, for example, Lord Justice Ormrod said, in a divorce case before the Court of Appeal, that in the relevant circumstances 'it seems to me quite impossible for any court to find that the refusal by a wife to have sexual intercourse more often than once a week is unreasonable'.[21] Because the wife was not acting unreasonably, the husband was not entitled to a divorce on that ground.

Obscenity cases may pose particular problems in this context. They can involve sophisticated defences based on the public good allegedly promoted by the impugned publication. 'No one has felt the full glory of a barrister's life who has not, in wig and gown, been called to the podium in the committee room of the House of Lords by an official in full evening dress and, on a wet Monday morning, lectured five elderly Law Lords in lounge suits on the virtues of masturbation'.[22] On such occasions, it may be wise for the judge to adopt the principle of adjudication stated by Chief Justice Vaughan in 1670: that he is a 'stranger [who] . . . knows no more of the fact that he hath learn'd in court . . . and consequently knows nothing'.[23] In deciding whether a publication is obscene, a judge may, despite his best endeavours to the contrary, be unable to define the legal rule with greater precision than that 'I know it when I see it'.[24] In such contexts, judges cannot win. 'It is difficult to know what judges are allowed to know, though they are ridiculed if they pretend not to know'.[25]

Despite the dangers of making fools of themselves, judges do sometimes choose to deliver themselves of broad propositions of social policy unnecessary to the determination of the case before the court. On reflection, judges may occasionally consider that such statements add little to the sum of human knowledge or understanding, other than to reveal in an unflattering light the attitudes and beliefs of members of the English judiciary. In 1978 Judge McKinnon informed a jury hearing a charge of incitement to racial hatred that he was nicknamed 'Nigger' at school and did not resent it.[26] His comments provided good newspaper copy.

When tempted to offer the benefit of his wisdom on extra-judicial matters, the judge should pause and consider the observation of Lord Justice Bowen made in 1888. Such 'obiter dicta'—statements not necessary to the decision in the case—'come home to roost sooner or later in a very uncomfortable way to the Judges who have uttered them, and are a great source of embarrassment in future cases'.[27] This is particularly so when moral and social views in the community develop at a greater pace than judicial thinking. In 1924 Marie Stopes, the birth-control pioneer, brought a libel action in relation to statements about books she had published in favour of birth control. In the House of Lords, Viscount Finlay announced that 'for my part I cannot doubt that [the books] are calculated to have a most deplorable effect upon the young of both sexes'.[28] In 1925 Lord Atkinson concluded that it was unlawful for a local council to provide equal pay for men and women doing like work. The council, he asserted, had acted unlawfully by becoming 'such ardent feminists' and by being guided 'by some eccentric principles of socialist philanthropy'.[29]

Whether a local authority needs to be reminded that 'the laws of this country are not like the laws of Nazi Germany'[30] or whether a woman really 'does not like [her hair] disturbed: especially when she has just had a "hair-do"'[31] are not matters on which judges have to pronounce or in respect of which they have special qualifications. They are not appointed for their competence as moral philosophers or social commentators. In the early decades of this century Mr Justice McCardie 'delivered himself freely of all sorts of aphorisms on many burning topics of the day'.[32] Judges ought to resist that temptation. It may be difficult to do so. In one of Theo Mathew's fables, a lawyer resolved that if he should ever be appointed to the Bench he 'would avoid the errors and failings of some of his predecessors. In particular he would not indulge in foolish jokes, give vent to irrelevant observations about men and things, or hint that the bar had sadly deteriorated since he had ceased to adorn its ranks.' The lawyer later became a County Court judge: 'Before the year was out the reporters in his Court had recorded that a Plymouth Brother could not be believed upon his oath; that it was common knowledge that a married woman was either a slave or a tyrant; ... that the moral standards of artists and literary men were extremely low ...'[33]

The Court of Appeal decided in 1985 that the women nuclear protesters living at Greenham Common were qualified to vote in that constituency. One paragraph of the decision was of particular importance to all those interested in judicial administration. Sir John Donaldson, Master of the Rolls, announced that the women 'all made a point of telling us that each is committed to the anti-nuclear cause and, in addition, [one of the women] made it very clear that she has strong views about the position of men in society. We record these facts because we feel sure that the ladies would wish them to be recorded, but we disregard them for all purposes.'[34] The reluctance of the court to express a view on the merits of the anti-nuclear cause or the role of men in society was a welcome retreat from the legendary enthusiasm of judges to state opinions on all manner of topics indirectly connected with the legal proceedings.

Some senior judges have been ignorant of non-legal issues. Lord Eldon (Lord Chancellor at the beginning of the nineteenth century) was 'conscious of his own deficiency in literary composition, from having read nothing but briefs for so many years'.[35] It was doubted 'whether he ever entered a theatre three times after he was called to the Bar'.[36] For similar reasons the conversation of Sir John Willes (Chief Justice of the Court of Common Pleas 1737–61) 'was either about law or lewdness'.[37] Lord Kenyon (Master of the Rolls 1784–8 and Chief Justice of the King's Bench 1788–1802) 'was unacquainted with every portion of human knowledge except the corner of jurisprudence which he professionally cultivated'.[38] Some judges have known as little about the law as they have about other matters. It was said of Lord Cranworth (Lord Chancellor 1852–8 and 1865–6) that the reason why he always sat with other Lords Justices in the Court of Appeal was a reluctance 'to be left alone in the dark'.[39]

Those who have wide gaps in their knowledge have occasionally made great judges. The force of their personality or their innate wisdom more than compensated for any other deficiency. Oliver Wendell Holmes, a distinguished US Supreme Court judge from 1902–32, did not read newspapers.[40] Sir Edward Coke, Chief Justice in the early seventeenth century and one of the fathers of the common law, 'never saw a play acted or read a play'.[41] Yet they were exceptionally good judges. Nowadays the ability of men and women to serve adequately as judges is likely to bear a closer relation to their knowledge and experience of life outside the courtroom.

The role of the judiciary continues to expand to cover the resolution of all manner of disputes, particularly in commerce and government, which previous generations did not consider to be justiciable. The judge can no longer hope to succeed as an amateur relying on legal learning alone to arrive at an adequate solution to disputes with important implications for the quality of other people's lives. In 1883 Lord Bramwell confessed his ignorance of the issues which Parliament had asked him to resolve by a statute controlling the fairness of commercial terms in a contract. 'Here is a contract made by a fishmonger and a carrier of fish who know their business, and whether it is just and reasonable is to be settled by me who am neither fishmonger nor carrier, nor with any knowledge of their business . . .'[42] Since then, the circumstances in which judges have been required to apply such vague values or criteria on subjects outside their experience have expanded dramatically.

At present, judges 'are not in a position to decide whether the climate of opinion has changed. Their very lives and backgrounds usually would make it impossible for them to know what went on in offices and factories all over the country.'[43] Until judges are helped to know more about what goes on outside the courtroom, they should be encouraged to stick to the legal point in court.

III

One subject in which judges rarely claim any great expertise is jurisprudence (the philosophy of law). Like Lord Chancellor Eldon, some judges take as much interest in 'abstract metaphysical calculations' as does 'the ox that stands staring at the corner of the street'.[44] In 1932 Harold Laski introduced Mr Justice Macnaghten to the theory of Oliver Wendell Holmes, the US Supreme Court Justice, that behind every judgment lies an 'inarticulate major premise'. Macnaghten explained to Laski 'with something like passion that he had no such premises, that he "simply applied the law, looking neither to the right nor to the left". I suggested that his mind might be slightly more complex than he knew, to which he retorted that he was a simple and honourable man and that no damned nonsense about complexity was going to obscure his motives.'[45]

Mr Justice Macnaghten had a narrow view of judicial bias. He understood it to cover only the judge who decides the case in a dishonourable fashion, knowingly by reason of his partiality (or dislike) for one litigant or his cause. In the past, some such judges have disgraced the Bench. Robert Louis Stevenson modelled his Lord Hermiston, the Lord Justice-Clerk in Scotland's criminal court, on the infamous Lord Braxfield. Lord Hermiston 'did not affect the virtue of impartiality; this was no case for refinement; there was a man to be hanged, he would have said, and he was hanging him'.[46] The eighteenth-century English judge, Mr Justice Buller, 'was said always to hang for sheep-stealing, avowing as a reason that he had several sheep stolen from his own flock'.[47]

Such partiality no longer stains the Bench. Few judges could hope to emulate the impartiality of Chief Justice Mansfield: he presided, fairly, at the trial of Lord George

Gordon in 1781 for alleged treason despite the fact that his own house had been burnt down in the riots provoked by Gordon. The trial resulted in Gordon's acquittal.[48] But all judges would now decline to sit in judgment on a case where their personal feelings or interests made it impossible for them to act in an impartial manner.

A judge who has a financial interest in the outcome of a case should not sit in judgment on it. A decision of Lord Chancellor Cottenham was quashed by the House of Lords in 1852 because he was a shareholder in a company which was a party to the action.[49] A judge who considers himself unable to decide a case impartially for other reasons will not sit in judgment. There are many types of judicial interest in a case which may preclude participation. A bizarre example of this type of judicial self-denial occurred in Texas in 1925. The entire membership of the State Supreme Court excused themselves from hearing a case involving a Masonic-style organization called Woodmen of the World. All the judges were members. The Governor appointed a special court of three women, presumably in the confident expectation that such an organization would decline to admit females to membership.[50] Mr Justice Clark resigned from the US Supreme Court in 1967 when President Johnson appointed the judge's son to be Attorney-General (a job involving frequent appearances before the Court).[51] In England 'it is not considered improper for a barrister to appear before his father or near relative in the High Court, Court of Appeal, or in the House of Lords'.[52] No judge whom a journalist had specifically criticized 'would dream of sitting' on a case involving that journalist.[53]

In exceptional cases the judge may excuse himself because he cannot be sure of controlling his emotions. In 1952 the US Supreme Court was asked to decide whether it was unconstitutional for a street railway company to install loudspeakers in its passenger vehicles for the transmission of music and advertisements. Mr Justice Frankfurter took no part in the case because his 'feelings were so strongly engaged as a victim of the practice in controversy that I had better not participate in judicial judgment upon it'.[54]

Occasionally a litigant objects to the involvement of a particular judge on the ground that previous judgments cause the litigant to doubt whether the judge would decide the case impartially. In 1978 Lord Denning acceded to such an application. He said that 'if the Church of Scientology felt that its case would be a little disturbed by his sitting on it, that was the last thing he would wish to do and he would see that it came before a court in which his Lordship was not sitting'.[55] In 1984 Lord Chief Justice Lane stood down from the court of three judges assigned to hear a case concerning the use of road blocks by the police to prevent striking miners reaching picket lines. Counsel for the miners had argued that Lord Lane would be influenced by comments he had made, adverse to the miners' legal claim to conduct such activities, in a previous case. Lord Lane said that he could see no reason why he should not hear the case, but that he was willing to stand down.[56] The case was heard and decided, in favour of the police, by the other two judges.[57]

Lord Denning and Lord Lane were over-generous in their response to these applications. Judges are there to decide cases, not to excuse themselves whenever a litigant doubts, without cause, the judicial qualities of those assigned to sit in judgment. Litigants should not be encouraged to treat judges like members of a jury whom they can challenge off the case, with or without cause. Some litigants have met with a harsher judicial response in this respect. In 1975 a US District Court female judge refused to accede to the request of a defendant in a sex discrimination case that she should

41

disqualify herself on the ground of bias because she was of the same sex as the plaintiff and had argued civil rights cases as a lawyer before her appointment to the Bench.[58] A barrister charged with professional misconduct was similarly unsuccessful in his complaint that a disciplinary tribunal, 'the majority of the members of which are practising barristers, is incapable of considering fairly a charge of misconduct brought against a fellow barrister'.[59]

In 1873 Thomas Castro, otherwise known as Arthur Orton, otherwise known as Sir Roger Charles Doughty Tichborne, Baronet, more popularly known as the Tichborne Claimant, addressed a public meeting on the subject of his forthcoming trial for perjury based on the evidence given by him at an earlier trial that he was indeed the Baronet. He told the meeting that Lord Chief Justice Cockburn, who was to be the trial judge in the perjury proceedings, should himself 'answer for contempt of court' because he had allegedly prejudged the issue in an associated case by having 'publicly denounced me as a rank imposter at his club'. Proceedings for contempt of court were then commenced not against the Lord Chief Justice, but against Castro. At the hearing of the charge of contempt, Mr Justice Blackburn said that the Chief Justice would not play any part in the contempt case. The alleged contempt 'partly consisted of personal attacks upon the Lord Chief Justice; and where that is the case there is a risk, of course, that his feelings might cause him to be vindictive, but there is a very much greater risk that, from his anxiety that his feelings should not lead him to give an excess of punishment, he would be too lenient'. However, despite the wish of Castro that Chief Justice Cockburn should not preside at the perjury trial, Blackburn J explained that 'there is not the slightest doubt, and never has been the slightest doubt in the mind of any one individual in the Court, that it would have been a great dereliction of duty if we were in the slightest degree to alter the arrangement in consequence of [the criticisms]; and the Lord Chief Justice himself was of opinion that it was his duty to preside at the trial, and every individual member of the Court agrees with him'.[60]

Because judges live in society, they are bound to be affected by the result of many cases that come before the courts. In one of A. P. Herbert's *Misleading Cases*, Sir Ethelred Rutt KC persuaded three Court of Appeal judges that neither they nor any other judges could properly hear an income-tax appeal because the judiciary, being paid by the Crown, had a direct interest in increasing the sums due to the Inland Revenue.[61] In the non-fictional Court of Appeal, a rather more realistic approach is necessarily taken. When the legality of a policy of cheaper public transport in London was challenged in the Court of Appeal in 1981, Lord Denning explained that

all three members of this court are interested on all sides. We are all fare-paying passengers on the tubes and buses and benefit from the 25 per cent cut in fares. My wife and I also have the benefit of senior citizens to travel free. We are all ratepayers in the area of Greater London and have to pay the increase in rates [to cover the revenue lost by reducing the fares]. No objection is taken by any party to our hearing the case. Any Court of Appeal would be likewise placed.[62]

What Mr Justice Macnaghten failed to appreciate in his rejection of the 'damned nonsense' of jurisprudence[63] was that a more pervasive and less easily remediable form of judicial bias occurs when judges do indeed strive to decide cases simply and honestly without partiality. Because 'judges are men, not disembodied spirits',[64] their judgments are inevitably influenced by the judicial character and experience. Such 'bias' necessarily affects all judges. In 1978 Judge Sir Gerald Fitzmaurice (from the United Kingdom) dissented from the judgment of the European Court of Human Rights that birching young offenders in the Isle of Man was degrading treatment or punishment contrary to Article 3 of the European Convention on Human Rights. He admitted 'that my own view may be coloured by the fact that I was brought up and educated under a system according to which the corporal punishment of schoolboys . . . was regarded as the normal sanction for serious misbehaviour, and even sometimes for what was much less serious'.[65] Aristotle was aware, many centuries earlier, that for those who decide cases 'love, hate or personal interest is often involved, so that they are no longer capable of discerning the truth adequately, their judgment being obscured by their own pleasure or pain'.[66] Such influences on judicial thinking do not justify criticism of the judge: he cannot alter his identity. Judges are necessarily 'subject to human limitations. . . . The great tides and currents which engulf the rest of men do not turn aside in their course and pass the judges by . . .'[67] Those who sit in judgment strive, usually with success, to control their emotions. If one were to define 'bias' and 'partiality' to mean 'the total absence of preconceptions in the mind of the judge, then no one has ever had a fair trial and no one ever will'.[68]

The partiality that inevitably affects judges has been noted in cases with a political flavour. In 1911 Winston Churchill (then Home Secretary) told the House of Commons that 'where class issues are involved . . . it is impossible to pretend that the courts command the same degree of general confidence [as in other cases]. On the contrary, they do not, and a very large number of our population have been led to the opinion that they are, unconsciously no doubt, biased.'[69] In 1920 Lord Justice

Scrutton made a similar point. He noted that judicial impartiality is difficult to attain. He was 'not speaking of conscious impartiality; but the habits you are trained in, the people with whom you mix, lead to your having a certain class of ideas of such a nature that, when you have to deal with other ideas, you do not give as sound and accurate judgments as you would wish'.[70] It has been suggested that the unconscious partiality of the English judiciary has resulted in the development and application of a distinctive conception of public policy: 'It concerns first, the interest of the State (including its moral welfare) and the preservation of law and order, broadly interpreted; secondly, the protection of property rights; and thirdly the promotion of certain political views normally associated with the Conservative Party.'[71]

Judges certainly do not all think alike. Nor does each judgment apply a uniform or consistent theory of the public interest. Nevertheless, the judgments of English courts, taken as a whole, are seen and understood as indicating a particular set of values. In striving to do justice according to law, the judge is very likely to be attracted to what he thinks is right and proper. All of this matters because the man who does not share these judicial values wants to know why he should have them imposed on him by the courts.

In 1902 the Divisional Court heard an application to quash a conviction before the Worthing Justices for driving a car at a speed of more than 12 miles per hour. The application was made on the ground that 'the Chairman of the Worthing bench, Lieutenant-Colonel Wisden, had on this and other summonses against motor-car drivers exhibited great bias against motors and their drivers'. During the hearing he had said, among other things, that 'it would be a good thing if the motor-car industry were destroyed'. Dismissing the application, Mr Justice Willis commented that a 'magistrate is at liberty to entertain strong views on a subject, though it were better if he kept his views to himself'. The court was satisfied that the facts of the individual case had been properly considered at the hearing before the magistrates.[72] Today the courts apply somewhat stricter standards in relation to ensuring that justice is seen to be done. For this reason, amongst others, 'the conscientious judge will, as far as possible, make himself aware of his biases of this character.'[73] Self-knowledge in this respect will prevent the judge from wrongly imagining that his decisions always pronounce universal truths.

However knowledgeable judges may be about their biases, we cannot expect them to give other than an informed and intelligent but nevertheless subjective view of the facts and the law. It is therefore a matter of some importance who is appointed to the Bench.

CHAPTER 3

Appointment and Training

I

I N 1884 a yacht, the *Mignonette*, sank on a voyage
from England to Australia. The crew of four clam-
bered into an open boat in the South Atlantic
nearly 2,000 miles from land. They had no fresh water and
no food except for two tins of turnips and a turtle caught on
the fourth day. On the twentieth day Captain Dudley, with
the agreement of the mate, Edwin Stephens, killed the 17-
year-old cabin boy, Richard Parker, who was very weak
through drinking salt water. This was done to enable the
three remaining sailors to feed off the victim's flesh and
blood and so have a chance of survival. Dudley, Stephens,
and the other crew member, Ned Brooks, were rescued by a
passing ship on the twenty-fourth day.

As every law student knows, the ordeal of Dudley and
Stephens did not end with their rescue. They were then
prosecuted and convicted of the murder of Richard Parker.
A bench of five judges ruled that, in Professor Simpson's
words, 'one must not kill one's shipmates in order to eat
them, however hungry one might be'.[1] After being sentenced to death, Dudley and Stephens were reprieved. Their
punishment was reduced to six months' imprisonment.

The case of Dudley and Stephens is a leading authority on whether necessity is a defence to the charge of murder and other serious crimes. It serves to introduce each new generation of undergraduates to the peculiarities of legal reasoning. The researches of Professor Simpson added flesh to the bones of the story. After being rescued, Dudley explained, in a particularly unhappy phrase, that 'their hearts were in their mouths'. The day after the rescue, Dudley sat on a chamber pot which broke, lacerating his buttocks and making it impossible for him to sit down during his trial two months later.[2]

The discreditable judicial response to the predicament of Dudley and Stephens is the richest vein that can be identified in this saga. 'Killing and eating cabin boys', as Professor Simpson observed, 'was not a practice likely to recommend itself to Her Majesty's judges.'[3] Baron Huddleston, the judge assigned to try the case, was typical in this respect. So anxious was he to ensure the conviction of the defendants, and so concerned was he to deny the jury an opportunity to acquit them, that he persuaded the jury to adopt the unusual device of entering a 'special verdict', stating the facts of the case, concluding that as to whether these facts established the offence of murder 'the jurors are ignorant', and leaving it to a Court of the Queen's Bench Division to rule on that issue.

The law reports preserve the pompous and supercilious judgment delivered by Lord Chief Justice Coleridge for a bench of five judges to find Dudley and Stephens guilty of murder. The defendants were informed that they had the duty 'not of the preservation, but of the sacrifice of their lives for others, from which in no country, least of all it is to be hoped in England, will men ever shrink, as indeed they have not shrunk. . . . It is enough in a Christian country to remind ourselves of the Great Example whom we profess to follow. . . .'[4] It is reassuring to learn that these pious homilies did not receive universal acclaim even in Victorian England. The *Daily Telegraph* leader writer cynically observed that judges were perhaps not ideally suited to lecture their fellow human beings on acceptable conduct in conditions of extreme deprivation: 'It is a trial of the judicial temper if lunch be too late . . .'[5]

When they arrived back in England after their terrible adventures at sea, Dudley and Stephens were treated by the public as heroes. The brother of Richard Parker exonerated them. Yet Lord Coleridge and his fellow judges created a legal consensus which demanded a conviction for murder. Often 'the simplest of facts give rise to the most complex questions of law'.[6] In such cases, judges are not much more adept today than they were in 1884 at giving judgments that are informed as to the values of people who work outside the law courts. Those who find it necessary to bring forward, or who have brought forward against their will, the detritus of their lives for public examination and judgment in courts of law are entitled to be heard by judges who understand and reflect the values and concerns of contemporary society. That litigants do not invariably enjoy such a benefit is not the fault of the judges. It is the inevitable consequence of our system of appointing and training the judiciary.

II

In his thirteenth-century treatise, *The Mirror of Justices*, Andrew Horn explained that 'women . . . serfs . . . those under the age of twenty-one, open lepers, idiots, attorneys, lunatics, deaf mutes, those excommunicated by a bishop [and] criminal persons' were ineligible for appointment to the Bench.[7] By 1915 little had changed. On the appointment of

Buckmaster as Lord Chancellor, the Master of the Rolls, Cozens-Hardy, wrote to say that 'all the judges, without exception, are members of the Athenaeum [club], and I presume you will wish to be a member'.[8]

Our judiciary still consists almost exclusively of middle-aged to elderly men who worked as barristers for twenty years or more prior to their appointment. No one may become a judge of the High Court unless he is a barrister of at least ten years' standing. To become a Court of Appeal judge one needs to be either a High Court judge or a barrister of at least fifteen years' standing.[9] To be eligible for appointment as a Law Lord, one must first have served for at least two years in another judicial office or have practised at the Bar for at least fifteen years.[10] The eligibility criteria for appointment as a Circuit Judge[11] are slightly more flexible. To become a Circuit Judge one must be a barrister of at least ten years' standing or a Recorder[12] who has held that office for at least three years.[13] A barrister or a solicitor of at least ten years' standing is eligible to be appointed a Recorder.[14] So a solicitor can, by first serving as a Recorder, become a Circuit Judge. As yet 'relatively few solicitors have applied to be made recorders, and relatively few of these graduated to Circuit Court status'.[15]

The exclusive right of barristers to judicial appointment at the level of the High Court and above, and the predominance of barristers amongst those appointed to the Circuit Bench, have certain advantages to the public interest (in addition to the obvious benefits accruing to barristers). The system results in a judiciary with a common professional background in and around the courts. That background has educated and trained the aspiring judge on the rules and conventions of court life which play so vital a role in the administration of justice.

There are, nevertheless, important detriments to the

public interest in selecting the judiciary predominantly from the ranks of practising barristers. There are few such barristers, particularly those of the appropriate age, who are willing and able to serve on the Bench. Many otherwise eligible barristers have practices which do not involve much, if any, court work and who therefore cannot claim any expertise in court conventions. In recent years, firms of solicitors have had great success in attracting more of the brighter law students away from the Bar. As the number of judges continues to expand,[16] it will become increasingly difficult to find sufficient barrister candidates with the necessary judicial skills. If the eligibility criteria are not eased, the quality of the judiciary is very likely to suffer.

As Felix Frankfurter (a US Supreme Court judge from 1939 to 1962) recognized, a good judge needs to have three qualities, each of which is disinterestedness.[17] Yet the barrister has spent his professional life in 'fierce partisanship. To practise the latter for half a lifetime is almost to preclude the acquisition of' the necessary judicial impartiality.[18] This was the problem which Lord Chief Justice Hewart could not overcome earlier this century. He displayed 'a tendency to take sides in cases that came before him. Lawyers ... said it was to be expected in a first-class advocate and that the failing would pass.' It did not. 'Hewart had been all his life a partisan, in politics as well as in the courts, and it was not easy for him to lose the habit of seeing one side of the picture more clearly than the other.'[19]

The jobs of barrister and judge self-evidently require very different skills. To have the ability to argue a proposition is not necessarily to have the qualities required fairly to decide the same issue according to law. At the end of the eighteenth century, Lord Chancellor Loughborough 'was not very lucky in the Judges whom he made; but he might be without blame, for they had enjoyed some eminence at the bar, and no-one can certainly foretell how the most distinguished advocate will conduct himself on the Bench'.[20] By recruiting the judiciary almost exclusively from amongst barristers, our legal system wrongly implies that because someone is a successful advocate he will therefore make a similar success of being a judge and that no one can be a good judge who has not been an eminent barrister.

There is a further disadvantage in using barristers as the raw material for the judiciary. So intense is the pressure of work for successful barristers that many other activities have to be sacrificed. Virginia Woolf observed that their daily toil 'leaves very little time for friendship, travel or art. . . . That explains why most successful barristers are hardly worth sitting next [to] at dinner—they yawn so.'[21]

In the course of his professional activities, the barrister will come into contact with many aspects of the seamier side of life. A case load of crime, divorce, bankruptcy, commercial double dealing, road accidents, unfair dismissal, and the deportation of immigrants will undoubtedly lead him to realize that there are vast numbers of people worse off than himself. But his perspective on these matters will necessarily remain a limited and abnormal one, confined to part of the relevant story. The barrister may miss out on much vital information. When Sir Thomas Inskip, Attorney-General 1928–9 and 1932–6, informed the Law Lords during the course of his argument in one case that 'roulette was played with cards', he had the indignity of 'suffering a devastating monosyllabic correction from the Woolsack'.[22] (He later became Lord Chancellor and, thereafter, Lord Chief Justice.)

The rules of professional conduct inhibit the barrister from direct contact with his client. They require the client only to approach the barrister through a solicitor. This inevitably shields the barrister from detailed knowledge and

concern as to how his clients live. The great defect of much
of the fiction written about legal life is that the barrister
there discovers what really happened. The reality is that the
adversary process of a trial more often leaves the truth
mysteriously hidden, covered over by the evasions and
half-truths of competing contentions. The busy life of the
barrister and the rules of his profession result in his
acquiring a less than ideal knowledge and experience of the
context of the problems which the judge is asked to resolve.
Plato thought that 'good judges are those who have mixed
with all sorts of people'.[23] Too often the barrister has
remained professionally cocooned in his chambers and at
court from the realities of non-legal life.

It is, then, not surprising that a Bench composed almost
entirely of former barristers should lack expertise and
knowledge of many of the matters which are central to the
lives of those people who come into court as litigants or
witnesses. Nor is it surprising that a Bench so composed
should display a fairly uniform set of social values or should
have a homogeneous independent school and Oxbridge
educational background.[24]

Judges have considerable power to make and apply the
law. They are not elected to office by the people whom
they govern in these respects. Other than in very exceptional circumstances judges are not required to leave office
until they reach the retirement age of 75 for High Court and
other leading judges[25] or 72 for Circuit Judges.[26] If it would
not result in an unacceptable diminution in the quality of
our judges, basic principles of representative government
suggest that the judiciary should cease to reflect the values,
background, and interests of so narrow a slice of society.
One important way to encourage respect for the law is to
show those whose behaviour it regulates that the law is
made by those whom it binds, not by a remote group

whose attitudes and ideals are foreign to those of ordinary people. The judiciary can claim many virtues. But it cannot pretend to be representative of the populace. A broadening of the judicial base would do much to strengthen the rule of law.

Solicitors should be made eligible for appointment to all judicial posts. They are lawyers, skilled and experienced in practical litigation in and around the courts. Of course many solicitors—like many barristers—will not have the requisite judicial qualities. But that is no justification for making all solicitors—irrespective of their individual quali-ties—ineligible for appointment. In 1962 R. E. Megarry (who later became a High Court judge) suggested that it was obvious that solicitors should remain off the Bench: 'Should a man be appointed to the Bench of the High Court when he has never argued a case there? The question answers itself.'[27] The answer no longer seems so obvious. Many solicitors do have experience of advocacy in the lower courts, if this is considered a relevant qualification for a judge. The main reason they lack such experience in the higher courts is because they are denied a right of audience.[28]

If being a solicitor is no longer a complete bar to appointment as a Circuit judge, it is difficult to see why it should prevent appointment to the High Court Bench, however well qualified to be a judge the solicitor is in other respects. Such a prohibition is especially absurd in the case of a Circuit judge who has shown great ability on the Bench. Circuit judges are sometimes promoted to the High Court Bench. But a Circuit judge cannot be so promoted if he was a solicitor rather than a barrister prior to becoming a Circuit judge.

It is not good enough to argue, as did Lord Chancellor Hailsham when the matter of the promotion of Circuit judges was raised during the Committee Stage of the Supreme Court Bill in 1981, that 'the royal road of promotion to the High Court bench for a solicitor is to practise in the High Court, which he can do perfectly easily by transferring to the Bar'.[29] The question is rather whether the legal system loses something by ignoring the qualities of potential High Court judges. To make solicitors who have served as Circuit judges eligible for promotion to the High Court would hardly impose great administrative burdens on the Lord Chancellor's Department. What it might do, of course, is to 'create ill-feeling between the two branches of the profession',[30] that is to say barristers might resent the removal of their monopoly. The denial to otherwise qualified solicitors of the opportunity to become judges is explicable only as a restrictive practice for the benefit of barristers. The practice imposes a serious detriment to the public interest by unnecessarily limiting the pool of eligible candidates for appointment to high public office.

There is a gulf between the academic and the practising lawyer in England. When Rumpole 'applied a torn-off page of the *Criminal Law Review* to the electric fire and lit the small cigar',[31] the value of academic legal writings to the practitioner was effectively demonstrated. Law review articles are usually ignored by solicitors, barristers, and judges. Academic lawyers are not appointed to the Bench. The contrast with the influence of academic lawyers in other legal systems, both in continental Europe and in North America, is striking.

In 1934 Harold Laski suggested to Lord Chancellor Sankey that he might appoint an academic lawyer to the Bench. Sankey explained that opposition within the legal profession prevented him from doing so.[32] There is no good reason for such a prohibition on the appointment of an academic lawyer who has the necessary qualities. That the academic lawyer has had no experience of litigation may well render him unsuitable for appointment as a Circuit judge or as a High Court judge. But his skills and expertise in the analysis of complex questions of law may well make him qualified to sit in the Court of Appeal or in the House of Lords.

It may be true that 'daily practice in the courts strengthens and develops not only the innate qualities of intellect and character but also those of patience, temper and resilience which are so important in the practice of the law'. It would be wrong to think that only barristers possess such qualities. R. E. Megarry opposed the appointment of academic lawyers to the Bench because the academic's 'tempo of life is quite different. It is one thing for ideas and theories to evolve and be tested over the years in the study and the lecture-room, and another thing to judge competing theories in the hot-house of the court room'.[33] No academic would be appointed unless he had the required qualities for adjudication. That academics do occasionally possess such qualities is shown by the experience of other legal sytems. In any event, the academic lawyer would feel at home in the slow and deliberate procedures of the Appellate Committee of the House of Lords, in which all messy issues of fact have already been resolved and the questions of law carefully defined and refined in advance of the hearing.

Similar arguments apply in respect of lawyers who chair administrative tribunals[34] and lawyers employed by companies, trade unions, or other organizations. If they have the qualities required of a judge they should not be excluded from the Bench merely because they have not worked as barristers for the appropriate number of years.

It is, of course, important to ensure that a more representative Bench does not become a less able Bench. In 1970 President Nixon nominated Judge G. Harrold Carswell to serve on the US Supreme Court. Carswell's obvious inadequacy was claimed to be a virtue by a Nixon supporter in the Senate: 'Even if he is mediocre', enthused Senator Roman Hruska, 'there are a lot of mediocre judges and people and lawyers. They are entitled to a little representation, aren't they . . .?'[35] In April 1970 the Senate indicated their disagreement with such a doctrine by rejecting the nomination of Carswell. Widening the pool from which judges are chosen would be unlikely to lower the high standards of the English judiciary. Barristers have a monopoly on appointments to the High Court Bench, but they have no monopoly on wisdom and legal learning. Such a reform would do much to dissipate the oppressive atmosphere of social and professional exclusivity that renders our courts so remote and daunting to the layman.

The distinctive contribution of President Nixon to jurisprudence is further seen in his approach to the lifestyle of candidates for high judicial office. In 1970 Harry Blackmun was interviewed by Nixon who was considering nominating him to fill a vacancy on the US Supreme Court. Nixon did not want to know about Blackmun's judicial philosophy but rather about his 'three daughters in their twenties. Nixon asked if any were "hippie types". Blackmun assured him that none was.'[36] Blackmun was nominated and thereafter confirmed by the Senate.

In England there has been a similarly irrelevant concern with the private life of an aspiring judge. As late as 1972 divorce was considered an impediment to appointment to the Bench. At that time, 'persons whose conduct in private life gives rise to a suspicion that they might not maintain the strict standards expected from judges are not promoted to the Bench. Bachelors who are known for leading "wild" lives would not be appointed to the Bench. Likewise, married barristers who do not exercise the required degree of self-control in their private life are likely to end their careers at the Bar.' One barrister is said to have been 'excluded from the Bench on the grounds that he was a most frequent visitor to a public house near the Law Courts. Having been involved unduly in racing activities would also damage the chances of a barrister with aspirations to judicial office.'[37] In 1970 Henry Cecil (a County Court judge) commented that 'one of the finest lawyers in the country used regularly to go to greyhound meetings and, I think, even owned a greyhound. There was nothing illegal or immoral in that. But was it the sort of life which a judge should lead? He was never made a judge, though otherwise eminently fitted for the Bench.'[38] For many barristers who aspire to judicial office, the principles (real or perceived) applied by the Lord Chancellor serve a valuable social function. They are a powerful inducement to a chaste family life. Rumpole's head of chambers, Guthrie Featherstone QC, is terrified that his marriage is under threat. 'I mean, a divorce just plays havoc with your chance of getting your bottom on to the Bench.'[39]

Judges are appointed to decide cases according to law. They are not moral tutors to the rest of the population. If a man has a criminal record, this may (depending on the nature of his crime) be a good reason for keeping him away from a job which involves enforcing the law. The fact that his personal conduct, although lawful, is unusual or even morally offensive to other people is as irrelevant to whether he should be appointed to the Bench as are his political views.[40] The requirement that English judges should satisfy such tests of their moral character is one reason why the Bench has traditionally failed to be representative of and to have empathy with the layman. To the extent that similar criteria continue to be applied (and one of the problems is to know what criteria are applied),[41] they should be abandoned.

The English judiciary includes few women, even fewer blacks, and nobody under the age of 40. English judges tend to be elderly gentlemen most of whom have had a public school education. It is disturbing that our judges come from so narrow a range of the community. To adjudicate cases is to exercise discretion in fact-finding, sentencing, applying the law, and awarding costs. Such powers should be exercised by judges of disparate backgrounds, ages, races, and sexes. This is for two main reasons. First, it is inequitable in a democratic society that one set of values should so predominate on the Bench. Secondly, there is a danger that minority groups and women faced by a Bench on which they see few, if any, of their number will lose respect for the law. A more diverse judiciary is unlikely to be attained while appointment is confined to practising barristers. There are few blacks, women, and Labour Party supporters among the ranks of senior barristers.

The Sex Disqualification (Removal) Act 1919 made sex discrimination in the professions unlawful. The first woman barrister joined the Inner Temple in 1922. Forty years later, Elizabeth Lane became the first female County Court judge. In 1965 she was promoted to become the first woman to sit on the High Court Bench. A handful of other women have followed her lead. In 1979 England's first Sikh judge was appointed. We have yet to follow the example of Governor Brown of California. In 1979 he appointed America's first openly homosexual judge and in 1981 the country's first admitted lesbian judge.[42] President Carter adopted a positive action programme from 1976 to 1980 which resulted in the appointment of nearly 100 women, blacks, and Hispanics to the Federal Bench.[43] President Johnson, a decade earlier, was influenced by the fact that Thurgood Marshall was black when he appointed him Solicitor-General in 1965. Johnson, a dedicated opponent of racism, told Marshall that he wanted 'folks to walk down the hall at the Justice Department and look in the door and see a nigger sitting there'.[44] Johnson had similar considerations in mind when he successfully nominated Marshall to be the nation's first black Supreme Court judge in 1967.

The paucity of women and blacks at the Bar helps to explain (though it cannot justify) their absence from the Bench under the existing practice of looking for judicial candidates only amongst barristers. There is no such excuse for the fact that judges are commonly appointed not at their intellectual zenith but at an age when their contemporaries are planning for retirement. A judge is never less than 40 years old on his appointment, rarely less than 45 (Lords Hodson and Devlin were aged 42 when appointed to the High Court in 1937 and 1948 respectively), and is usually over 50.

Lord Radcliffe was appointed a Law Lord direct from the Bar in 1949. Lord Greene was appointed a Judge of the Court of Appeal direct from the Bar in 1935. (He later recalled that he was 'sitting quietly at Monte Carlo with a glass of champagne in my hand, ready to relax at last after being appellant in the last five cases in the Privy Council, when I got a telegram. It asked me to go direct to the Court of Appeal. I couldn't refuse, could I? But I don't know how many years it's going to take me to sort out my income tax and surtax. They really ought to give you some warning, don't you think?')[45] Lord Wilberforce was promoted to be a Law Lord from the High Court Bench in 1964. Nevertheless, the usual pattern[46] is for the very distinguished English judge to serve at least three years in the High Court and a similar period in the Court of Appeal before reaching the House of Lords. It is, then, rare for the English judge to sit as a Law Lord before he is 60. (Scottish judges often reach the Appellate Committee of the House of Lords at a younger age). Since judges are not required to retire until the age of 75 (or 72),[47] and are sometimes invited to remain on the Bench after retirement age, the average age of the English judiciary, particularly in the appeal courts, is around the normal retirement age (60 to 65) of other workers.

Prior to the introduction of a compulsory retirement age, some judges were able to resist hanging up their wig and gown until well after their seventy-fifth birthday. Salathiel Lovell was 'on the verge of ninety years of age' when *appointed* a Baron of the Court of Exchequer in 1708. 'He sat for the next five years but from his extreme age could not be of much use to his colleagues.' He was 'distinguished principally by his want of memory'.[48] Vice-Chancellor Bacon retired at the age of 88 in 1886.[49] At the age of 92, Lord Halsbury sat in a case heard by the Appellate Committee of the House of Lords in 1916.[50] Lord Denning was appointed to the Bench prior to 1959 so he was not bound by the compulsory retirement age introduced in that year.[51] He resigned as Master of the Rolls in 1982 at the age of 83.

Henry Cecil expressed surprise in 1970 that it should be suggested that we have 'elderly judges'. On the contrary, he argued, 'the average age on appointment is 53 and the average age of all judges sitting today is 60'.[52] By the standards of other professions, that is indeed 'elderly'. There are distinct disadvantages in having an elderly judiciary. Oliver Wendell Holmes (who himself sat on the US Supreme Court until after the age of 90) observed that 'judges commonly are elderly men, and are more likely to hate at sight any analysis to which they are not accustomed, and which disturbs repose of mind, than to fall in love with novelties'.[53] Judges will apply to their job principles and values which they learnt forty or fifty years earlier. A judiciary composed predominantly of senior citizens cannot hope to apply contemporary standards or to understand contemporary concerns. Aristotle wisely doubted whether judges of important causes should hold office for life for 'the mind grows old no less than the body . . .'[54]

There are those who insist that wisdom arrives with old age and that youthful exuberance is no substitute for experience. They cite Plato's argument that a 'good judge must not be a young man . . . but an old one' who has learnt about wickedness by watching it in other people.[55] There is also the unfortunate precedent of King Rehoboam. With disastrous consequences—the division of the Kingdom of Israel—he 'rejected the advice which the elders had given him and spoke to the people as the young men had advised'.[56]

But this is no justification for present policies. Candidates for office—judicial or otherwise—should be assessed on their merits and not ignored simply because they are younger than 45. In past centuries younger judges were appointed. Mr Justice Buller became a judge of the King's Bench in 1778 at the age of 32.[57] Judge Jeffreys (admittedly not the happiest example)[58] was Chief Justice at the age of 35 in 1683. Ralph de Hengham was appointed Chief Justice of the King's Bench in 1278 when 'he was little more than thirty years of age'.[59] When Solomon decided which of two women should have custody of a baby, he was, in his own estimation, 'a mere child'.[60] On occasions in the past, steps have been taken, or threatened, to reduce the average age of the judiciary. In Talmudic law a man who had reached the age of 60 was prohibited from sitting as a judge in a capital trial (except where the charge was inciting idolatry, so serious a matter that the stern attitude typical of the elderly judge was welcomed).[61] In 1381 one of the demands made by the rebellious Wat Tyler and his followers was that 'old justices should be hung'.[62]

The legal system survived Wat Tyler's threat. It continues to venerate old age. When the future Lord Chancellor Guildford was appointed one of His Majesty's Counsel in 1668, the Benchers of the Middle Temple were outraged: he was only 31. They refused to make him a Bencher and so recognize his status but had to back down at the insistence of the King.[63] Trollope's Mr Younglad 'was a promising common-law barrister, now commencing his career, of whom his friends were beginning to hope that he might, if he kept his shoulders well to the collar, at some distant period make a living out of his profession. He was between forty and forty-five years of age, and had already overcome the natural diffidence of youth in addressing a learned bench and a crowded court.'[64]

Once he has about ten years' experience of the law in action, a lawyer may be as fit to sit as a judge as he will ever be. To prevent the potential Solomon from serving as a judge until his late middle-age is an unjustifiably inefficient use of scarce human resources. What a waste of talent that those who are admirably suited to dispense justice should spend the years when they are at the height of their intellectual powers awaiting a letter from the Lord Chancellor's Department.

III

'Nothing can be more fantastical than the distribution of prizes in the lottery of legal promotion.'[65] Yet, as Lord Hailsham recognized, 'the selection and appointment of the judiciary [is] one of [the] most important responsibilities' of a Lord Chancellor.[66] 'No one can calculate the aggregate amount of evil inflicted on the community' by a bad decision.[67] In 1986 Lord Hailsham attempted 'to dispel any lingering sense of mystery or obscurity that there may be' about how judges are appointed by publishing a guide to his policies and procedures.[68]

The guide explains in bland terms the criteria for appointment: 'The Lord Chancellor's policy is to appoint to every judicial post the candidate who appears to him to be the best qualified to fill it and to perform its duties ...' It outlines the process of gathering information and 'broadly based' consultations which precede an appointment. Lord Hailsham had earlier described how the practice in all High Court appointments is to hold a meeting between the Lord Chancellor and the Heads of Division (the Lord Chief Justice, the Master of the Rolls, the President of the Family Division, and the Vice-Chancellor) at which a 'number of names is always discussed. There is never a vote, but a consensus is usually arrived at ... I never remember a case in which the decision, when made, was not in fact a collective one.'[69]

Grateful as one is for any information about the working practices of the Lord Chancellor's Department, it is unlikely that the published guide will satisfy the growing number of people concerned about, first, the extent of the patronage in the hands of the Lord Chancellor and, secondly, the absence of mechanisms to ensure that decisions are made on adequate information and proper criteria.

The Queen appoints Circuit and High Court Judges on the recommendation of the Lord Chancellor. Law Lords, Lords Justices of Appeal (who sit in the Court of Appeal), the Lord Chief Justice, the Master of the Rolls, the President of the Family Division, and the Vice-Chancellor are appointed by the Queen on the advice of the Prime Minister (though in practice the views of the Lord Chancellor carry great weight with the Prime Minister).[70]

Some barristers have not sought to disguise their eager-
ness to be selected for appointment. When a vacancy
occurred in the Appellate Committee of the House of Lords
in 1909, Thomas Shaw was arguing a case in a Scottish
court. He 'abandoned his client at a critical stage of the
proceedings, and departed to London in order to urge
personally upon the Prime Minister his claims to the vacant
office'. His efforts were not in vain.[71] Until Lord Chancellor
Cowper abolished the custom in 1706, it was the practice of
all the counsel who appeared in the Chancery Court to
bring to a breakfast with the Lord Chancellor on New
Year's Day 'a pecuniary present, according to their genero-
sity or their means, or their opinion of his venality or of his
stability . . . in the hope of being raised to the Bench, or of
obtaining silk gowns, or of winning "the Judge's ear"'.[72]

In the past, some judges were appointed for corrupt or
other improper motives. In 1684 Robert Wright was
promoted to the Bench while in a destitute state. His
patron, Chief Justice Jeffreys, suggested to him that 'as you
seem to be unfit for the bar or any other honest calling, I see
nothing for it but that you should become a judge yourself'.
Despite the opinion of Lord Chancellor Guildford that
Wright was 'the most unfit person in England to be made a
judge . . . a dunce, and no lawyer; who is not worth a groat,
having spent his estate by debauched living; who is without
honesty . . .', the King was persuaded by Jeffreys to appoint
Wright to the Bench. Wright became so pronounced a
favourite of James II that in 1687 he was promoted to Chief
Justice, 'greatly accelerating and furthering the Revolution'
in 1688 by his decisions. In all his judicial functions he
displayed himself by his 'ignorance, stupidity and immorality' to be one of 'the most sordid wretches' ever to sit on
the Bench in England.[73]

Lord Halsbury, who held office as Lord Chancellor at the

turn of the last century, appointed many undistinguished men to the Bench because of their political services to the Conservative Party. As Lord Salisbury, the Prime Minister, wrote to Halsbury in 1897, 'the judicial salad requires both legal oil and political vinegar; but disastrous effects will follow if due proportion is not observed'.[74]

Today, judicial appointments are not made on a corrupt or politically partisan basis. But the methods adopted continue to suffer from major defects which harm the public interest. Judges are appointed by a process that resembles a pre-1965 Conservative Party leadership contest or a Papal Conclave rather than the choice of law-makers in a modern democracy. Judges are chosen without any public discussion of their identity, let alone of the merits or defects of the candidates. Their appointment receives little, if any, public comment.[75] The reasons why one candidate, rather than another, has been recommended to the Queen remain hidden in the files of the Lord Chancellor's Department or concealed within the breasts of those senior judges amongst whom 'soundings' have been taken. All of this serves to deter public discussion of the criteria of good judges and to perpetuate gossip (most of it untrue) about the reasons for the rejection of certain candidates and the success of others. El Vino's wine bar in Fleet Street is 'the source of many false rumours which have dashed the hopes of many an aspirant to a High Court appointment'.[76] If he wants to find out more about such rumours, the aspiring judge cannot take advantage of the Data Protection Act 1984 to discover what information is holding up the progress of his career. The Act contains an exemption for personal data held by a government department which consists of 'information which has been received from a third party and is held as information relevant to the making of judicial appointments'.[77] The system has the considerable danger that a person whose views are unattractive to judges or to leaders of the profession may fail to achieve the judicial status which his talents deserve.

In the USA the President has the power to appoint Supreme Court Justices with the consent of the Senate. A Presidential nominee has to undergo a Senate examination of his record and jurisprudential beliefs. This serves a valuable function in helping to articulate the criteria of a good judge, in publicizing the beliefs of the nominee, in rejecting inadequately qualified candidates, and in focusing public attention on the process of appointment. The Senate has declined to confirm twenty-seven of the nearly 140 Supreme Court nominees placed before it since 1789.[78] Other federal US judges are similarly appointed by the President, subject to confirmation by a vote of the Senate. The tasks of the President and the Senate are facilitated by the practice of the American Bar Association of assessing whether the nominee is qualified to be a judge.

The more open, more critical American procedure of judicial appointments could be imitated in England to great advantage. At present we work on the doubtful principle that the Lord Chancellor and senior judges will know the candidates for judicial office, professionally or otherwise. Hence Rumpole's head of chambers searches through his letters 'in the hope of finding an invitation to play golf with the Lord Chief Justice'.[79] Such principles become less and less satisfactory as the Bar expands in size. They will be obviously inadequate if lawyers other than barristers become eligible for appointment to the Bench.

In 1972 the Justice Sub-Committee which reported on the judiciary wisely recommended that the Lord Chancellor should be helped in his task by an appointments committee. This would 'allow for interested bodies to make recommendations, or for interested persons to apply . . . The appointments committee could comprise representatives of the Law Society, the Bar, academic lawyers, the judiciary, and perhaps some lay members, for example highly trained and experienced personnel officers skilled in selection procedures.'[80] The Committee would not fetter the decision of the Lord Chancellor on whom to appoint. Nor would it introduce party politics into the process. It would, however, add an element of professionalism into what is still an amateur exercise. When judges are appointed to the Court of Appeal or the House of Lords, the Committee could usefully publish a report on the qualifications of the nominee. In this and other ways (such as the publication of an annual report on judicial appointments) the Committee would introduce a much needed public eye into what has hitherto been a private appointment process.

Radically different methods of selecting judges operate in some other countries. Many European nations have a career judiciary which candidates enter after university and in which judges are promoted, in theory, according to their talents. Some States in America elect their judges. Our present method is, as Lord Salisbury observed in 1897, 'perhaps ... not an ideal system—some day no doubt the M[aster of the] R[olls] will be appointed by competitive examination in Law Reports, but it is our system for the present'.[81] It remains our system, and it remains less than ideal—if preferable to the alternatives of a career judiciary or an elected judiciary.

The lottery of legal promotion continues to be as mysterious as when John Aubrey wrote his seventeenth-century note on Mr Brograve of Hamel in Hertfordshire. The young Brograve was riding in the country one day when he 'had a blow given him on his cheek (or head). He looked back, and saw that no body was near behind him; anon he had such another blow; I have forgot if a third. He turned back and fell to the study of the law; and was afterwards a Judge.'[82] However a Judicial Appointments Committee were to approach the task of helping the Lord Chancellor, it could hardly fail to improve on the unarticulated criteria, acts of God, and secret processes of nature which currently govern judicial appointments.

IV

That middle-aged men starting a new career as judges might need some job training does not seem a controversial proposition. Nevertheless, Lord Chancellor Hailsham stated in 1983 that he regarded 'with a degree of indifference verging on contempt the criticism of judges that demands for them a type of training which would render them more like assessors or expert witnesses than judges of fact and law'.[83] The topic of judicial training is evidently a sensitive one.

An amateur approach to judicial training was traditionally adopted by the English legal system. Lord Devlin recalled that when he was appointed to the High Court in 1948, 'I had never exercised any criminal jurisdiction and not since my early days at the Bar had I appeared in a criminal court. I had never been inside a prison except once in an interviewing room. Two days after I had been sworn in, I was trying crime at Newcastle Assizes ...'[84] Such blissful innocence is not confined to criminal cases. Sir Neville Faulks explained how, after a successful libel practice at the Bar, he was appointed to be a Judge in the Probate, Divorce and Admiralty Division of the High Court. The only training he had was to spend the Christmas vacation 'reading very carefully' the leading textbook on divorce law. As the vacation judge deciding all types of legal dispute, it was, he remembered, 'fun trying Chancery matters of which I had no experience at all'.[85] The litigants may not have been so amused. There is more than a little truth in Theo Mathew's *Forensic Fable* about the Regius Professor who describes to the King of the Upper and Lower Cannibal Islands how divorce cases 'were usually tried by lawyers who had been trained exclusively in the Admiralty Court, for reasons which he would subsequently explain; and questions relating to the cost and quality of female garments were referred to bachelor judges'.[86]

In recent years important developments in judicial training have taken place. When the Duke in *Measure for Measure* expresses his wish to appoint Angelo to be a judge in the Duke's absence, Angelo asks: 'Let there be some more test made of my metal, / Before so noble and so great a figure / Be stamp'd upon it.'[87] Today, the new judge invariably has experience as a Deputy or as a Recorder prior to appointment. The Judicial Studies Board, created in 1979, established the principle of judicial training in the criminal jurisdiction. From October 1985 the Board's valuable role was expanded to cover the provision of training in the civil and family jurisdictions.[88] These developments are very welcome. The new judge needs training in three distinct areas. First, gaps may have to be filled in his knowledge of the substance and procedure of the law by reason of the specialized nature of the work he has done as a barrister. Secondly, he will, in some cases, benefit from a broadening of perspective. Chambers in the Temple are not the best vantage point for a full understanding of industrial relations, prisons, local government finance, and the workings of the supplementary benefits system, all matters which may come before the court. Thirdly, practice in deciding cases may be advisable before a new judge is let loose on the public. 'We would not allow a man to perform a surgical operation without a thorough training and certification of fitness. Why not require as much of a trial judge who daily operates on the lives and fortunes of others?'[89]

Attendance at a Judicial College for a course lasting one or two months would not be an excessive requirement for new judges. Lectures and seminars could be supplemented by mock trials. This would help the judge to avoid learning his craft at the expense of the first few litigants to appear in his court. Time could usefully be spent visiting factories, boardrooms, and prisons. In industry and commerce, senior employees consider it essential to attend regular refresher courses to help them to act on new information and methods. Judges would similarly benefit from sabbatical leave at regular intervals to enable them to attend a Judicial College to study legal and non-legal developments 'particularly in the actuarial, sociological and psychological fields. No one could expect expertise in such a range of subjects, but a familiarity with the basic terminology and concepts, coupled with a knowledge of trends, is essential.'[90]

The great US Supreme Court judges have been 'widely read and deeply cultivated men whose reading and cultivation gave breadth and depth to their understanding of legal problems and infused their opinions'.[91] Indeed, Judge Learned Hand of the US Court of Appeals argued that it can be as important to a judge 'to have at least a bowing acquaintance with Acton and Maitland, with Thucydides, Gibbon and Carlyle, with Homer, Dante, Shakespeare and Milton, with Machiavelli, Montaigne and Rabelais, with Plato, Bacon, Hume and Kant, as with the books which have been specifically written' on the area of the law which he is considering.[92] A period of training prior to ascending the Bench will help to repair some of the gaps which may have been created by the demands of life at the Bar.

There remain those who resist the idea of training for judges. Despite his own experiences, Lord Devlin expressed a series of typical objections to judicial training.[93] He argued, first, that the judge is 'the juryman writ large' and so should 'reflect the attitude of the ordinary man applying an intelligent mind to technical questions'. But eminent barristers are not appointed to the Bench because they are ordinary men with intelligent minds. They are appointed because of the legal expertise they already possess. The question is whether we should enhance that expertise. Secondly, Lord Devlin contended that to have trained judges would deny open justice: everything that influences the court's judgment should be presented by way of evidence or argument in court. But judges necessarily bring with them to court a bundle of ideas and information. The debate cannot concern how to keep judges immune from personal views on whether trade unions compel their members to strike or whether short sharp shocks deter crime. Rather the issue is whether the judicial perspective on such topics is to be based on robing-room gossip or on lectures, seminars, and visits to the institutions involved. Finally, Lord Devlin was worried by the danger of an 'official' view being imposed on the judge. The role of a Judicial College is to provide information, not doctrine. It would not reflect well on the intelligence and independence of mind of judicial appointees were they unable to identify and reject propaganda pushed in their direction.

In 1903 Lord Macnaghten asked: 'With the light before him, why should he shut his eyes and grope in the dark?'[94] Judicial training is not the only illumination which is within reach of our judges. Unlike their counterparts in the USA, English judges have no law clerks to help them with research. (F. E. Smith, Lord Chancellor Birkenhead, was, in this respect as in so many others, unusual. The principal function of his secretary was 'to do the necessary devilling and drafting for F. E.'s judgments—even on occasion to write them where the question at issue did not engage F. E.'s interest'.)[95] English judges have very limited secretarial assistance. In court the English judge is not given any great help in understanding the social implications of the alternative decisions he could reasonably make in hard cases. The English legal system knows nothing of the Brandeis brief (pioneered by the future US Supreme Court judge, Louis Brandeis, as a lawyer in the early years of this century) in which written submissions contain a wealth of non-legal material relevant to the determination of the issue before the court. Also very rare here is the *amicus curiae* (friend of the court) brief. The US Supreme Court is well aware that any decision it makes will affect the welfare not only of the parties to the case but also of a wide variety of other people. It therefore admits written argument from vitally concerned groups. English courts prefer to act on the doubtful wisdom of Lord Eldon's aphorism that 'truth is best discovered by powerful statements on both sides of the question'.[96]

The amateur approach which the English legal sytem adopts in this context hinders the effective performance of the judicial function.

V

'Law is too serious a matter to be left exclusively to judges.'[97] But because judges necessarily have an important role to play in making and applying the law, there is every reason for ensuring that their selection, training, and working practices facilitate rather than frustrate their ability to decide cases wisely on behalf of the community.

CHAPTER 4

Performance and Discipline

I

I F (as occasionally happens) a judge errs in law, an appeal to older, wiser judges will usually provide a remedy. But if a judge acts in an injudicial manner, there is often much less that an aggrieved person can do.

Mr Justice Jackson of the US Supreme Court observed in 1952 that 'men who make their way to the bench sometimes exhibit vanity, irascibility, narrowness, arrogance and other weaknesses to which human flesh is heir'.[1] It would be surprising, indeed alarming, if some of the eminent legal minds that constitute the English judiciary did not, on their rare off days, act injudiciously. This was recently recognized by Lord Chancellor Hailsham. Those who sit in judgment occasionally become subject to what he called 'judges' disease, that is to say a condition of which the symptoms may be pomposity, irritability, talkativeness, proneness to obiter dicta [that is, statements not necessary for the decision in the case], a tendency to take short-cuts'.[2]

A 'judge may grow unfit for his office in many ways'.[3] It is therefore important to consider what sanctions exist in relation to judges who are unable to act in a judicial manner. The unfortunate reality is that in England judicial performance very much depends on judicial self-restraint and self-control. When these qualities fail, or when litigants believe them to have failed, there is a need for an independent forum in which complaints about judicial performance can be considered.

II

In all societies throughout history, judges have occasionally been adversely affected by their power. An early example occurs in the biblical story of Daniel and Susanna. Two elders of the community were appointed to serve as judges. They saw Susanna walking in her husband's garden 'and they were obsessed with lust for her'. When she resisted their advances they falsely accused her of infidelity to her husband. 'As they were elders of the people and judges, the assembly believed them and condemned her to death.' A young man named Daniel protested that an inquiry should be made into the judges' allegations. He accused them of giving 'unjust decisions, condemning the innocent and acquitting the guilty'. Under his careful cross-examination, the judges were proved to be liars.[4]

The English Bench has had its fair share of bad judges. Their faults have ranged from extreme impropriety to mildly irritating behaviour. In the seventeenth century, the Bench 'was cursed by a succession of ruffians in ermine [most notably Jeffreys and Scroggs], who, for the sake of court favour, violated the principles of law, the precepts of religion, and the dictates of humanity'.[5] At the other extreme, Lord Thankerton (a Law Lord from 1929 to 1948) 'irritated some counsel by practising his hobby of knitting while on the bench'.[6]

A wide variety of judicial malpractices has occurred. Not all judges have complied with the basic obligation to remain in court. One High Court judge 'left the court and also the precincts' on a Friday afternoon while a jury was considering their verdict in a case heard before him. He had instructed the usher to deal with the formalities. In the Court of Appeal, Lord Justice Singleton remarked that 'the parties, and the jury, are entitled to expect that the judge will remain if they have to do so; that is, in the absence of unforeseen circumstances'.[7]

Judges who remain in court occasionally fall asleep during the proceedings. Plato mentioned the problem.[8] In the seventeenth century, Mr Justice Doderidge 'had the habit of shutting his eyes while sitting on the bench, for the purpose of concentrating his attention on the argument, without being distracted by surrounding objects, and was thence jocularly called the Sleeping Judge'.[9] In the eighteenth century Lord Chancellor King 'often dozed over his cases when upon the bench'. However, 'it was no prejudice to the suitors', because two eminent barristers, Sir Philip Yorke and Mr Charles Talbot, were invariably briefed for the opposing parties in the court and they 'were both men of ... good principles and strict integrity and ... were sensible on which side the right lay'. They would instruct the registrar of the court what order it was appropriate to record.[10] During an 1891 slander case, involving an allegation that an acquaintance of the Prince of Wales had cheated at cards, the wife of the trial judge, Lord Chief Justice Coleridge, 'sat close to her husband's right hand, and had the duty of checking the occasional inclination to sleep which had at this time become noticeable'.[11]

Earlier this century, Mr Justice Finlay, 'when his court resumed after lunch, used to walk up and down the bench behind his chair because he was afraid of going to sleep'.[12] In the Court of Appeal, Lord Justice Birkett was 'often ... asked by his fellow judges on the bench to follow a case

77

closely while they had a half-hour nap after the lunch adjournment—sitting on the bench beside him'[13]. Mr Justice Cave regularly had an afternoon snooze at work. 'Flippant young barristers dropped heavy volumes on the floor or banged the flaps of the seat.'[14]

In 1972 the Court of Appeal rejected an appeal against a murder conviction brought on the ground that the judge was, or appeared to be, asleep during part of the trial. The defence solicitor stated in an affidavit that at certain times during the trial 'the judge was sitting with his head resting on his hand, his eyes shut and his head nodding'. The Court of Appeal concluded that the judge's notes of the trial showed that he had not been asleep. As to the complaint that the judge had appeared to be asleep, the Court said that, if true, this was 'a matter which the court would certainly deplore'. However, they added astonishingly, it 'was not a sufficient ground for saying that justice was not seen to be done'. The Court noted that 'none of the experienced counsel present found it necessary to take steps to awaken the judge or to acquaint him with the fact that his appearance seemed to be less alert than it should have been'.[15] In 1980 the High Court held that the Chairman of a bench of magistrates should have withdrawn from a case when a solicitor complained to the clerk that the Chairman appeared to be asleep. In fact she was not asleep, but 'it was her custom ... to close her eyes and to look down rather than to look directly at a witness'. The High Court remitted the case to be heard by another bench of magistrates.[16]

If a judge remains awake in court, he may fail to concentrate adequately on the proceedings. Lord Campbell recalled in 1868 that he had seen a judge 'indulge his curiosity by turning over the unwieldy pages of *The Times* while a counsel has been opening, in a condensed manner, a very important and complicated case—requiring the closest attention of a Judge'.[17] Towards the end of Lord Brougham's period of office as Lord Chancellor from 1830 to 1834, 'he became careless and heedless on the Bench, and it was common talk how he would write letters, correct proofs, read the newspapers, do anything, in short, but follow the arguments or listen to the affidavits'. When a barrister confronted Brougham with his inattention—by stopping his argument in the middle of a sentence and waiting for Brougham to put down his private correspondence—Brougham rejected the complaint: 'You may as well say that I am not to blow my nose or take snuff while you speak.'[18] Lord Hewart, Lord Chief Justice from 1922 to 1940, wrote letters while sitting in court, although his biographer reassures us that 'nothing passed over his head'.[19] The Scottish judges appointed prior to 1800 distracted themselves, and others, in a different manner. 'Black bottles of strong port were set down beside them on the Bench, with glasses, caraffes of water, tumblers and biscuits ... There was a comfortable munching and quaffing to the great envy of the parched throats in the gallery ... Not that the ermine was absolutely intoxicated, but it was certainly sometimes affected.'[20]

Judges who observe what is going on in court may disrupt the proceedings by irrelevant comments. Such comments may not affect the decision in the case being tried but they can promote a sense of grievance and dissatisfaction with the legal process which will last long after the court's decision has been announced and enforced. This is particularly true of judicial comments about irrelevant aspects of a litigant's character or behaviour. In November 1985 a woman pleaded guilty to a drunken-driving charge and explained that on the day the offence had taken place her doctor had informed her that she only had six months to live. The magistrate remarked, 'Well, we've all got to die sometime.' In October 1986 the same gentleman commented on a Portuguese defendant who had been living in England for ten years before being convicted of evading bus and train fares: 'They all get jobs, just like the illegal immigrants who come here . . . council houses, jobs, the lot.'[21] Sport is often the stimulus for irrelevant judicial utterances. During an important criminal trial in 1977, Judge Alan King-Hamilton told the jury that 'the Australians are 4 for 1 wicket'.[22] In 1986 Judge Michael Argyle told a jury trying a tax fraud case that the lack of Test Match cricket on television was 'enough to make an Orthodox Jew want to join the Nazi party'.[23]

In 1986 the Court of Appeal held that a Mr Swati was not entitled to challenge by way of judicial review the decision of an immigration officer to refuse him permission to enter the United Kingdom. Sir John Donaldson, Master of the Rolls, explained at the beginning of his judgment that Mr Swati 'arrived at Heathrow Airport from Pakistan. He sought leave to enter for one week in order "to spend some time visiting places of interest in the UK which has been my long term ambition". The venture', continued Sir John, 'has not been a success, because he was refused permission to enter and the only places of interest which he has been able to visit were the airport and the Ashford Remand Centre.'[24] Judicial humour is sometimes a necessary form of light relief from the stresses and strains of court business. Occasionally it becomes a misuse of power by holding up to ridicule the unfortunate and defenceless butt of the joke. Different senses of humour may well place the same example of judicial wit, such as that mentioned above, at different positions on the scale of acceptability.

Humour takes a variety of forms in court. The absurdity of many of the events on which courts are asked to pronounce and the implausibility of some of the explanations presented by litigants or their lawyers are often extremely funny. A skilful barrister can sometimes laugh his opponent's case out of court. But deliberate jokes are rarely amusing in the formal atmosphere of court proceedings unless they tend to deflate the pomposity of the occasion.

Some judges have disrupted the legal process by striving for comic effect. Mr Justice Darling (appointed to the Bench in 1897) 'would lie back in his chair staring at the ceiling with the back of his head cupped in his hands paying scant attention to any argument but waiting until some footling little joke occurred to his mind. When this happened he would make the joke, the court would echo for about thirty seconds with sycophantic laughter, and then the process would start over again.'[25]

The nature of much 'laughter in court' was similar a century earlier in proceedings before Lord Eldon (Lord Chancellor 1801–6 and 1807–27). 'Whenever it was indicated, by a peculiar elevation of his eye-brow, that he meant to be jocular, it is said that the gentlemen of the Chancery Bar were thrown into an ecstasy of mirth, and those most anxious to have the "ear of the Court" were guilty, by premeditation, of seemingly involuntary indecorum.'[26] During a House of Commons debate in 1906 on the injudicious conduct of Mr Justice Grantham, the Attorney-General, Sir John Walton, stated some eternal truths about much judicial humour. It 'proverbially occupies a very low place in the classification of wit. Its scintillations gain immensely by their setting and surroundings. They are emanations from a superior sphere, and are accepted and enjoyed and condoned by those who are compelled to listen to them. They are very seldom enjoyed by both parties to a cause. The wit is generally exercised at the expense of the party, or the witnesses of the party who is supposed at the time not to have the favourable consideration of the Court.'[27]

If a judge is tempted to perform a stand-up comic routine while sitting on the Bench, he should remember that the Strand courts are a long way in purpose, although close in distance, from the old Holborn Empire. He should bear in mind that the litigants cannot give the traditional responses of a dissatisfied audience: they can neither boo nor walk out nor decline to book seats for the next show, even though, from their point of view, the jokes may be in very poor taste. In Henry Fielding's *Tom Jones*, Lord Justice Page was the judge at the trial of a man charged with stealing a horse. When the judge made a joke, 'everybody fell a-laughing, as how could they help it? ... The fellow was hanged.'[28] The layman's view of much judicial humour is indicated by Evelyn Waugh's description of the response of a jury hearing a libel claim brought by him in 1957. The jury 'were not at all amused by the judge. All the £300 a day barristers rocked with laughter at his sallies. [The members of the jury] glowered. That was not what they paid a judge for, they thought.'[29] They may well not have found the jokes particularly funny. According to his biographer, 'the best joke ... ever heard in a law court' by Sir Edward Marshall Hall (one of the legendary advocates of this century) occurred in 1913. A jockey who had failed to weigh in after a race left the witness box before F. E. Smith (one of the counsel) had the chance to question him. 'Wait a moment,' said the judge, Mr Justice Darling, 'Mr Smith has not weighed in yet.'[30]

When judges are themselves the victims of such behaviour, they appreciate its disruptive effect. During a hearing before the Judicial Committee of the Privy Council in 1926, Lord Darling (as the judge had by then become) 'interrupted the closely woven argument of [a barrister], which he did not appear to have been following, with a quotation from *The Compleat Angler*. Lord Sumner was so cross that he threw the book he was looking at onto the floor.'[31]

Judicial humour can turn into judicial scorn. The eighteenth-century Scottish judge, Lord Braxfield, was 'a disgrace to the age'. He took pleasure in 'tauntingly repelling the last despairing claim of a wretched culprit, and sending him to Botany Bay or the gallows with an insulting jest'.[32] Robert Louis Stevenson based Lord Hermiston upon Braxfield. In court, Hermiston 'took his ease and jested, unbending in that solemn place with some of the freedom of the tavern; and the rag of man [the defendant] was hunted gallowsward with jeers'.[33] Braxfield and his contemporaries have a special place in the annals of judicial misbehaviour. They were 'cynically indifferent to the proprieties of the Bench to an extent which now may well seem incredible. Uncouth in appearance, profane in speech, frequently harsh and contemptuous in the discharge of their judicial functions, addicted to the wildest eccentricities, and exhibiting at all times a decided penchant for deep potation and the coarse and boisterous jocularity of the tavern . . .', they lacked all judicial qualities.[34]

A judge may disrupt proceedings by saying too much of relevance to the case before him. Mr Justice Roxburgh sat in the Chancery Division of the High Court from 1946 to 1960. His obituary mentioned that 'his many interruptions and interlocutory observations often hampered and embarrassed counsel in the conduct of a case'. It then surprisingly suggested that 'the difficulties might well have been overcome had he been promoted to a higher Court'.[35] In extreme cases appeal courts will intervene in relation to such a judge. Mr Justice Hallett 'was not a good listener, either in private or in public'.[36] He became known as 'the judge who talked too much'.[37] In one case the Court of Appeal ordered a new trial after complaints that the nature and extent of the judge's interruptions during the hearing of the evidence had made it impossible for the barristers to present their case properly.[38] Occasionally, members of the judiciary will attempt to remedy the loquacious nature of their colleague. In 1935 Lord Dunedin wrote to tell Lord Chancellor Hailsham that Lord Thankerton, a Lord of Appeal, was 'making himself a veritable nuisance by excessive talking. I was asked to speak to him, and did quite lately. He took it quite well, but I hear . . . that instead of being better he is worse than ever.'[39]

There are many other ways in which judges can disrupt the fair administration of justice. At the end of the last century Mr Justice Hawkins habitually shut down his Court on Derby Day.[40] When his Court was open he had 'no notion of what justice meant or of the obligations of truth and fairness'.[41] Lord Chief Justice Saunders (who held that office in 1683) 'was a fetid mass that offended his neighbours . . . in the sharpest degree. Those whose ill-fortune it was to stand near him were confessors, and in summer-time almost martyrs.'[42] Lord Birkett described how in 1942 Mr Justice Charles 'smokes in the [assize] procession . . ., belched from beer' in the assize sermon, and was generally 'a domineering, vulgar, unjust and decrepit old man who is a blot on the administration of justice'.[43] At the end of the nineteenth century, Mr Justice Ridley 'had a perverse instinct for unfairness'.[44] Lord Hewart 'lacked only the one quality which should distinguish a judge: that of being judicial . . . The opening of a case had only to last for five minutes before one could feel—and sometimes actually see—which side he had taken; thereafter the other side had no chance.'[45]

A long day in court can make the judge very irritable. Sir John Leach (Master of the Rolls 1827–34) was so habitually rude to the Bar that a delegation of leading barristers protested to him.[46] Lord Chancellor Campbell (who held that office from 1859 to 1861) was sometimes unable to control his irritability. 'Wearied out by the prolixity of an eminent and imperturbable counsel, and having exhausted his usual phrases of disgust, he got up from his seat and marched up and down the Bench, casting at intervals the most furious glances at the offender.'[47] Mr Justice North was appointed to the Queen's Bench Division of the High Court in 1881. 'After some ill-judged observations on the conduct of a member of the North-Eastern Circuit, the members of the [Bar] mess decided not to appear before him until he had withdrawn his remarks.' In 1883 he was transferred to the Chancery Division (where the barristers were presumably more tolerant).[48] Mr Justice Scrutton was so rude to barristers and to solicitors' clerks just after his appointment to the Bench in 1910 that the main City solicitors briefed a barrister to make a protest to him in Court. 'Scrutton listened without comment but showed proof of his penitence in his subsequent conduct.'[49] Sir Edward Marshall Hall KC was often irritated by judicial conduct into losing his temper in court. Some of the judges with whom he quarrelled 'were equally to blame for their inconsiderate behaviour and hasty words, and one of them at least was thought at the time to be animated by malice'.[50]

Goaded beyond endurance by Lord Chief Justice Hewart in 1928, Serjeant Sullivan threw down his papers and walked out of Court, followed by junior counsel and his client.[51] Barristers should be cautious in following such a precedent. The Court of Appeal has emphasized that 'only a very strong case indeed would justify a refusal by a party to continue to take part in the trial'.[52] Appeal courts are not always willing to impose sanctions on judges who indicate their irritation with barristers. In 1968 the Court of Criminal Appeal heard an appeal against a conviction and sentence in the Middlesex Quarter Sessions. Lord Justice Widgery noted that when one barrister was about to begin a protracted speech, the Chairman 'observed in a loud voice, "Oh, God", and then laid his head across his arm and made groaning noises . . . It is said that throughout the speech the Chairman kept sighing and groaning'. The Court of Criminal Appeal held that, although 'we could not possibly condone' the conduct of the Chairman, it was not conduct which could cause the conviction to be unsafe or unsatisfactory. So the appeal was dismissed.[53]

Judges occasionally lose patience with the careful deliberations of a jury. In 1960 the Court of Criminal Appeal quashed the convictions of three defendants because the trial judge had made a 'threat (and we regret we can call it nothing else)' to the jury. After the jury had been considering its verdict for over two hours, the judge called them back into court and told them that he had 'disorganized my travel arrangements out of consideration for you pretty considerably already. I am not going to disorganize them any further. In ten minutes I shall leave this building and if, by that time, you have not arrived at a conclusion in this case you will have to be kept all night and we will resume this matter at quarter to twelve tomorrow.' The jury returned with verdicts of guilty six minutes later.[54]

Other judges are unwilling or unable to give judgment on matters argued before them. In 1823 Lord Eldon was asked to give a decision in a case he had heard in 1817. He had 'entirely forgotten it' and so it had to be reargued.[55] He began his judgment in another case by remarking that 'having had doubts upon this will for twenty years, there can be no use in taking more time to consider it'.[56] Eldon's defence for such delay was that he 'always thought it better to allow myself to doubt before I decided, than to expose myself to the misery, after I had decided, of doubting whether I had decided rightly and justly'.[57] William Hazlitt was unconvinced. He described Eldon as a judge who 'hugs indecision to his breast and takes home a modest doubt or a nice point to solace himself with it in protracted, luxurious dalliance. Delay seems, in his mind, to be of the very essence of justice. He no more hurries through a question than if no one was waiting for the result and he was merely a *dilettanti*, fanciful judge, who played at my Lord Chancellor, and busied himself with quibbles and punctilios as an idle hobby and harmless illusion'.[58]

Some judges strive hard to perform their job fairly and properly but are unable to do so because of infirmity. In March 1890 Sir James Fitzjames Stephen became incapable of acting in a judicious manner by reason of mental illness. 'It was even said that he once started to sum up at a criminal trial without calling on the defence.'[59] He resigned in April 1891. More recently, a few judges have been unable adequately to perform their duties because of physical or mental illness.[60] When a High Court Judge 'lost his faculties' in the 1950s and resisted the 'pressure . . . put on him by his brethren to retire from the bench . . . no work was assigned to him'. He had no alternative but to resign.[61] On a more mundane but equally unfortunate level, deafness sometimes inhibits the proper performance of the judicial role. In 1826 an Irish barrister petitioned the House of Commons complaining that an 85-year-old Irish judge, Lord Norbury, was 'so deaf that he could hardly hear anything that passed in his court'. Since the judge was about to retire, the House of Commons declined to act.[62]

The student of the judiciary inevitably concludes that there have been many bad and some appalling judges, with all manner of defects, administering justice over the centuries. Macaulay rightly explained that 'the earlier volumes of the State trials are the most frightful record of baseness and depravity in the world. Our hatred is altogether turned away from the crimes and the criminals, and directed against the law and its ministers. We see villanies as black as ever were imputed to any prisoner at any bar daily committed on the bench and in the jury-box'.[63]

Of course, standards have much improved. But whatever methods of judicial appointment we adopt, it is inevitable that in each generation some incapable or inadequate judges will sit on the Bench. The 1972 Report of a Justice Sub-Committee commented that 'it would be inappropriate to particularise instances of alleged [judicial] misbehaviour, although we all have no doubt that instances occur suffi-ciently often to justify our consideration of the problem . . . Every practising member of the [legal] profession is familiar with a number of bad cases'.[64] Contemporaneous published accounts of judicial imperfections are rare. Private com-ments by lawyers and litigants become public only in memoirs which appear long after they could have any beneficial effect on the conduct of the particular errant judge. Even if judges were all blessed with the wisdom of Solomon and the patience of Job, there would always exist aggrieved litigants whose confidence in the legal system depended on the existence of independent complaints procedures.

III

Some judges have received more than their just deserts for injudicious behaviour. In the thirteenth century, Andrew Horn alleged that in one year (four centuries earlier) King Alfred caused forty-four judges to be 'hanged as homicides for their false judgments'.[65] In 1381 a mob pursued the Lord Chancellor, Simon de Sudbury, and cut off his head.[66] One year later, Lord Chief Justice Cavendish was killed after being apprehended by a mob and subjected to a mock trial in which he was sentenced to death.[67] In 1688 the infamous Judge Jeffreys, by then the Lord Chancellor, went into hiding when James II fled the country. Jeffreys was captured in Wapping when he was recognized in a tavern by a man who had been a dissatisfied litigant in his court. (The man had won his case but Jeffreys had been rude to him and kept him waiting.) Jeffreys was put in the Tower of London, where he died in 1689.[68] At the summer assizes in Oxford in 1577, during the trial of a bookseller for uttering scandalous words about the Queen, Chief Baron Bell and everyone else in court became fatally ill, 'arising, it was believed, from the stench of the prisoners'.[69] Baron Flowerdew suffered a similar fate at the Exeter assizes in 1586, as did Baron Pengelly at Taunton in 1730.[70] Gaol fever killed a number of judges at the Old Bailey sessions in 1750.[71]

Such examples of the litigant's revenge have been rare in English history. Judges have been removed from office on very few occasions. The judicial scandal of the late thirteenth century involved the corruption, due to low pay, of many officials. Edward I appointed a commission of inquiry which led to the dismissal of two out of three judges of the Court of King's Bench and four out of five judges of the Court of Common Pleas.[72] Sir William De Thorpe, Chief Justice, was convicted of accepting bribes in 1350 and removed from office.[73] Lord Chancellor Bacon suffered the same fate for similar reasons in 1621. In 1725 Lord Chancellor Macclesfield resigned after being convicted of selling offices in the Court of Chancery. Lord Chancellor Westbury resigned in 1865 after abuses in the administration of bankruptcy were revealed.[74]

Judges of the High Court and Court of Appeal 'hold that office during good behaviour, subject to a power of removal by Her Majesty on an address presented to Her by

both Houses of Parliament'.[75] Similar provisions apply to
Law Lords.[76] Such protection of judicial tenure dates from
1700. 'The object of all this was to protect the Judges, not
from Parliament, but from the arbitrary and uncontrolled
discretion of the Crown.'[77] Sir Jonah Barrington, a Judge of
the High Court of Admiralty in Ireland, was removed from
office by these means in 1830 after being convicted of
appropriating for his own use funds paid into court. Since
1830 several other judges have been accused in the Houses
of Parliament of misconduct, but no judge has been
removed from office by these means since that date.[78]

Some judges have been required to resign in less than
satisfactory circumstances. After Mr Justice Hallett had
been criticized by the Court of Appeal for asking too many
questions,[79] Lord Kilmuir, the Lord Chancellor, 'sent for the
Judge. It was arranged that he should continue to sit for a
little while and then resign. That he did at the end of the
summer term.'[80] The resignation of Lord Atkinson as a Law
Lord in 1928 'was brought about in a strange way ... The
[Lord] Chancellor asked me to call upon him. I did call. He
said the scurrilous press of Quebec had abused the Privy
Council and said the members were all old fogies, that I was
the oldest of the old fogies and had better resign ... I did
so.'[81]

In one of the most extraordinary episodes ever involving
the English judiciary, the 77-year-old Mr Justice A. T.
Lawrence was appointed Lord Chief Justice in 1921 to
replace Lord Reading, who became Viceroy of India.
Gordon Hewart, the Attorney-General, wanted the post of
Chief Justice for himself, but (for political reasons) Lloyd
George, the Prime Minister, could not spare him. So a
shabby deal was done. Hewart remained in the House of
Commons, with the promise from Lloyd George that the
post of Chief Justice would be made available to him when

political considerations so allowed. To his credit, Lord Birkenhead, the Lord Chancellor, wrote to the Prime Minister explaining that such an arrangement 'would make the Lord Chief Justice a transient figure, subject to removal at the will of the Government of the day, and the creature of political exigency. I do not think that if such an arrangement were publicly discussed, it would be found capable of reasoned defence.' Lloyd George was not impressed by such reservations. He replied to Birkenhead, rather missing the point, that 'if it is contrary to the Judicature Acts to stipulate that high legal functionaries should not cling to their posts into years of decrepitude then it is high time these Acts were amended'.[82] A year after his appointment as Lord Chief Justice in 1921, Lawrence (by then Lord Trevethin) resigned to make way for Hewart. 'Trevethin, abandoned without ceremony, read of his own resignation in *The Times* . . .'.[83]

At the lower levels of the judicial hierarchy, security of tenure is less well protected by the law. Circuit judges sitting in County Courts and Crown Courts may be removed from office by the Lord Chancellor 'on the ground of incapacity or misbehaviour'.[84] Lay magistrates are appointed by the Lord Chancellor on behalf and in the name of the Queen, 'and a Justice so appointed may be removed from office in like manner'.[85]

In September 1985 a magistrate failed in her attempt to obtain judicial review of the Lord Chancellor's decision to dismiss her from the Bench for taking part in a Campaign for Nuclear Disarmament demonstration outside the court in which she dispensed justice and for refusing to promise not to do so again.[86] In principle, judicial review is available in respect of the Lord Chancellor's exercise of such powers. In 1852 Chief Justice Campbell considered the powers of the Lord Chancellor to remove a County Court judge from office. Lord Campbell said that the Lord Chancellor is 'subject to the control of this Court'. The Court would give relief if the victim judge could 'show that he was removed without notice of any charges against him, or without an opportunity of being heard in his defence, or that no evidence was adduced to support the charges, or that the complaints against him were not for inability or misbehaviour in his office, and were of such a nature that, if proved or admitted, they could not disqualify him for his office, or amount to inability or misbehaviour, within the meaning of the Act of Parliament'. However, as in other cases of judicial review, it is not for the Court to substitute its judgment for that of the authority empowered by Parliament. Furthermore, 'it is possible that a man may have valuable qualities and may be amiable in private life, and yet may be justly removed for inability and misbehaviour as a Judge'.[87]

The Lord Chancellor has specific powers to secure the removal from office of an infirm judge. Section 11 of the Supreme Court Act 1981 applies to High Court and Court of Appeal judges. It provides that if the Lord Chancellor is satisfied by means of a medical certificate that such a judge is disabled by permanent infirmity from the performance of the duties of his office and is for the time being incapacitated from resigning his office, then the Lord Chancellor may declare that judge's office to have been vacated. Such a declaration needs the concurrence of at least one other senior judge.[88] There are similar provisions relating to the infirmity of a Law Lord.[89] The Lord Chancellor was given such powers after the illness of a Court of Appeal judge who was so seriously incapacitated in 1970 that he was not able to resign for nearly a year.[90]

All judges appointed after 1959 are obliged to retire by the age of 75.[91] This has undoubtedly led to an improvement in the mental and physical vitality of the judiciary.

Much has changed in these respects in this century. When, in the 1860s, Lord Westbury asked Sir William Erle, who had recently retired from being Chief Justice of the Common Pleas, why he did not sit on the Judicial Committee of the Privy Council, Erle replied, 'Oh, because I am old and deaf and stupid.' Westbury was not convinced by this answer: 'But that's no reason at all,' he said, 'for I am old, and Williams is deaf and Colonsay is stupid and yet we make an excellent Court of Appeal.'[92]

The Lord Chancellor occasionally delivers a public reprimand to a judge who has acted foolishly. In November 1983 a Recorder sitting at a London Crown Court condemned as a 'public disgrace' a private prosecution of a woman accused of shoplifting. Lord Hailsham, the Lord Chancellor, wrote to the Chairman of the department store which had brought the prosecution to say that the Recorder's conduct was 'intemperate and made before he had heard the evidence in the case. It follows that his remarks should not have been made. I have written to him to this effect.'[93] More frequently, a complaint to the Lord Chancellor about judicial misbehaviour will bring no satisfactory remedy. Lord Hailsham explained that 'in a number of cases, although I seldom told the complainant that I had done so, I showed the complaint to the judge concerned. I thought it good for him both to see what was being said about him from the other side of the court, and how perhaps a lapse of manners or a momentary impatience could undermine confidence in his decision'.[94] Such a private discussion, uncommunicated to the complainant, would be unlikely to remove his sense of grievance.

The aggrieved litigant's remedies for injudicious behaviour by a judge are virtually non-existent. Judges do sometimes feel the need to speak out, without fear or favour and occasionally without adequate information or common sense, on issues which nobody has asked them to decide. The most notorious example in a criminal case in recent years was the attack made in 1970 by Mr Justice Melford Stevenson in sentencing Cambridge students convicted of criminal offences in relation to a demonstration at a hotel. The judge told the defendants that the sentences he was imposing 'would have been heavier had I not been satisfied that you have been exposed to the evil influence of some senior members of your university, one or two of whom I have seen as witnesses for the defence.'[95] In an indignant letter to *The Times*, six dons who had appeared as witnesses for the defence expressed their 'profound astonishment' at the charge which they 'emphatically denied'.[96]

What, then, can you do if a judge blames you for the ills of the world, with which you have not been formally charged and to which you would (if given the opportunity) plead not guilty? You certainly have no legal remedy against the unfair judge. You cannot appeal to the Court of Appeal since you were not a party to the case heard and decided by the judge and since he has not imposed any legal sanction on you. In any event, the appeal court would not deal with the substance of a complaint against an unfair judge. In 1970 the Court of Criminal Appeal stressed the 'very important distinction' between 'conduct on the part of the presiding judge which may be regarded as discourteous and may show signs of impatience—and, indeed, conduct which cannot be commended in any way', but which does not of itself give grounds for an appeal, and conduct which makes the Court proceedings so unsatisfactory that an appeal should be allowed.[97] The appeal court may well have difficulty in appreciating the extent of any injudicious behaviour by the trial judge. As counsel pointed out to the Court of Criminal Appeal, 'the transcript would not help, as the grimaces, gestures, sighs, groans and other asides do not appear on the record'.[98] The judicial performance of Lord Braxfield was malevolent in the extreme, but 'his misconduct was not so fully disclosed in formal decisions and charges, as it transpired in casual remarks and general manner'.[99]

You will be unable to bring a legal action against the rude or unfair judge. Lord Denning explained in a 1974 Court of Appeal decision that 'ever since the year 1613, if not before, it has been accepted in our law that no action is maintainable against a judge for anything said or done by him in the exercise of a jurisdiction which belongs to him. The words which he speaks are protected by an absolute privilege. The orders which he gives, and the sentences which he imposes, cannot be made the subject of civil proceedings against him. No matter that the judge was under some gross error or ignorance, or was actuated by envy, hatred and malice, and all uncharitableness, he is not liable to an action.'[100] Judges of a superior Court are so protected even when acting outside their jurisdiction, so long as it is a good-faith exercise of the office in the belief that the judge has jurisdiction over the matter. Judges of an inferior Court are not so immune if they act outside their jurisdiction, or if they act within their jurisdiction maliciously and without reasonable and probable cause.[101] We are a long way from the recent development in judicial liability in the USA. Some American judges have taken out malpractice insurance because of an increase in claims against them based on their Court decisions.[102]

The Ombudsman has no jurisdiction to consider a complaint of public humiliation and vexation by the antics of an unfair judge. The Parliamentary Commissioner Act 1967 states that among the matters not subject to investigation by the Ombudsman is 'the commencement or conduct of civil or criminal proceedings before any court of law in the United Kingdom'.[103] You may therefore be in the unhappy position of having had your personal or professional reputation damaged by judicial comments which you believe to be unjustified, which have been made in breach of the most elementary principles of natural justice (in that you had no notice of the charge and no chance to answer it), and which have received widespread publicity. Yet you have no effective remedy.

The English judiciary is, thankfully, now free from the type of scandals which continue to afflict the legal systems of other nations. In 1980 an Ohio judge was jailed for corruption in dispensing lenient sentences to women defendants in return for sexual favours.[104] In 1986 the Government of Ghana dismissed two High Court judges and a Circuit Court judge for alleged corruption, drunkenness, and incompetence.[105] In England people who come to Court, whether as litigants, witnesses, or lawyers, have different concerns about the quality of justice and the standards of the judges who dispense it. They want to be sure that they will be attentively listened to by a courteous tribunal which will not pass judgment except on the subject-matter of the case.

IV

In many parts of the world, individuals who are dissatisfied with judicial conduct have a right of access to a Judicial Ombudsman or a Judicial Performance Commission. The vast majority of American States have such mechanisms. The relevant bodies have the power to investigate whether the judge has acted in other than a judicial manner. In some jurisdictions they have the power to impose sanctions, including dismissal, on an errant judge. Many of these States give the accused judge the right of appeal to the

State Supreme Court, which has the power to reconsider any finding made and any sanction imposed. In 1980, for example, the Supreme Court of Wisconsin upheld the decision of the State judicial conduct panel that Christ T. Seraphim, a Circuit judge in the County of Milwaukee, had engaged in judicial misconduct. He was found guilty of, among other matters, 'unprivileged and nonconsensual physical contacts with offensive sexual overtones, the totality of which is gross personal misconduct' and of 'a temperament unsuited for judicial office', as illustrated by 'his berating and disparagement of defence counsel and defendants, his use of bail as an instrument of retaliation, his disrespect for other trial and appellate courts, his refusal to listen to defence arguments . . .'. The Supreme Court of Wisconsin suspended him from judicial office for three years without pay.[106]

The commissions or tribunals in different States vary in the scope of their jurisdiction, the procedure they adopt, the powers they possess, and the efficiency and competence they display. But they share four important objectives: to deter injudicious conduct; to provide a means by which judges can be disciplined in appropriate cases; to vindicate by an independent report a judge who has been unfairly criticized; and, most important of all, to enable aggrieved litigants or others to air their complaints.[107]

The English legal system would benefit from the introduction of a Judicial Performance Commission to carry out such functions. The existing mechanisms for considering complaints of injudicious behaviour on the Bench are plainly inadequate. Resistance to such a reform would not be based on the absence of such complaints or the adequacy of existing procedures. Rather, it would be said, such a reform would damage the independence of the judiciary.

Until the reign of George III, all judges were removable

from office on the death of the monarch. Such a principle was 'not without its advantages'[108] in ridding the courts of unsatisfactory judges. Indeed, Dr Johnson regretted the abolition of this principle. He believed that 'there is no reason why a Judge should hold his office for life, more than any other person in public trust ... It was desirable that there should be a possibility of being delivered from him by a new King.'[109]

Today, it is the received wisdom that judicial independence requires a large measure of judicial immunity from sanctions for injudicious conduct. The rationale for the present immunity of judges from legal sanctions for their conduct has been explained in the leading cases. In 1863 Mr Justice Crompton dismissed as stating no cause of action a claim brought against his colleague, Mr Justice Blackburn, by a dissatisfied litigant. Crompton J said that 'it is a principle of our law that no action will lie against a Judge of one of the superior courts for a judicial act, though it be alleged to have been done maliciously and corruptly ... The public are deeply interested in this rule, which, indeed, exists for their benefit, and was established in order to secure the independence of the Judges, and prevent their being harassed by vexatious actions.'[110] In 1974 Lord Denning suggested that judicial immunity from actions for damages exists 'not because the judge has any privilege to make mistakes or to do wrong. It is so that he should be able to do his duty with complete independence and free from fear.'[111] Lord Bridge gave a similar explanation in 1984: 'If one Judge in a thousand acts dishonestly within his jurisdiction to the detriment of a party before him, it is less harmful to the health of society to leave that party without a remedy than that nine hundred and ninety-nine honest judges should be harassed by vexatious litigation alleging malice in the exercise of their proper jurisdiction.'[112]

Such arguments are entirely unconvincing. The value of the principle of judicial independence is that it protects the judge from dismissal or other sanctions imposed by the Government or by others who disapprove of the contents of his decisions. But judicial independence was not designed as, and should not be allowed to become, a shield for judicial misbehaviour or incompetence or a barrier to examination of complaints about injudicious conduct on apolitical criteria. Lord Bridge failed to appreciate that a remedy for the injured party may be the best protection for other litigants who will come before the same judge in future cases. We should apply to judges the standards which they have, rightly, applied to other professional people. 'Numerous other professional men may fairly say that fear of a law-suit could impede their work and delay their making of crucial decisions. So far this suggestion has not impeded the judges from demanding reasonable standards of competence from solicitors, architects, surveyors and a host of others.'[113] That a man who has an arguable case that a judge has acted corruptly or maliciously to his detriment should have no cause of action against the judge is quite indefensible.

Nor can judicial independence be a reason in principle for rejecting a Judicial Performance Commission. The dangers of impeding the judicial function should not be exaggerated. Judges are experienced individuals, unlikely to be deterred from carrying out their job in a proper manner (which may well include trenchant criticisms of parties or their lawyers or witnesses) by the knowledge that a complaint may be made about them. In any event, the dangers of judicial pusillanimity are outweighed by the potential advantages of subjecting judicial conduct to the assessment of the outside observer. The layman's willingness to accept the result of his trial, civil or criminal, is a pre-condition for the survival of the rule of law. Such acceptance by the layman depends as much on the diligence, politeness, and fairness he believes he has received from the judge as it does on the legal quality of the decision made by the judge in his case. It therefore seems perverse to give one or more rights of appeal against the legal decision in the case, but no means by which the litigant's dissatisfaction with judicial conduct can be publicly ventilated and considered. In an age when people are less willing than ever before to accept uncritically the exercise of public powers, the reputation of the judiciary can only benefit from the creation of a Judicial Performance Commission.[114]

Judges are already vulnerable (in theory) to removal from office for bad behaviour or for infirmity. Subject to the law of contempt of court and the law of libel,[115] it is already open to the press and the public to state their dissatisfaction with a judge. Judicial performance is occasionally criticized by the Lord Chancellor. The operation of a Judicial Performance Commission would not create any further impediment to judicial independence provided two limitations were imposed on the powers of such a body.

First, the powers of a Judicial Performance Commission should be limited to considering complaints of injudicious conduct. It would be prohibited from investigating whether the judge reached the correct decision on a point of law. Appeal courts exist to analyse the decisions of the judge. But where the judge clearly erred in law, the Commission might be entitled to consider a complaint of judicial incompetence. In a 1982 case, a Crown Court judge fined a business man £2,000 for the offence of raping a 17-year-old girl, rather than sending him to prison, because the victim had been 'guilty of a great deal of contributory negligence' by hitch-hiking alone at night.[116] The sentence and the comments of the judge quite rightly provoked almost universal condemnation and repudiation by lawyers and by politicians of all parties. When a judge makes such a fundamental error of law, outraging professional and public opinion, he could usefully be asked to explain his conduct to the Commission.

A second limitation on the powers of the Commission would be that it could not impose any sanction. The Commission would carefully investigate complaints. It would then report its findings to the Lord Chancellor. This report would be published. Like the Ombudsman, the Commission would have no power other than the respect accorded to its published report by professional and lay opinion. The publication of a report would in most cases be sufficient to remedy and deter injudicious conduct. With these basic limitations, the Judicial Performance Commission would reconcile the preservation of judicial immunity from improper interference with the need for an independent forum for ventilating and examining complaints about judicial behaviour.

No doubt considerable discussion would be needed to determine the composition of a Judicial Performance Commission, the procedures it would adopt, and the matters with which it would be concerned. One difficult problem is what role such a Commission should play in respect of the out-of-court conduct of judges. The disciplinary powers of the Lord Chancellor over the minor judiciary necessarily extend to out-of-court behaviour which is incompatible with the holding of judicial office. It is as complex to assess what out-of-court conduct by a judge makes him unfit for office as it is to decide when judicial conduct in court is injudicious.

A habitual disregard for the law of the land, even on grounds of conscience, would make a judge unsuited for office. Isolated violations of the law might disqualify a judge, depending on the seriousness of the offence. No judge who commits a murder or a rape is likely thereafter to be fitted to dispense justice. That a judge is convicted for a parking offence is irrelevant to the performance of his job. It is the criminal offences between these extremes that pose difficulties, for example drunken driving or, even more seriously, causing death by dangerous driving. Whatever the appropriate sanction for such criminal offences, it does seem harsh to impose a principle of vicarious liability: in the mid-1970s, 'three women magistrates whose husbands had been convicted of offences ... were required to resign'.[117]

As difficult is the question what, if any, conduct which is not criminal but is contrary to moral conventions makes a person unfit to be a judge. Dr Johnson believed that a judge 'may play a little at cards for his amusement; but he is not to play at marbles or at chuck-farthing in the Piazza'.[118] In 1970 Henry Cecil (himself a County Court judge) suggested that a high standard of conduct was required of a judge. 'Plainly he must not visit disorderly houses or striptease shows or entertainments of that kind . . .'[119] According to a character in a Henry Cecil novel, 'a judge shouldn't be seen regularly at night clubs'.[120] Even after the decriminalization in 1967 of homosexual conduct between consenting male adults in private, 'in the few cases of this kind that were brought to [the Lord Chancellor's] attention the [magistrate] resigned'.[121] Similarly, 'a male transvestite who masqueraded in public in female clothing was required to resign because public confidence in the courts was likely to be weakened if it were known that justices behaved in this way, although transvestism is not an offence and may be regarded as a harmless activity'.[122]

Judges are responsible for interpreting and applying the law. They are not moral guardians to the community. It is therefore wrong that a judge can be required to resign for lawful practices of which the majority of people may morally disapprove.[123] In any event, what we lack at present are any consistent and open principles concerning the standards required of judges in their out-of-court conduct. Decisions are made within the Lord Chancellor's Department by reference to unpublished criteria which are not thereafter publicly explained or justified.

The Judicial Performance Commission could serve a valuable function in these respects. Litigants should have the power to refer to the Commission a complaint about the conduct of a judge. The Lord Chancellor should have such power, and should be obliged to exercise it prior to dismissing a judge. (This would not prevent a judge resigning to avoid publicity on the matter.) In May 1986 Lord Hailsham expressed support for the introduction of an independent complaints board to investigate the facts and make recommendations to the Lord Chancellor prior to the dismissal of a Circuit judge. He said (understandably) that he was troubled by the absence of a fair procedure at present.[124]

The jurisdiction of the Commission would need to cover all members of the judiciary and should not be confined to cases where the Lord Chancellor is contemplating dismissal. Whoever the complainant may be, and however high the judicial status of the investigatee, the value of the Commission would be in the presentation of a reasoned, public, and objective analysis of the relevant criteria and of the facts of the case.[125]

V

For Francis Bacon (himself one of the few judges in English history to bring disgrace to the Bench),[126] 'the place of justice is an hallowed place; and therefore not only the bench, but the foot-pace and precincts and purprise thereof, ought to be preserved without scandal and corruption'.[127] The creation of a Judicial Performance Commission, with limited jurisdiction and powers, would serve this important goal without threatening the independence of the judiciary. The overwhelming majority of our judges do a difficult job extremely well and have nothing to fear from the existence of a Commission. The case for such a Commission is that it would help to ensure that all judges truly did hold office 'during good behaviour' and were seen and recognized to do so.

CHAPTER 5

Criticism

I

IN 1527 Serjeant Roo, 'a great lawyer of that time, more eager to show his wit than to be made a Judge', composed a satire on the abuses of the law for which Lord Chancellor Wolsey was responsible. The satire was delivered in the presence of the King. Roo was summarily dispatched to prison.[1] Nowadays a more tolerant attitude is taken towards critics of the judiciary. Nevertheless, lawyers and non-lawyers remain reluctant to emulate the critical approach of Serjeant Roo.

Laymen treat judges as a priestly caste to whom they are reluctant to apply the standards of criticism imposed on other public servants. Lawyers tend to be conservative in their attitudes in this as in other respects. The iron of the doctrine of precedent has entered into their souls. If they do have suggestions for reform of the judiciary, or comments to make on judicial performance, they whisper them to each other over lunch in the Middle Temple or in professional journals remote from the public gaze. Such heresies are expressed cautiously, in deferential language: 'in my respectful submission, the learned Judge erred as to fact or law.'

In one case, after Lord Mansfield (Chief Justice of the King's Bench 1756–88) had given judgment for a Bench of four judges, he asked Serjeant Hill, who appeared for the unsuccessful party, to 'tell us your real opinion and whether you don't think we are right'. Hill replied that 'he always thought it his duty to do what the Court desired and . . . he . . . did not think that there were four men in the world who could have given such an illsounded judgment . . .'.[2] More often, it is only in fiction that the conventions of politeness to judges are defied. The judges before whom John Mortimer's Rumpole appears are perverse and malign. They are ignorant of the ways of the world. They are deferential or rude to witnesses depending on the social status of those who have the misfortune to give evidence in their courts. Typical of the judges with whom Rumpole comes into daily contact is His Honour Judge Bullingham: he has unpleasant 'personal habits such as picking his teeth and searching in his ear with his little finger while on the Bench' and he has an 'unreasoning prejudice against all black persons, defence lawyers and probation officers'.[3] Only a barrister of Rumpole's experience (and lack of ambition) can afford to reply in kind to the discourtesy emanating from that fictional Bench.[4]

There is, by custom, a Judicial Secrets Act, imposing a twenty-year rule. Only after the expiry of that period is it considered appropriate to discuss in public the inadequacies of those non-fictional judges who have long since handed down their final judgments.

II

The use of vigorous language may cause problems for critics of the judiciary. For accusing two judges of 'oppression' and because he already had a criminal record, Nathaniel Redding found in 1680 that 'the gentlemen at the Bar did pray that his gown might be pulled over his ears (he having been formerly a practiser at the Bar) which was ordered and executed in Court, and he was also condemned in Court to pay the King £500 and lie in prison till he paid it'.[5] Two centuries later a Nova Scotia lawyer wrote a letter to the Chief Justice complaining (as many lawyers have privately believed before and since) that 'I can't help thinking that I am not fairly dealt with by the Court or Judges, and that the well-beaten track is often departed from for some bye-way to defeat me . . .'. He added that he 'could also recall cases where the decision was, I believe, largely influenced, if not wholly based, upon information received privately from the wife of one of the parties by the Judge. Is this justice?' Lord Westbury replied, in the Judicial Committee of the Privy Council, that this 'undoubtedly was a letter of a most reprehensible kind . . . a contempt of court, which it was hardly possible for the Court to omit taking cognizance of'.[6]

If a barrister is going to write to a judge concerning a case in which he has appeared, he would be wise to avoid 'using expressions in the letter which no gentleman could permit to be used towards himself' and making a 'threat, the object of which is to induce the [judge] to alter the opinion he was supposed to have formed'. In 1837 such conduct was held by Lord Chancellor Cottenham to be 'a contempt of the highest order'. The unfortunate barrister was sent to prison. He remained there for three weeks, no doubt restraining the expression of his true feelings in deference to the Lord Chancellor's judgment that 'every insult offered to a Judge in the exercise of the duties of his office is a contempt'.[7]

Critical lawyers have had a variety of sanctions imposed on them. When in the early nineteenth century the barrister Henry Brougham persisted in his proposals for law reform, solicitors threatened him with a professional boycott.[8] He survived to become Lord Chancellor. In the early years of the nineteenth century, Lord Chancellor Eldon denied the rank of King's Counsel to eminent barristers for political reasons.[9] In 1953 a barrister was suspended from practice for four months by the Benchers of his Inn for 'conduct unbecoming a barrister' in suggesting (as was indeed the case) that many lawyers believed Lord Chief Justice Goddard to be other than 'a model of courtesy, fairness and impartiality' in his conduct of criminal trials.[10]

Hazlitt records how Lord Eldon was irritated by a newspaper report of criticism of him in the House of Commons. He came into court, 'fire in his eyes and a direct charge of falsehood in his mouth, without knowing anything certain of the matter, without making any inquiry into it, without using any precaution or putting the least restraint upon himself'.[11] Eldon took the view that Parliamentary criticism of the courts was intolerable. In 1825 two barristers who were Members of Parliament brought forward a motion criticizing the Chancery Court. Eldon wrote to the Home Secretary, Peel, asking

can it possibly be endured that a barrister, because he happens to be a member of the House of Commons, . . . is to hold a surveillance over the highest court of justice in the kingdom and . . . to attack the characters of the Judges of that court? And call upon the Judges annually to explain their conduct, which he can't possibly understand? Can any man remain a Judge in that court under such circumstances? . . . It is impossible to submit, with any comfort, to this sort of degradation . . .[12]

There remain strict limits to the 'degradation' which can be imposed on a judge by criticism in Parliament. In 1973 the Speaker of the House of Commons ruled that 'it can be argued that a judge has made a mistake, that he was wrong, and the reasons for those contentions can be given, within certain limits'. The limits are that 'no charge of a personal nature can be raised except on a motion. Any suggestion that a judge should be dismissed can be made only on a motion.'[13] Therefore when, in 1980, a Member of Parliament called Lord Diplock (a Law Lord) 'a Tory judge', the Speaker intervened. 'It is wrong', he pronounced, 'for any of us to attribute to any judge a bias. . . . I deprecate calling judges by anything other than "the judge". . . . I have made it clear that I consider, and in future I shall so rule, that it is offensive to refer to a judge of the High Court in any way other than as a judge of the High Court. It is not for us to add an adjective. Otherwise we shall be lowering our parliamentary standards.'[14]

In previous decades the branch of contempt of court known as 'scandalizing the judiciary' served to inhibit criticism of the courts by laymen. To a limited extent it remains a fetter on freedom of expression about judicial performance. 'Any act done or writing published calculated to bring a Court or a judge of the Court into contempt, or to lower his authority, is a contempt of court.'[15] Scottish law has a similar offence of 'murmuring judges'.

In an early case, a pamphleteer was accused of contempt for describing Lord Mansfield as acting 'officiously, arbitrarily and illegally' in court. Mr Justice Wilmot (in an opinion which was undelivered because the prosecution was dropped) explained the purpose of this law:

The arraignment of the justice of the Judges is arraigning the King's justice; it is an impeachment of his wisdom and goodness in the choice of his Judges, and excites in the minds of the people a general dissatisfaction with all judicial determinations and indisposes their minds to obey them; and whenever men's allegiance to the laws is so fundamentally shaken, it is the most fatal and most dangerous obstruction of justice, and, in my opinion, calls out for a more rapid and immediate redress than any other obstruction whatsoever; not for the sake of the Judges, as private individuals, but because they are the channels by which the King's justice is conveyed to the people.[16]

In 1788 Mr Justice Buller expressed similar sentiments:

Nothing can be of greater importance to the welfare of the public than to put a stop to the animadversions and censures which are so frequently made on courts of justice in this country. They can be of no service, and may be attended with the most mischievous consequences. . . . When a person has recourse . . . by publications in print, or by any other means, to calumniate the proceedings of a Court of justice, the obvious tendency of it is to weaken the administration of justice, and in consequence to sap the very foundation of the Constitution itself.[17]

The grandiloquent fear that criticism of the courts may endanger civilization has, in the twentieth century, continued to lead to the punishment of persons who have insulted members of the judiciary or impugned their impartiality.

In 1899 the Judicial Committee of the Privy Council heard a case concerning a newspaper the columns of which had accused the Acting Chief Justice of St Vincent of not deciding cases honestly and impartially, and described him as a 'briefless barrister, unendowed with much brain'. The Privy Council sensibly announced that 'committals for contempt of court by scandalising the court itself have become obsolete in this country. Courts are satisfied to leave to public opinion attacks or comments derogatory or scandalous to them.' (Less sensibly, the court added that 'in small colonies, consisting principally of coloured populations, the enforcement in proper cases of committal for contempt of court for attacks on the court may be absolutely necessary to preserve in such a community the dignity of and respect for the court'.)[18] It was soon demonstrated that the judgment of the Privy Council as to the obsolescence of the offence of scandalizing the judiciary was over-optimistic. English law remained unwilling to leave it to public opinion to assess whether criticism of the judiciary had any basis.

Mr Justice Darling was the presiding judge at the Birmingham Spring Assizes in 1900. Before the start of a trial for obscene libel, he warned the press that they should not publish indecent accounts of the evidence. After the conviction and sentence of the defendant in the criminal case, Mr Gray wrote and published in the *Birmingham Daily Argus*, of which he was the Editor, an article entitled 'A Defender of Decency'. The Law Reports say, sanctimoniously, 'it is thought unnecessary to set forth this article'.[19] Fortunately, a rival set of reports did not agree.

In his article, Gray described how Mr Justice Darling,

having so few prisoners to try in Birmingham, and feeling the inspiration strong upon him to be a terror to evildoers, filled in a pleasant five minutes yesterday. . . . If anyone can imagine Little Tich upholding his dignity upon a point of honour in a public-house, he has a very fair conception of what Mr Justice Darling looked like in warning the Press against the printing of indecent evidence. His diminutive Lordship positively glowed with judicial self-consciousness. . . . He felt himself bearing on his shoulders the whole fabric of public decency. . . . The terrors of Mr Justice Darling will not trouble the Birmingham reporters very much. No newspaper can exist except upon its merits, a condition from which the Bench, happily for Mr Justice Darling, is exempt. There is not a journalist in Birmingham who has anything to learn from the impudent little man in horsehair, a microcosm of conceit and empty-headedness. . . . One of Mr Justice Darling's biographers states that 'an eccentric relative left him much money'. That misguided testator spoiled a successful bus conductor. Mr Justice Darling would do well to master the duties of his own profession before undertaking the regulation of another.[20]

This splendid piece of invective effectively punctured the

vain pretensions of Mr Justice Darling whose injudicious behaviour on the Bench was frequently a disgrace. It was well known that 'in charges of less gravity he often allowed himself to behave with a levity quite unsuited to the trial of a criminal case. ... [He] frequently lost the respect of the jury to such an extent that they ignored or paid little attention' to him.[21]

Mr Gray's prose was not appreciated by the courts. He was brought before the Queen's Bench Division charged with contempt of court. He swore a grovelling affidavit of apology, no doubt on sensible legal advice that otherwise there would be even more serious consequences for him. He acknowledged that he had 'used language referring to Mr Justice Darling in terms which were intemperate, improper, ungentlemanly and void of the respect due to his Lordship's person and office'. He explained that he deeply regretted the publication of the article 'and the inexcusable and insulting language in which it referred to one of Her Majesty's Judges, and I humbly apologize to his Lordship and to the Court for my conduct, which I now upon consideration see reflected not only upon the individual judge but upon the Bench of judges and the administration of the courts and I submit myself to the merciful consideration of the Court'.

Lord Russell, the Lord Chief Justice, did not appreciate that it was these legal proceedings, rather than the original newspaper article, that brought discredit to the law. He gave a solemn judgment, noting that it was 'an article of scurrilous abuse of a judge in his character of judge — scurrilous abuse in reference to the conduct of a judge while sitting under the Queen's Commission, and scurrilous abuse published in a newspaper in the town in which he was still sitting under the Queen's Commission'. He concluded that there was no doubt that the article amounted to a contempt of court. But for the contrition of the defendant and his affidavit expressing regret, the judges thought that it would have been their 'duty to send Howard Alexander Gray to prison for a not inconsiderable period of time' for writing and publishing such a 'personal scurrilous abuse of a judge as a judge'. Instead, he was fined £100 and ordered to pay the costs.[22]

Another five successful prosecutions in England show the vitality of the offence of scandalizing the judiciary in the early decades of this century. There can be little doubt that the bringing of such prosecutions had an inhibiting effect on newspaper and magazine reporting of judicial affairs generally.

In 1922 a dissatisfied litigant who believed that the President of the Probate, Divorce and Admiralty Division of the High Court was a party to a conspiracy against him walked up and down outside the Law Courts with a placard accusing the judge of being 'a traitor to his duty'. He was sentenced to four months' imprisonment.[23] In 1925 another dissatisfied customer sent a letter to Mr Justice Roche, who had decided a case against him, accusing the judge of being 'a liar, a coward, a perjurer'. He too was held to be in contempt of court.[24]

In 1928 an article in the *New Statesman* accused Mr Justice Avory of 'prejudice' against the aims of Dr Marie Stopes (the birth-control pioneer) when presiding over a libel action brought against her. The article alleged that 'an individual owning to such views as those of Dr Stopes cannot apparently hope for a fair hearing in a Court presided over by Mr Justice Avory—and there are so many Avorys'. Lord Hewart, the Lord Chief Justice, held in the Divisional Court that the article was a contempt of court because it 'imputed unfairness and lack of impartiality to a judge in the discharge of his judicial duties. The gravamen of the offence was that by lowering his authority it interfered with the performance of his judicial duties.' Because the editor apologized, and because the article had been written in haste, the editor was not imprisoned and no fine was imposed.[25] In 1930 an article in the *Daily Worker* led to a sentence of imprisonment for contempt. It had stated that 'Rigby Swift, the judge who sentenced Comrade Thomas, was the bewigged puppet and former Tory Member of Parliament chosen to put Communist leaders away in 1926. The defending counsel, able as he was, could not do much in the face of the strong class bias of the judge and jury.'[26]

The most recent conviction in England for contempt by scandalizing the judiciary occurred in 1931. The editor of a magazine was fined for publishing an article alleging that 'Lord Justice Slesser . . . can hardly be altogether unbiased about legislation of this type'. The judge had, as Solicitor-General, steered the relevant legislation through Parliament.[27]

More recently, courts have emphasized that only in very exceptional cases will charges of contempt of court be brought against those who criticize the judiciary. Lord Atkin explained in a 1936 Privy Council decision that

whether the authority and position of an individual judge, or the due administration of justice, is concerned, no wrong is committed by any member of the public who exercises the ordinary right of criticising, in good faith, in private or public, the public act done in the seat of justice. The path of criticism is a public way: the wrong-headed are permitted to err therein; provided that members of the public abstain from imputing improper motives to those taking part in the administration of justice, and are genuinely exercising a right of criticism, and not acting in malice or attempting to impair the administration of justice, they are immune. Justice is not a cloistered virtue: she must be allowed to suffer the scrutiny and respectful, even though outspoken, comments of ordinary men.[28]

The Privy Council there allowed an appeal against a conviction for contempt by the editor of a newspaper which had published an article criticizing the disparity in sentences given in the courts for comparable offences.

Very similar comments were expressed by the Court of Appeal in 1968. A private individual began contempt proceedings against Mr Quintin Hogg MP (later Lord Chancellor Hailsham) in respect of an article he had written in *Punch* magazine criticizing decisions of the Court of Appeal on gaming law. He had written that the governing legislation was 'rendered virtually unworkable by the unrealistic, contradictory, and, in the leading case, erroneous, decisions of the courts'. The article suggested that the Court of Appeal should apologize for the expense and trouble to which it had put the police. The Court of Appeal held that this was not a contempt of court. 'We do not fear criticism, nor do we resent it,' said Lord Denning. 'It is the right of every man, in Parliament or out of it, in the Press or over the broadcast, to make fair comment, even outspoken comment, on matters of public interest.'[29]

Although 'nothing really encourages courts or Attorneys-General to prosecute cases of this kind in all but the most serious examples, or courts to take notice of any but the most intolerable instances',[30] the offence of scandalizing the judiciary does survive as an unjustifiable impediment to freedom of speech about the judiciary. The continued existence of the offence, and the memory of successful prosecutions, inhibits journalists, who wrongly suspect that they have a legal obligation to speak respectfully and cautiously when discussing the judiciary. In fact, there is little danger of a prosecution nowadays for criticizing the judiciary, irrespective of the ferocity of the language used, unless one suggests that the court lacks impartiality. The principle of tolerance formulated by Lord Atkin carefully extends only to those who 'abstain from imputing improper motives to those taking part in the administration of justice'.[31]

The offence of scandalizing the judiciary has remained very much alive in Commonwealth countries. In 1935 the High Court of Australia held in contempt a newspaper article which had criticized High Court decisions as, amongst other things, displeasing 'everybody except the Little Brothers of the Soviet and kindred intelligentsia'. Mr Justice Rich said that 'such imputations, if permitted, could not but shake the confidence of litigants and the public in the decisions of the Court and weaken the spirit of obedience to the law'. The editor was fined £50 and the newspaper company was fined £200.[32] In 1969 the New Brunswick Supreme Court, Appeal Division, in Canada, held that an article in a student magazine was in contempt because of its 'malignment' of a judge and its 'most uncalled for attack on the integrity of the Courts of New Brunswick'. The article had alleged that the impugned judge's court was 'a mockery of justice' and that the courts in New Brunswick were 'simply the instruments of the corporate elite'.[33]

In 1970 the Supreme Court of India upheld the contempt conviction of the Chief Minister of Kerala. He was found guilty of 'lowering the prestige of Judges and Courts in the eyes of the people' by telling a press conference that

judges are guided and dominated by class hatred, class interests and class prejudices and where the evidence is balanced between a well-dressed pot-bellied rich man and a poor ill-dressed and illiterate person the Judge instinctively favours the former . . .[34]

Other critics of the judiciary have come uncomfortably close to conviction. In 1950 a newspaper article criticized the appointment of a particular lawyer to the Supreme Court of Victoria, Australia: 'He is a die-hard tory. . . . Such an appointment throws a clear light upon the nature of the judiciary—namely an institution forming an integral part of the repressive machinery of the State.' In dismissing the consequent contempt charge, O'Bryan J generously concluded that he was not satisfied that the purpose of the article was to suggest bias or to lower the authority of the court.[35] In 1970 a law lecturer was charged with contempt for writing an article published in the South African Law Journal suggesting that large numbers of advocates believed that judges deliberately took race into account in sentencing on capital charges. Claassen J, in the Transvaal Provincial Division, held the article not to be in contempt (although 'the representative of the State cannot be blamed for having brought this matter to Court') because he accepted the defendant's evidence 'that at no time did he have any intention of reflecting improperly on the Judges or the administration of justice and that he had always held them in the highest esteem'.[36]

The real dangers of alleging judicial bias, even in the 1980s, are demonstrated by a recent decision of the High Court of Australia. The secretary of a trade union was imprisoned for contempt of court. His appeal to the Federal Court succeeded. He immediately gave a press conference in which he expressed his appreciation for the support shown by the members of his trade union. He added that he believed that the strikes which had occurred in support of his appeal 'had been the main reason for the court changing its mind'. The Federal Court held this to be a further contempt and sentenced him to three months' imprisonment. The High Court refused him leave to appeal on the ground that he was clearly guilty of contempt. He was 'insinuating that the Federal Court had bowed to outside pressure in reaching its decision . . . What was imputed was a grave breach of duty by the court. The imputation was of course unwarranted.'[37]

In the absence of an allegation of bias, or other improper motive, the offence of scandalizing the judiciary is obsolete in England. Mr Gray's attack on Mr Justice Darling would not now lead to a prosecution. If it did, it would be unlikely to lead to a conviction. Gone are the days of the early seventeenth century when 'a Catholic gentleman nearly eighty years old' received a sentence that he 'should be fined £1000, lose his ears, stand on the pillory at Westminster and Lancaster, and suffer perpetual imprisonment, for merely presenting a respectful petition to the King, praying for inquiry into the conduct of one of the Judges of assize, who had condemned to death a neighbour for entertaining a Jesuit'.[38]

Although criticizing judges out of court may now be less dangerous, contempt of court still has its penalties for those who are unable to control their emotions in court.[39] When a jury found a defendant not guilty of high treason in 1796, 'there was a considerable shout in the Hall; and a man of the name of Thompson jumping up in the middle of the court waving his hat and hallooing was taken into custody and fined £20'.[40] In 1888 a solicitor was held to be in contempt of court for interrupting a judge while he was giving judgment by saying, 'That is a most unjust remark.'[41] In 1893 Lord Chief Justice Coleridge ordered the detention of a youth for disturbing a court hearing by applauding from the public gallery. (The youth was released at the end of the day's proceedings.)[42] In 1964 a litigant whose submissions had not found favour with the Court of Appeal decided it would be more persuasive to remove all his clothes except his shirt and to lie down on a bench at the front of the court. He was imprisoned for a week.[43] A defendant in a criminal trial was held to be in contempt of court in 1974 for shouting from the dock, on his conviction, that it was a 'carve up'.[44]

Minor judges have been known to abuse the contempt of court jurisdiction in an attempt to enhance their own dignity. In 1926 a County Court judge fined a man who had inadvertently failed to remove his hat on entering the court.[45] In 1972 a witness in a Scottish trial returned to the public benches in court after giving his evidence. When the prosecutor summed up the evidence, the witness shook his head, without making any noise. The judge told him: 'It is not for you to shake your head at what you hear in this court.' He was fined £10 for contempt. The High Court of Justiciary allowed an appeal, concluding that no contempt had been committed.[46]

In 1970 the Court of Appeal, New South Wales, Australia, declined to interfere with a sentence of fourteen days' imprisonment imposed by a magistrate on defendants who, on entering the courtroom to answer a criminal charge of trespass, 'made a gesture by raising [their] left arm with the hand or fist clenched'. The magistrate found this conduct to be a contempt of court, despite the defendants' explanation that the gesture was 'an international symbol of solidarity in the oppression of justice'. The Court of Appeal was unsympathetic to such a display. Awarding the defendants' silent and peaceful conduct a significance it could not otherwise have claimed, the judges asserted that the gestures 'were of a kind that has been in the past and, perhaps, is now associated with philosophies and attitudes which have consistently denied the rule of law which forms the basis of a truly democratic society'. Such 'gestures of defiance to the authority of the Court [may] ... have a tendency to lower the authority of the courts and to weaken the spirit of obedience to the law'.[47]

Courts should be wary of requiring an abnormal degree of self-control from those who attend proceedings. There was an astonishing episode in 1981 when a Durham Crown Court judge ordered a man to spend the weekend in gaol for contempt of court by throwing up his arms to celebrate his acquittal by a jury on two theft charges. The man was committed for contempt despite apologizing and explaining that 'it was just the excitement of getting off. I've been in custody for five months.' The judge took a stern view: such behaviour was an 'insolent contempt'.[48] Perhaps the judge had taken seriously one of A. P. Herbert's *Misleading Cases* where the 'editor' makes a footnote reference to '*Marrable v Rowntree*, where the jury, on being discharged, sang "For he's a jolly good fellow", and were committed for contempt'.[49]

Not everyone will share the belief of Chief Justice Erle, expressed in an 1861 judgment, that 'the personal feelings of the Judges have never had the slightest influence in the exercise of these powers entrusted to them for the purpose of supporting the dignity of their important office; and so far as my observation goes they have been uniformly exercised for the good of the people'.[50]

III

Despite the perils of contempt of court, criticism of the judiciary was often fierce in previous decades. On the appointment to the Bench of Mr Justice Lawrance in 1890, the *Law Times* wrote that this was 'a bad appointment, for ... Mr Lawrance has no reputation as a lawyer, and has been rarely seen of recent years in the Royal Courts of Justice'. On the promotion of Mr Justice Ridley to the Bench in 1897, the *Law Journal* said that 'the appointment can be defended on no ground whatsoever'. As with appointments, so with the continuation on the Bench of judges who were no longer up to the job. In the 1890s the *Law Times* wrote of Mr Justice Hawkins that 'we do not hesitate to say that a judge who is of advanced age and crippled health rendering necessary neglect of his duty in order to recover in foreign climes should accept the pension which the law provides and give place to an efficient successor'.[51]

Legal journals refrain from expressing such views nowadays. This is not because all those appointed to the Bench are blessed with the requisite skills. Nor is it because judges always retire before they lose their judicial faculties. Even when a judge dies, 'the imperfections of his conduct on the bench will seldom be mentioned in his obituary, the biographer discreetly side-stepping the subject by recalling what a keen cricketer he was in his youth, how kind he was to animals, and how assiduously he collected Toby jugs or used postage stamps'.[52] Reticence overcomes the press in its coverage of the judiciary. It would consider laughable such treatment of Parliament, business, the Royal Family, or even the Church.

Perhaps because cogent criticism of the judiciary is now so rare, its appearance causes disproportionate excitement and leads otherwise sensible people to behave in irrational ways. Lord Goddard, Lord Chief Justice 1946–58, was a controversial judge and an unusual man. His biographer reports, without comment, that as a judge on the Northern Circuit

he was a frequent and popular guest in the Circuit Bar Mess and after dinner it was his wont to say, 'Now boys! What about a boat race?'. Whereupon seventeen members of the Circuit would arrange themselves sitting with him on the floor in the formation of two eights, each with a cox, in which positions to the great detriment of the seats of sixteen pairs of trousers (including the judicial trousers whose wearer always occupied the position of Stroke of one of the 'boats'), the competing eights shuffled backwards across the floor until one of them crossed as victors the imaginary finishing line.[53]

In court, Goddard's behaviour was even more extraordinary. His enthusiasm for capital punishment, corporal punishment, and the moral values of the Victorian age in which he had grown up made him a symbol of the establishment's losing battle against social change in the post-war world.

Yet even Lord Goddard's eminence can hardly account for the fact that after a critical article by Bernard Levin in the *Spectator* in 1958, the Attorney-General, Sir Reginald Manningham-Buller (later Lord Chancellor Dilhorne), wanted to prosecute Levin for contempt of court or for criminal libel.[54] Almost as astonishing was the outrage caused by a critical article on Lord Goddard written by Levin and published in *The Times* soon after Goddard's death in 1971. Levin wrote (with justification) that in one notorious murder case, Goddard's animus (as the trial judge) against the defendants 'was as undisguised as it was unjudicial ... Goddard not only behaved with vindictiveness, but injected a crude emotionalism into the case ... Goddard as Lord Chief Justice', concluded Levin, 'was a calamity . . . Goddard's influence on the cause of penal reform was almost unrelievedly malign'.[55] Angry letters to *The Times* from a number of senior judges (typified by the complaint of Lord Parker, who had succeeded Lord Goddard as Lord Chief Justice in 1958, about 'the shock and distress' he had suffered at reading the article)[56] suggested that judges are unaccustomed to critical comments on the public performance of their duties. In her autobiography, published in 1985, Dame Elizabeth Lane (Britain's first woman judge) announced that the article—she cannot bring herself to mention Levin by name—made her so furious that she 'vowed that I would never read another word the author wrote and I never have done'.[57]

In 1985 Lord Devlin wrote a book about the 1957 Old Bailey trial of Dr John Bodkin Adams, over which he had presided as the judge. Devlin's account was as much about Manningham-Buller, the Attorney-General who acted as prosecuting counsel, as it was about Bodkin Adams (who was acquitted of the charge of murdering one of his patients). Devlin explained that Dilhorne (as Manningham-Buller later became) had little discernible legal ability. Yet he became Lord Chancellor in 1962 and, surprisingly, in 1969 he was appointed as a Law Lord, which he remained until shortly before his death in 1980.

Devlin's critical assessment of Dilhorne's character ('what the ordinary careerist achieves by making himself agreeable, falsely or otherwise, Reggie achieved by making himself disagreeable'), his ability as a lawyer ('from the beginning a weak case was bungled'), and his temperament (he did not have 'a grain of judicial sense')[58] provoked strong criticism of Devlin by other judges. A former Court of Appeal judge, Sir Robin Dunn, wrote that Devlin's attack on Dilhorne's character and ability had caused much anguish to Dilhorne's family. Taking off the judicial gloves, he added that 'many of Lord Dilhorne's judgments will be remembered when the more obscure pronouncements of some who regarded themselves as his intellectual superiors are forgotten'.[59] Lords Scarman and Bridge, Law Lords, wrote a letter to the *Times Literary Supplement* stating that they had discussed Devlin's book with 'many lawyers who knew Lord Dilhorne' and that the 'unanimous opinion' of those lawyers (with whom Scarman and Bridge agreed) was that 'the posthumous attack on him by a former judicial colleague was deplorable'.[60]

As Devlin himself observed,[61] this defensive reaction to criticism of a judge is very odd. Dilhorne had died five years earlier. During his life he had spoken his mind, often in a controversial manner, and had expected others to do the same. No one would suggest that posthumous criticisms in similar terms—distressing though they may be to the subject's family—should not be expressed about a politician's public life and performance in a senior governmental position. Taking the judicial oath should give no immunity from criticism. Nor does it, especially twenty years after Devlin's retirement from the Bench in 1964, condemn someone who has been a judge to silence on a matter of public interest. In her autobiography Dame Elizabeth Lane suggested that there was an 'unbreakable tradition' that a judge, even after retirement, did not comment publicly on any other living judge.[62] The reaction to Devlin's book indicates that many judges would extend that restriction to comments on dead judges. Members of the judiciary should remember that they do not belong to a private club in which loyalty is the prime virtue. Nor are they members of a Cabinet with collective responsibility. They are independent, public figures with much to contribute in the public interest on many issues related to the administration of justice.[63] An enforced silence, restraining criticism of one judge by another, also has the regrettable consequence of devaluing the genuine praise of one judge for another. Why should we believe a laudatory obituary if we know that the author is prohibited by a binding convention from pointing to any blemishes?

Distinguished and otherwise sensible men and women continue to see criticism of judges as threatening to the good order of society. In 1971 Lord Shawcross (Attorney-

General 1945–51) was reported as defending the non-publication of a reasoned report by eminent lawyers and laymen critical of judicial administration and proposing reforms. The report[64] was by a Sub-Committee of *Justice* (the British Section of the International Commission of Jurists). The Sub-Committee was chaired by Peter Webster QC (now a High Court judge). Shawcross was concerned that the report could 'shake public confidence in the judiciary'.[65] The report was published with a foreword explaining that some members of the Council of *Justice* had strong reservations about the wisdom of 'engendering mistrust of the judiciary in those who, without reading the full Report, might draw unjustified inferences from the recommendations alone'.[66] The judiciary survived.

Academic lawyers should be in the forefront of reasoned criticism of the judiciary. Regrettably, many academics retain the conservatism of earlier generations of dons. In 1932 Harold Laski wrote to Mr Justice Holmes of the US Supreme Court about the views of the distinguished academic lawyer, William Holdsworth. According to Laski, Holdsworth had made a speech which 'went on the lines that the law teacher ought not to encourage criticism of the judiciary and its decisions in an age of scepticism, and produced the effect of a desire to fall flat on his face before a Law Lord'.[67]

Thankfully, some academics are prepared to say what they think about judicial decisions. In 1985 the House of Lords considered the issue of criminal liability for an attempt to commit an impossible crime (for example, when a pickpocket attempts to pick a pocket that is, unknown to him, empty).[68] The Law Lords produced such an inadequate judgment that Professor Glanville Williams, the leading academic authority in the field of criminal law, wrote a scathing attack on them:

The tale I have to tell is unflattering of the higher judiciary. It is an account of how the judges invented a rule based upon conceptual misunderstanding; of their determination to use the English language so strangely that they spoke what by normal criteria would be termed untruths; of their invincible ignorance of the mess they had made of the law; and of their immobility on the subject, carried to the extent of subverting an Act of Parliament designed to put them straight.[69]

In a judgment soon after, abandoning the approach which had been the subject of this rebuke, Lord Bridge grudgingly conceded that he had 'had the advantage' of reading the criticism, and that although the language used by Williams was 'not conspicuous for its moderation ... it would be foolish, on that account, not to recognise the force of the criticism and churlish not to acknowledge the assistance I have derived from it'.[70]

Criticism of judges by politicians produces the most extreme reaction from defenders of judicial sanctity. In 1979 a Sheriff Court in Scotland ruled that a young mother who had not taken a contraceptive pill should only receive £1 a week from the father of her illegitimate child because of her 'carelessness'. A Labour MP said that she would raise the matter with the Lord Advocate (the senior adviser to the Government on all matters of Scottish law). Mr George Younger, Secretary of State for Scotland, pronounced judgment: 'Once any politician, let alone a Minister, starts telling the Bench that it has done wrong on this or that or the other you are on the road to a police State.'[71] When a judge gave an unjustifiably lenient sentence for the crime of rape in February 1987, contravening the guidelines laid down by the Lord Chief Justice a year earlier, he was rightly criticized by all sectors of informed opinion—except the Government. Ministers declined to comment on the sentence because to do so might damage 'the independence of the judiciary'.

By far the most vigorous champion in recent years of judicial immunity from criticism by politicians has been Lord Hailsham. This is, to say the least, somewhat surprising in the light of his own record of forthright criticism of judicial imperfections[72] and his own willingness as Lord Chancellor (a political appointment) to make public criticisms of errant judges in certain circumstances.[73] In 1975 a defendant who pleaded guilty to two rapes was sentenced by a judge to a suspended sentence of six months' imprisonment. Some MPs put forward a motion in the House of Commons calling for the dismissal of the judge. Lord Hailsham wrote to *The Times* 'to warn against the encroachment on the independence of the judiciary'. He asserted that 'to substitute for a judicial process political pressures taking the form of savage denunciation of individual judges (even when, as of course they do, they make mistakes) is to introduce a new, and potentially extremely harmful element into judicial administration. It is, indeed, nothing but a modified and updated form of mob rule.'[74] In 1983 he wrote that judicial independence depends partly on 'immunity from attack either by Parliament or the executive or from the media'.[75] In a speech to the annual Mansion House dinner for the judges in July 1984, he suggested that 'to try and pick out, as politicians are beginning to do, individual judges for praise or blame for their real or supposed political opinions is subversive of the whole system and wholly contrary to truth'.[76]

So powerful is the idea that judges must not be criticized that it has even led to the rebuke of a judge who had commented adversely on the decision of other judges. In a 1971 case Mr Justice Lawson gave his reasons for doubting the correctness of an earlier decision of the Court of Appeal.

Nevertheless, he concluded, 'I am bound by the decision in [the earlier case], although I am compelled to say, again with the greatest respect, that I believe it to have been wrongly decided'.[77] The Court of Appeal was very unhappy. Lord Justice Davies replied, 'with the greatest respect to Lawson J.', that he thought that 'those observations were out of place. It is unusual, and, I am bound to say, undesirable, in my opinion, for a judge sitting at first instance . . . to express the opinion, although accepting that he is bound by it, that a decision, and a fairly recent decision, of this court was wrong.'[78]

'With the greatest respect', as they say in the law courts, one needs carefully to consider whether the deterrence and occasional punishment of criticism of the judiciary is in the public interest.

IV

Criticism of the judiciary is not the dangerous evil feared by those who would protect the courts. The benefits of freedom of expression are as strong in this context as in others. Criticism of the judges will not damage the rule of law. It may, by identifying defects in the legal system, promote the cause of justice. Where criticism is wrong or misguided, one should have confidence in the strength of the institution to demonstrate by its conduct that it serves a valuable function and does its job well. As was suggested by the 1969 Committee on the Law of Contempt as it affects Tribunals of Inquiry, chaired by Lord Justice Salmon, 'the right to criticize judges . . . may be one of the safeguards which helps to ensure their high standard of performance'.[79]

In 1974, however, the Phillimore Committee on Contempt of Court concluded that the offence of scandalizing the judiciary should be retained. It argued:

First, this branch of the law of contempt is concerned with the protection of the administration of justice, and especially the preservation of public confidence in its honesty and impartiality ... Moreover, some damaging attacks, for example upon an unspecified group of judges, may not be capable of being made the subject of libel proceedings at all. Secondly, judges commonly feel constrained by their position not to take action in reply to criticism and they have no proper forum in which to do so such as other public figures may have. These considerations lead us to the conclusion that there is need for an effective remedy ... against imputations of improper or corrupt judicial conduct.[80]

These remarks, although specifically directed at the offence of scandalizing the judiciary, contain a useful summary of the general objections to vigorous criticism of the judiciary. The reasons given are, on analysis, without substance.

In 1873 the Tichborne Claimant[81] was prosecuted for contempt of court after alleging at a public meeting that Lord Chief Justice Cockburn had, at his club and at a party, prejudged a case to be heard in his court. Mr Justice Blackburn said that 'it is not right that a judge, or a person occupying the position of the Lord Chief Justice, when personal attacks are made on him, should come forward and meet them and explain them, and that is well known to those who make the attack, and certainly that knowledge does in my mind render the conduct of those who attack a judge in that way, to use the mildest term, neither just nor decorous'.[82] It is true (though less so than in previous times) that judges tend not to reply to criticism.[83] But that is their choice. Much criticism of judges does not merit a reply. There are ample means—letters to newspapers, statements in court, or press conferences—by which a judge could, if he wished, reply to criticism. If judges decide not to respond, it is often because they are content to allow members of the public to assess whether the criticism has any justification. In the case brought against Quintin Hogg for alleged scandalizing of the judiciary, Lord Denning said that the court was willing to 'rely on our conduct itself to be its own vindication'.[84]

In appropriate circumstances, judges can and do bring libel actions to protect their reputations. When a journalist wrongly suggested that a Catholic had been appointed as a County Court judge in Northern Ireland because of his religion, and that his appointment had been criticized on this ground, the judge sued for libel.[85] There are old precedents for such legal action by judges. In the 1590s Julius Caesar (who later became Master of the Rolls) was awarded £200 against a man who asserted that Caesar had, as a judge of the Admiralty Court, 'pronounced a corrupt sentence against him'.[86] In 1638 a man shouted out in court, 'I accuse Mr Justice Hutton of high treason'. He was fined £5,000, imprisoned during the King's pleasure, and ordered to have 'a paper upon his head showing his offence, and go therewith to all the Courts of Westminster'.[87] Mr Justice Hutton brought an action against the man for defamation and recovered £10,000 damages.[88] Magistrates have occasionally resorted to the courts to protect their reputations. In 1725 a magistrate sued a man for calling him 'a rascal, a villain and a liar'. The Chief Justice held that 'though *rascal* and *villain* were uncertain, yet being joined with *liar*, and spoken of a Justice of the Peace, they did import a charge of acting corruptly and partially, and therefore there ought to be judgment for the [magistrate]'.[89] Seventeen years later it was held that to call a magistrate 'a rogue' (in the carrying out of his office) was actionable in law.[90] Those who are sued by a judge would be well advised to take note of the biblical warning: 'Do not go to law with a judge, for in deference to his position they will give him the verdict.'[91]

Public confidence in the judiciary is not strengthened by the deterrence of criticism. In Quintin Hogg's case, Lord Justice Salmon rightly explained that 'the authority and reputation of our courts are not so frail that their judgments need to be shielded from criticism'.[92] The US Supreme Court has well understood the dangers of inhibiting freedom of expression in this area. In 1941 Mr Justice Black for the Court reminded everyone that 'the assumption that respect for the judiciary can be won by shielding judges from published criticism wrongly appraises the character of American public opinion. For it is a prized American privilege to speak one's mind, although not always with perfect good taste, on all public institutions. And an enforced silence, however limited, solely in the name of preserving the dignity of the bench, would probably engender resentment, suspicion and contempt much more than it would enhance respect.'[93] In any event, 'judges are supposed to be men of fortitude, able to thrive in a hardy climate'.[94] For these reasons, American constitutional law applies in this context, as in others, a 'clear and present danger' test, that is 'a working principle that the substantive evil must be extremely serious and the degree of imminence extremely high before utterances can be punished'.[95] To justify the use of the contempt power, there must be shown 'a substantive evil actually designed to impede the course of justice'. In the absence of such an evil, 'men are entitled to speak as they please on matters vital to them; errors in judgment or unsubstantiated opinions may be exposed, of course, but not through punishment for contempt for the expression. Under our system of government, counterargument and education are the weapons available to expose these matters, not abridgement of the rights of free speech'.[96]

Judges should be able to ignore an 'uncouth insult', such

as that uttered by a young man to Mr Justice Melford Stevenson, who had just sentenced him to six months' imprisonment for contempt of court by planning to release laughing gas into a criminal court to disrupt the proceedings. 'You are a humourless automaton,' the young man told the judge. 'Why don't you self-destruct?'[97] A good judge pays no attention to unjustified criticism. Lord Mansfield announced in 1770 that he would 'not do that which my conscience tells me is wrong, upon this occasion, to gain the huzzas of thousands or the daily praise of all papers which come from the press: I will not avoid doing what I think is right, though it should draw on me the whole artillery of libels'.[98] More recently, in the Court of Appeal Lord Denning explained that 'no professional judge would be influenced in the least by any criticism that appeared in the newspapers, even if he read them, or on the television, even if he watched it'.[99] In the same case, Lord Salmon, in the House of Lords, expressed similar views. He had 'always been satisfied that no judge would be influenced in his judgment by what may be said by the media. If he were, he would not be fit to be a judge.'[100] Despite the fact that Viscount Dilhorne had 'some difficulty' in accepting this 'claim to judicial superiority over human frailty',[101] it seems clear that the continued existence of the offence of scandalizing the judiciary by criticism, however intemperate, cannot be justified by judicial susceptibility to outside pressure. At the very least, it should be necessary to establish that a person charged with such a contempt had, by his words, actually impeded the administration of justice. If his impugned statements were ignored by the court, no contempt would exist.

Even if criticism of the court could have an effect on a judge's action, the offence of scandalizing the judiciary should be abolished. Like other public servants, judges should accept criticism as an occupational hazard. Legal sanctions, even if rarely used, will inevitably deter plain speaking. Those with something valuable to say may well be scared into silence. Whatever the content of the criticism, even if it includes allegations of bad faith or corruption on the Bench, judges neither need nor deserve special legal protection. If the allegation is true, it is in the public interest for it to be made openly. If the allegation is false, other sanctions exist. A judge can answer back if he thinks it appropriate to do so. The law of libel provides an effective remedy to protect the reputation of the individual judge. The reputation of the Bench as a whole is well able to look after itself.

Because the judiciary enjoys a security of tenure rightly denied to politicians and unique among public servants,[102] it is especially important that the judges should be subject to free and open criticism of the performance of their duties.[103]

V

The insistence of the English judge on respect for his office is well illustrated by the farcical case of Sardar Tejendrasingh. For reasons of his own, Mr Tejendrasingh had 'no respect for this country or its civilization or its courts'. He therefore persistently refused to stand up while addressing the Cambridge County Court in support of his claims to be owed money. In August 1982 the Registrar of the Court ordered an action to be stayed until Mr Tejendrasingh purged his contempt of court in refusing to stand up. In September 1983 His Honour Judge Garfitt told Mr Tejendrasingh that until he gave an undertaking in writing that he would stand up, the court's position was that the action would not be heard.

Mr Tejendrasingh appealed. In November 1985 three

Court of Appeal judges, including Sir John Donaldson, the Master of the Rolls, wisely allowed Mr Tejendrasingh to address them sitting down (so as to avoid prejudging the fundamental issues raised by his case). But they decided that the County Court judge was entitled to stand on his dignity and require Mr Tejendrasingh to stand up.[104]

The Court of Appeal noted that it is customary to stand in court while presenting evidence or argument and that there are practical reasons for this: to preserve order in court and to assist audibility. In any event, the court held, 'if a court orders somebody to stand when addressing it or giving evidence, that order is no different from any other order of the court. It is something which has to be obeyed.'

The decision of the Court of Appeal echoes the approach taken by some judges in other jurisdictions. In 1965 the Supreme Court of British Columbia, Canada, declined to interfere with a sentence of three months' imprisonment imposed on a defendant for his refusal to stand up when the magistrate hearing a criminal charge against him entered the court. Branca J thought it 'sufficient for the purposes of this case to state that the public has been educated so to [stand] and has done so since time immemorial'. This is, he suggested, 'an inseparable attribute to court procedure and a mark of veneration or respect'. He explained that the defendant, by refusing to stand, had made 'a gesture . . . by way of conduct that can only be characterized as a marked insult to the court, which tended to limit the authority of the court by persistent disobedience'. The prison sentence was, he concluded, 'a necessary procedure to preserve order in the court over which [the magistrate] presided'.[105] In 1969 two women spectators at a US District Court refused to stand when the judge entered the courtroom. The judge sentenced them to ten days and thirty days in prison respectively. The Court of Appeals said that the judge was entitled to enforce 'the traditional rising in unison of persons present in a court' since it is 'a way of marking the beginning and end of the session'. Here, the Court of Appeals said, there was no need for more enforcement than was accomplished by excluding the women from the courtroom and taking them into custody until the judge had time to deal with them (4 hours and $2\frac{1}{2}$ hours respectively).[106]

The enforcement of respect for the judiciary by sending to prison, or in Mr Tejendrasingh's case not listening to, those who will not stand up has little to recommend it. The disrespect indicated by Mr Tejendrasingh could hardly be described as extreme. It involved no physical assault. It involved no words of abuse. It did not impede the ability of the court to hear the evidence and decide the issues. It is no doubt true that a witness who stands up can be more easily seen and heard. But many tribunals dispense justice with everyone sitting down. At the opening of the National Industrial Relations Court in 1971, the President, Sir John Donaldson, announced that 'the parties and their advisers will sit at tables and will probably wish to address the court seated'.[107] Infirm or elderly witnesses (or lawyers) are not required to stand in court. So there is no rule of procedure requiring such conduct. In any event, the Cambridge County Court ordered Mr Tejendrasingh to stand not because the judge would otherwise have been unable to see or hear him, but because the man's insistence on sitting down indicated disrespect for the court.

Since Mr Tejendrasingh was willing to address the court in a manner that would not have impeded the court's ability to determine the issues, he should have been heard standing up, or sitting down, or standing on one leg, or standing on his head, or with a funny hat on. Courts exist to dispense justice, not to demand respect from litigants as the price of admission. The decision of the Court of Appeal that Mr Tejendrasingh did not have a leg to stand on did nothing to enhance respect for the law. It unfortunately encouraged judges to think that their dignity is more important than getting on with the job of deciding cases.

It is rare for a litigant to challenge the court's demand for respect. Many of those who attend courts would, however, share the feelings of one litigant in person that 'she deplored the fact . . . that she had had to look up to members of the court' by reason of the elevation of the Bench.[108] Dressed in wig and gown, seated on an elevated throne, addressed by barristers who await every gesture, deciding the fate of nervous litigants, and accountable to no one but the appeal court, the judge may well conclude that 'a Bench, no matter what you may say, is a damned fine thing to sit on', as Lord Chancellor Westbury acknowledged in the mid-nineteenth century.[109]

It is said that prior to the opening of the Royal Courts of Justice in 1882, Lord Chancellor Selborne called a meeting of the judges at which the draft of an address to be made to Queen Victoria was discussed. The draft included the words, 'Your Majesty's Judges are deeply sensible of their own many shortcomings . . .'. Sir George Jessel, Master of the Rolls, objected: 'I am not conscious of "many shortcomings", and if I were I should not be fit to sit on the bench.'[110] Despite this objection, Lord Selborne included the phrase in his speech, on behalf of himself and the judges, on being handed the key to the building[111] (which had been paid for 'out of the funds left by litigants in the Chancery Court, who had despaired of ever seeing their cases concluded').[112] There is a risk that, in the absence of criticism, the judge will be drowned in veneration and self-satisfaction. There will always be people, like Sir Leicester Dedlock in *Bleak House*, who regard the court of law even if it should involve an occasional delay of justice and a trifling amount of confusion, as a something, devised in conjunction with a variety of other somethings, by the perfection of human wisdom for the eternal settlement (humanly speaking) of everything. And he is upon the whole of a fixed opinion, that to give the sanction of his countenance to any complaints respecting it, would be to encourage some person in the lower classes to rise up somewhere—like Wat Tyler.[113]

Lord Hewart told the Lord Mayor's Banquet in 1936 that 'His Majesty's Judges are satisfied with the almost universal admiration in which they are held'.[114] It is difficult to believe that such were the true feelings of many of the customers of Hewart's own court.[115] More vigorous criticism of judicial conduct would have disabused Lord Hewart of his fictional ideas. More recently, Lord Devlin was similarly misinformed in suggesting that 'the English judiciary is popularly treated as a national institution . . . and tends to be admired to excess'.[116] The absence of public criticism should not be taken to imply private admiration. The layman does not have a high opinion of lawyers, whatever their seniority or status. Shakespeare ranked 'the law's delay' amongst 'the whips and scorns of time'.[117] Dickens said of the Court of Chancery that 'there is not an honourable man amongst its practitioners who would not give—who does not often give—the warning, "Suffer any wrong that can be done you, rather than come here"'.[118] Such literature accurately reflects the mood of the layman.

Without criticism of the courts, the judge will remain ignorant of the true feelings of his customers. Few litigants are going to write personally to members of the judiciary when 'every private communication to a Judge, for the purpose of influencing his decision upon a matter publicly before him . . . is a high contempt of court'.[119] Thomas

Martin so discovered in 1747 when he wrote to the Lord Chancellor 'making mention of a bill in Chancery ... and enclosing a bank note for £20, which he thereby desired his Lordship's acceptance of'.[120] Some judges have rejected valuable opportunities for learning the true views of laymen. One County Court judge complained that some of his colleagues 'had to share the same lavatory as the litigants and witnesses. Many people who have seen a judge in court do not recognize him without his wig. It is highly undesirable, in my view, that the judge standing next to a man in the lavatory should have the opportunity of hearing himself described as a "cock-eyed old so-and-so ...".'[121]

Sometimes litigants make even more plain their feelings about the court. Judges have had a variety of objects thrown at them. The man who threw a brickbat in 1631 was 'immediately hanged in the presence of the Court'.[122] In 1877 Malins V-C had an egg thrown at him while he was leaving the court. He remarked that it 'must have been intended for his brother Bacon V-C, who was sitting in an adjoining court'[123] (though this story has been doubted on the ground that 'no one will seriously believe that a judge could have perpetrated such an unseemly jest from the bench').[124] The culprit, a Mr Cosgrave, was imprisoned for five months. Disappointed litigants have thrown at the bench whatever came to hand (and paid the appropriate penalty for contempt): apples at a Scottish judge at the beginning of the century;[125] tomatoes at the Court of Appeal in 1938;[126] and law books at the Court of Appeal in 1970.[127] Mr Justice McKenna recalled in 1969 that 'in one of the first cases that I tried, a temperamental Irish lady flung her handbag in my direction after I had sentenced her delinquent brother to a period of training. I gave her the benefit of the doubt; I assumed that her target was the Clerk of the Court sitting beneath the throne, and not myself.'[128]

Disappointed litigants occasionally need to be reminded that it 'would . . . undoubtedly be contempt to assault [a] . . . judge in protest against his judgment'.[129] In 1898 a Manchester County Court judge, Sir Edward Parry, was shot and seriously injured in court.[130] In 1973 a Criminal Court of Appeal judge was attacked by a man whose appeal had been rejected. The man was sentenced to nine months' imprisonment for the assault.[131] In 1982 Justice Byron White of the US Supreme Court was punched at a meeting of the Utah Bar Association by someone protesting against the Court's decisions on pornography.[132] While sitting on the bench in October 1983, Judge Gentile of Cook County Circuit Court, Chicago, was shot and killed by an angry litigant in a divorce case.[133] It is treason to 'slea' one of Her Majesty's judges 'being in their places, doing their offices . . .'.[134] How much better if litigants could be encouraged to use words as the only weapon of attack.

CHAPTER 6

Mysticism

I

At 10.30 p.m. on a December evening in 1891, Miss Daisy Hopkins was arrested by the Revd F. Wallis, a Pro-Proctor of the University of Cambridge. She was charged with 'walking with a member of the University'. On her conviction by the University court she was ordered by the Vice-Chancellor to be detained for fourteen days in the University gaol.

Miss Hopkins applied to the Queen's Bench Division of the High Court.[1] Her lawyers argued that the charge disclosed no offence known to the common law, statute, or the Charter of the University. It was explained on behalf of the University that the charge was in the usual form for such cases and was 'always understood to mean that the woman charged was in company with an undergraduate for an immoral purpose'. The Revd Wallis told the court that he knew Miss Hopkins 'to be a reputed prostitute'.

Lord Coleridge, the Lord Chief Justice, observed that 'nobody would suppose that a person simply walking with a member of the University, who might be that member's mother, or sister, or wife, or friend, was guilty of an offence against the law which would justify the Vice-Chancellor in imprisoning him or her'. Mr Justice Smith similarly had 'not the slightest doubt that this woman was tried upon a charge of immorality; that there was ample evidence to justify that charge of immorality ... What is more,' he added, 'she and [her lawyer] knew perfectly well she was being tried upon that.' Nevertheless, the judges concluded, the conviction must be quashed because Miss Hopkins had been charged with something which did not constitute an offence. The Vice-Chancellor, or anyone else, 'could not use a form of words which did not give jurisdiction, and yet give themselves jurisdiction by saying, "Oh, we meant them in a sense which would have given us jurisdiction, and they are words which we have for a long time used, and which we understood to give us jurisdiction"'.

Lord Coleridge and Mr Justice Smith stubbornly refused to recognize the validity of the euphemism adopted by the University. It would be an error of interpretation of their decision as disastrous as that made by Miss Hopkins (who, in 1892, sued the Revd Wallis for false imprisonment and failed because he was found to have had reasonable cause for arresting her)[2] to conclude that the law respects and requires common language and nullifies any barrier to the proper understanding of legal rights and duties.

II

Each year the New Year's resolutions of many actual and potential litigants echo the oath of Dick in Shakespeare's *Henry VI, Part II*: 'The first thing we do, let's kill all the lawyers.'[3] There are many reasons why lawyers are not the most universally popular of men and women. But it is not the exorbitant cost of legal proceedings, the intolerable delays, the unpredictable judgments, the lawyers' ignorance of life outside the courts, or the indefensible restrictive practices (that would bring envious tears to the eyes of the toughest trade union official) which most infuriate litigants.

They can take all of that. What irritates and annoys them beyond endurance is the ridiculous habit of lawyers of dressing up for the occasion in wigs and gowns and using language that laymen cannot understand.

What Trollope described as 'the paraphernalia of the horsehair wigs'[4] engenders misunderstanding and a deep distrust of all those who earn their living in courts of law. Why are these people who are sending me to prison, or ruining my business, or throwing me out of my home, dressed up for a pantomime and speaking in a foreign language?

The separate development of lawyer and layman in a country that contains them both is aided by the fanciful costumes in which judges and other lawyers dress and by their extraordinary procedures, including the practice of bowing before each other. Alexander Herzen, visiting an English court for the first time in 1853, was struck by 'the comicality of the medieval mise-en-scène', the climax of which was the appearance of the judge 'wearing a fur coat and something like a woman's dressing-gown'.[5]

The adverse effects of traditional judicial attire are obvious. First, the wig and gown isolate judges from litigants, falsely suggesting that the law is a mystical process that cannot possibly be understood by people not trained in the priesthood. Secondly, judicial dress hinders the work of the courts by making witnesses strained and hesitant when giving evidence in the unusual, theatrical atmosphere of the court. Dickens was well aware that 'life in a wig is to a large class of people much more terrifying and impressive than life with its own head of hair'.[6] Thirdly, court attire promotes what the distinguished American judge, Jerome Frank, called 'the cult of the robe'.[7] Wigs and gowns, and other types of legal ceremony, encourage legal pomposity and distance courts from common standards and common sense. They imply to outsiders (and to insiders) that judges are not ordinary human beings whose conduct and statements are subject to normal standards of assessment and criticism. The protective clothing of the judge deters all but the most persistent critic. As one of Dickens's characters put it: 'Would you care a ha'penny for the Lord Chancellor if you know'd him in private and without his wig?—certainly not.'[8]

Judicial dress is, then, a barrier to communication with the public which courts exist to serve. It is scarcely surprising that judges are misunderstood, unfairly criticized, and undeservedly praised when their working clothes shield and disguise their attributes and performance.

If the country folks of those assize towns on his circuit could see him now! No full-bottomed wig, no red petticoats, no fur, no javelin-men, no white wands. Merely a close-shaven gentleman in white trousers and a white hat, with sea-bronze on the judicial countenance, and a strip of bark peeled by the solar rays from the judicial nose, who calls in at the shell-fish shop as he comes along, and drinks iced ginger-beer![9]

The case for the fancy dress is said to be that it is 'an indication of the functions of those engaged in the proceedings and as enhancing the formality and dignity of a grave occasion. In their appearance they also lessen visual differences of age, sex and clothing, and so aid concentration on the real issues without distraction.'[10] Lewis Carroll's Alice had 'never been in a court of justice before, but she had read about them in books, and she was quite pleased to find that she knew the name of nearly everything there. "That's the judge", she said to herself, "because of his great wig".'[11] It would be a sad comment on the quality of the judiciary if our ability to identify the judge, or our respect for judicial proceedings, or the capacity of lawyers to concentrate on the issues in the case, really did depend on the wearing of particular clothes. As Mr Justice McKenna argued in 1969, the 'scarlet formalities' of judicial attire are not necessary to ensure order in court.[12]

Lawyers do not dress up when dispensing justice in tribunals, or in magistrates' courts, or in High Court cases heard in private. The Law Lords, sitting in the highest court in the land, do not wear wigs and gowns, merely ordinary suits. Such proceedings presumably attain the requisite degree of dignity and majesty (and, incidentally, spectators are able to identity those who sit in judgment) without the presence of legal costume. The unhappy fate of the National Industrial Relations Court (charged with the duty of administering the industrial relations legislation of the Conservative Government of 1970–4 and abolished by the Labour Government in 1974) does not make less impressive the concern of its President, Sir John Donaldson (now Master of the Rolls, presiding judge in the Court of Appeal), to avoid legal mysticism. At the opening of the NIRC on 1 December 1971, he announced that hearings would take place in surroundings which in no way resembled a traditional courtroom. Members of the court would not wear robes. Their chairs would be in a portion of the room which was elevated by 9 inches solely in order that they could see and be seen.[13]

If, as was the case, such a procedure best served the interests of justice, why adopt different arrangements for other courts of law? Indeed, as Mr Justice Megarry stated in 1973, 'robes are not essential, and the court may dispense with them where there is good reason. Jurisdiction is neither conferred nor excluded by mere matters of attire'. He referred to 'the numberless occasions upon which judges have exercised a variety of judicial functions in unusual places without the aid of robes for them or for counsel, from

Lord Lyndhurst L. C. in a box at the opera, to Sir Lancelot Shadwell V-C while bathing in the Thames and Sir Samuel Evans P. in a dressing-gown in his bedroom'.[14] Lord Chancellor Shaftesbury sat on the bench in 1672–3 defying the conventions as to dress. To the annoyance of the other judges, he wore 'an ash-coloured gown, silver-laced, and full-ribboned pantaloons displayed, without any black at all in his garb'.[15] In the 1890s the *Law Times* noted that 'Baron Huddleston, being confined to his bed at Lewes by an attack of gout, charged the grand jury from that comfortable position'.[16]

There are many things wrong with the English legal system. A large proportion of them can be explained by our reverence for the doctrine of precedent. We do things not for any rational reason but because they have previously been done that way. The wearing of wigs and gowns in court has no other explanation and justification. 'Wigs are simply a fashion in headdress that was once universal for gentlemen, and was given up by all of them except Bishops, Judges and barristers towards the end of the eighteenth century. Bishops, with the permission of William IV, gave them up in 1832: Judges and barristers retain them still.'[17] The legal process is not a pageant to be admired by tourists for being old and quaint. It is, rather, a vital organ of government to be assessed by reference to its ability to further the goal of justice under the law.

The masquerade of the law tends to make judges and barristers objects of ridicule. Judges cannot expect to be taken as seriously as they deserve, and cannot hope to be properly respected and understood, until they abandon the priestly garments that separate them from ordinary men and women. The law has an unfortunate preoccupation with court dress. While cross-examining during a criminal trial, Rumpole receives a note from the judge, Mr Justice Prestcold. '"Dear Rumpole. Your bands are falling down and showing your collar-stud. No doubt you would wish to adjust accordingly". What was this, a murder trial, or a bloody fashion parade?'[18] Annex 11 to the Code of Conduct for barristers lays down that, in court, men must wear waistcoats, shoes must be black, and shirts should be predominantly white or some other unostentatious shade. This goes further than Lord Brightman suggested (in deciding that a woman barrister was not entitled to deduct for income tax purposes the expense of buying court dress): 'What sort of clothes a barrister should wear in court . . . is a matter of good taste and common sense, the criterion being that they should be appropriate to the dignity of the occasion.'[19]

There will always be malcontents amongst lawyers, their shoes brown, their shirts not predominantly white. However, they deserve to be listened to by judges if they state loudly and clearly that wigs and gowns epitomize all the defects of English law, its remoteness, its uncritical reverence for tradition, its absence of rationality, and its inability to see obstacles in the way of the understanding of the legal system by laymen. Furthermore, as any barrister or judge will agree, a wig makes your head itch.

III

The most important element of judicial mysticism is not the fancy dress worn by judges but the language in which judges, like other lawyers, communicate. Lawyers have, as Jonathan Swift observed, 'a peculiar cant and jargon of their own, that no other mortal can understand'. They take care to ensure that all legal business is conducted in this language 'so that it will take thirty years to decide whether the field left me by my ancestors for six generations belongs to me or to a stranger three hundred miles off'.[20]

This language, condemned by Jeremy Bentham as 'lawyers' cant' and 'flash language',[21] serves various purposes, none of them in the public interest. It unites lawyers, distinguishing them from laymen. It makes the law mysterious and incomprehensible to those laymen, thus ensuring a steady supply of work for lawyers who are needed to interpret the language they have invented.[22] The language of the law fosters the illusion that legal problems are remediable only by the application of the medicine of the specialist. Only a lawyer can resolve the complexities of the problem: better see a lawyer; 'don't trust Whatsisname', as the memorable Law Society advertisement warned consumers. Legal language also enshrouds the law, hiding it from the public. The idiom of the law leads to public ignorance of the content of the law (which paradoxically refuses to recognize ignorance of the law as a defence). It provokes the indifference of too many laymen towards the law and the contempt of so many litigants for a system which they do not understand. Legal jargon also helps to make sound acceptable what in plain terms would be seen as outrageous: 'In law, what plea so tainted and corrupt / But, being season'd with a gracious voice, / Obscures the show of evil?'[23]

To avoid the adverse consequences of the legal vernacular, in Thomas More's *Utopia* the populace

have no barristers to be over-ingenious. . . . They think it better for each man to plead his own cause, and tell the judge the same story as he'd otherwise tell his lawyer. . . . In Utopia everyone's a legal expert, for the simple reason that there are . . . very few laws, and the crudest interpretation is always assumed to be the right one. They say . . . the more ingenious the interpretation, the less effective the law, since proportionately fewer people will understand it . . .[24]

Sir Edward Coke (the seventeenth-century Chief Justice who was a founder of the modern law) claimed that the ancient Britons wrote their law in Greek 'to the end that their discipline might not be made common among the vulgar'.[25] Nowadays, 'proceedings before the court must be conducted in English and in no other language. In particular', according to Mr Justice Roxburgh in 1959, 'the proceedings could not be conducted in French, although his Lordship might be able to proceed with the hearing if the case were conducted in that language.'[26] When a group of students disrupted the proceedings of the High Court in 1970, Lord Justice Davies (considering an appeal against a sentence of imprisonment for contempt of court) said that he would 'pay no attention to their infantile rudeness in insisting on speaking in Welsh to a judge who, as they must have known, could not understand what they were saying, when they themselves were perfectly fluent in English'.[27]

It takes an exceptional layman to converse with lawyers, even in English. One such individual, Arthur Scargill, President of the National Union of Mineworkers, was complimented by Vice-Chancellor Megarry for having 'argued his case throughout with both courtesy and competence'. The judge added that he wanted to emphasize this, particularly 'in view of the number of occasions on which I found it necessary to interrupt his submissions, usually because he was going too fast for coherent note-taking'.[28]

In a 1966 Court of Appeal judgment Lord Justice Diplock suggested that

lawyers ... have been compelled to evolve an English language, of which the constituent words and phrases are more precise in their meaning than they are in the language of Shakespeare or of any of the passengers on the Clapham omnibus this morning. .... Non-lawyers are unfamiliar with the meanings which lawyers attach to particular 'terms of art' ...[29]

So complex is this language of the law that only certain lawyers can be granted the right of audience in the High Court. In 1867 Mr Justice Byles held that 'for the sake of members of the Bar' a mere solicitor could not stand up in court and consent to a verdict against his client.[30] Although a solicitor could be given a right of audience in exceptional cases, for example in the absence of the barrister who had been instructed,[31] until a 1986 Practice Statement[32] a judge could not allow a solicitor to read out in open court an agreed statement in settlement of a libel case.[33] In the past, the gods have indicated their displeasure at the unnatural practices of lawyers in these respects. In 1840, during the delivery of a judgment that the Serjeants (a superior caste of barristers from whose ranks judges were selected) had an exclusive right of audience in the Court of Common Pleas (thus preventing ordinary barristers from being heard in that court), 'a furious tempest of wind prevailed, which seemed to shake the fabric of Westminster Hall, and nearly burst open the windows and doors of the Court'.[34]

It is the speech of the lawyer which holds the legal charade together. This has been understood by perceptive laymen from Jesus ('Woe unto you lawyers. You have taken away the key of knowledge')[35] to the Marx Brothers ('The party of the first part shall be known in this contract as the party of the first part').[36] In the opening paragraphs of *Bleak House*, Dickens describes how the heart of the London fog rests in the High Court of Chancery. There the lawyers are 'groping knee-deep in technicalities, running their goat-hair and horsehair warded heads against walls of words'. In Kafka's *The Trial*, the commercial traveller explains to K that the petition to the Court drafted by his lawyer

was very learned but it said nothing of any consequence. Crammed with Latin in the first place, which I don't understand,

and then whole pages of general appeals to the Court, then flattering references to particular officials ... then some self-praise of the Advocate himself, in the course of which he addressed the Court with a crawling humility, ending up with an analysis of various cases from ancient times that were supposed to resemble mine.[37]

Only on isolated occasions have judges recognized that they, like all other lawyers, suffer from such afflictions. To his credit, Lord Justice Cumming-Bruce acknowledged in a 1979 decision that 'parts of this judgment I am afraid are still drafted in a kind of legal jargon which may later have to be translated into English, and I hope it is intelligible'.[38] It is one thing to spot the symptoms. It is more difficult to find a cure for the disease.

There are several distinguishing features of legal language. First, there is the extraordinary prolixity of legal speech. Lawyers are, as Swift explained, 'a society of men ... bred up from their youth in the art of proving by words multiplied for the purpose that white is black, and black is white, according as they are paid'.[39] Hence, Gulliver discovers, in Brobdingnag steps have been taken to restrain lawyers by a provision that no law of the country may exceed in words the number of letters in their alphabet, which is twenty-two.[40] Secondly, there is the frequent reliance on archaic forms, such as *aforesaid, heretofore,* and *thenceforth*. Thirdly, there is the common use of Latinisms, from *ab initio* to *ex post facto*, reducing the litigant, *ex parte*, to *in forma pauperis*. Fourthly, legal language delights in unnecessary repetition: *the truth, the whole truth, and nothing but the truth ... to have and to hold ... his last will and testament ... null and void*. Fifthly, it revels in clichés that are generally avoided in ordinary speech: *rack and ruin ... part and parcel ... safe and sound*. Sixthly, lawyers use language as a protective shell, designed to insulate them from the consequences of their words or actions: *without prejudice ... in my submission ... it would seem ... the alleged ... if any.* Seventhly, the language of the law welcomes the euphemism. It uses it for a variety of purposes including ceremony, obfuscation, and the avoidance of what might otherwise be distasteful.

All these linguistic devices help the lawyer to communicate in a tongue that cannot be understood by others. The legal profession is well aware that, in Bentham's words, 'the power of the lawyer is in the uncertainty of the law'.[41] None of this might matter except that, as an American judge, Justice Johnson, once pointed out, the vital interests of a party to legal proceedings 'may depend upon a comma'.[42]

IV

Cases come before the judge by means of a process which has made its own contribution to the euphemistic language of the law. Barristers prefer to be called *counsel*. This suggests that they act as a friend or confidant rather than in a mere professional capacity. For similar reasons, when appearing in court on behalf of a client (the date and time having been fixed *through the usual channels*, that is by the court telling the barrister's *chambers*—his offices—when the case will be heard), the barrister is paid a fee for the first day and a *refresher* (a term which implies a physical necessity for what is, after all, a financial transaction) for each subsequent day. Barristers leave the negotiation of such fees to their *clerks*, as their office managers like to be known. To explain why they feel obliged to represent rogues and scoundrels, barristers tend to refer to the *cab-rank principle*. This is a serious defamation of the ethics of taxi-drivers.

Once in court, the barrister begins to communicate with the judge in a language full of euphemisms. Barristers *make submissions* rather than present arguments. They introduce these arguments with an obsequious *May it please your Lordship*, when 'Hello, good morning judge' would do. The fictional Sir Cyril Tart QC does not stretch credibility too far when he opens a case before Mr Justice Squirrel with the words, 'If your Lordship pleases—as, may I add, your Lordship habitually does'.[43] The barrister presents his arguments *with respect, with great respect*, or, on difficult occasions, *with the greatest of respect*. The degree of respect voiced is, of course, in inverse proportion to the willingness indicated by the judge to agree with the arguments being advanced. Little has changed in these matters since the seventeenth century. After making his maiden appearance in court as a barrister, the future Lord Chancellor Cowper wrote to his wife to say that bystanders found fault with his performance only in that 'I did not interweave what I said with civil expressions enough to his Lordship, as "may it please your Lordship" and "I am humbly to move your Lordship" and the like'.[44] This formal language has infected foreign lawyers trained in England. When, in 1980, the Pakistan Government ordered lawyers and judges to discard their wigs, gowns, and legalisms as symbols of colonialism, the lawyers found it far from easy. 'I have been saying "my Lord" and "your Lordship" ... for so many years', a Lahore lawyer explained, 'that it is second nature to me.'[45]

A barrister acting for the opposing party is always *my learned friend* (as in *it may be helpful to your Lordship and my learned friend if I . . .*, meaning it will certainly be helpful to me; or *in all fairness to my learned friend . . .*, meaning that one is about to put the legal boot in). This is irrespective of the intellectual qualities of one's opponent and whether or not one has just made his acquaintance. Such euphemistic legal amity is again reflected in the practice of the judge of inviting argument from an *amicus curiae* (friend of the court), usually a barrister briefed by the State.

To avoid expressing the absurd rules that govern dress in court, a judge who is annoyed at a barrister for not wearing a waistcoat (or for being guilty of some similar heinous offence) will say to him *I cannot see you (or hear you), Mr X*. A barrister does not withdraw a bad argument. If a judge shows an argument to be nonsense, the barrister may *resile from it*. If a point assists, he will *pray it in aid*. If the judge sees a helpful argument hitherto ignored by the barrister, the latter will tell the former that *your Lordship puts the point far better than I could*. Applying the principle that it is easier to persuade a person of the truth of a proposition if one first leads him to express it, the phrase *it's your Lordship's point* is to be heard whenever the judge has shown the slightest understanding of the argument being developed. It is only to the trained observer of the law courts that Sir Ethelred Rutt KC reveals himself as a figment of A. P. Herbert's imagination when he responds to a comment from the judge with the words, 'Your Lordship is extraordinarily handsome and good'.[46] A judge does not directly tell a barrister that the latter has failed to convince him with an argument and that it is time to move on to another point. Rather the judge will inform the barrister that *I hear what you say*. The barrister, familiar with this code, acknowledges that the message has been received: *I will not improve my submission by repetition; your Lordship has the point*. By contrast, when a judge is already persuaded of the legal merits of a litigant's case, in whole or on a particular point, and so does not need to hear argument from the litigant's barrister, the judge will announce this with the phrase *I don't need to trouble you, Mr X*. The polite barrister has to resist the temptation to respond by explaining that it is no trouble as one is being paid to be there.

Occasionally, even the language of the law may be inadequate to capture the subtlety of the barrister's argument. After describing two grounds of appeal, Lord Justice Scrutton explained that 'there was also a third point, which [the barrister] said was difficult to express in words, but which, as he never made me understand what it was, I cannot deal with'.[47] Try as they do, lawyers cannot always escape the force of ordinary language. In the Court for Divorce and Matrimonial Causes in 1861, the judge explained that the respondent seemed to be in contempt of court because he had 'threatened a person who knew some of the facts of the case that, if she gave evidence, she should be indicted for perjury'. Dr Deane QC, for the respondent, was indignant on behalf of his client: 'His conduct is hardly open to that construction.' The judge's reply was persuasive: 'He says "that is a lie, and if you swear it I will give you six months for perjury". What other construction can you put upon it?'[48] Sometimes even a judge may have to admit defeat in the face of legal language. In 1920 Mr Justice McCardie said of an earlier decision of another judge: 'I confess I am unable to understand it.'[49]

Judges sometimes take offence when laymen understand legal language too well. In 1967 Lord Justice Winn gave judgment for the Court of Appeal in a criminal appeal brought by a 'scoundrel'. The appellant, a Mr Cox, had been interviewed by the police in relation to the crimes alleged against him. 'I do not propose', said Winn LJ,

to cause myself again the annoyance of reading and certainly not of reading aloud the impudent, arrogant and quite outrageous language used by Cox on that occasion. In substance it came to this: 'You cannot get me for the criminal offences which I admittedly committed in France. I know better than that. You cannot charge me here in England. It is only in France that I can be charged for those offences' . . . How much of the law he has read, one does not know. He probably will find himself in very grave trouble indeed if he goes on in the future relying on his very partial grasp of the law of this country.

The effect of this lecture was somewhat spoilt by the judge's recognition that 'unfortunately he [Cox] was right in this case . . .'. Therefore, to the regret of Winn LJ, 'it follows that so far as this matter is concerned, this man is free to go'.[50]

When laymen show a basic failure to understand legal language, the legal process may well be inconvenienced. In a New Jersey accident case in the early 1960s, when the foreman of the jury was asked by the judge, 'have you agreed upon a verdict, Mr foreman?', he replied, 'My name isn't Foreman. My name is Admerman.' The appeal court ordered a retrial, in part because of this 'basic confusion'.[51]

The law of libel is responsible for one of the most extraordinary examples of legal language: the statement in open court. London is the libel capital of the world. Society hostesses, faded ex-starlets, politicians with no sense of humour, and assorted nutcases with axes to grind into the shoulders of their sworn enemies sue each other for expressing facts and opinions which are of no conceivable interest to anyone else. The delay in bringing a case to court, the uncertainty of the outcome, and the enormous costs of fighting a libel action mean that the vast majority of cases are resolved before the trial. Those who are sued for libel often prefer to read out in open court a grovelling 'apology' which nobody could possibly take seriously but which is widely publicized, rather than contest the libel claim.

Judges prefer to be known as *my Lord* or *your Honour* or *your Worship* (the last of these being an anachronistic but revealing indication of the vanity that can afflict adjudicators in minor courts and tribunals). The precise form of address of each rank of judge is carefully prescribed by a Practice Direction.[52] The judges of the European Court of Justice—only one of whom is from the United Kingdom—must be baffled by the odd practice of English lawyers of calling them 'my Lords'.

To depersonalize the law, judges refer to themselves as *the bench*. One judge may agree with 'that which has fallen from'[53] another on the bench. To encourage a belief in their unity and amity, judges sit as *brethren* (a euphemism which gives a not wholly misleading indication of the frequency with which women are appointed as judges). It was, no doubt, an intentional piece of irony that the book which claimed to reveal the professional jealousies afflicting US Supreme Court judges was called *The Brethren*.[54]

The judgment of the court depends on euphemisms. Sometimes this is designed to avoid inflicting unnecessary pain. *While it is not for one moment suggested that Mr X is deliberately seeking to mislead the court, it is apparent to me that his memory, like that of many other people, has regrettably grown hazy with the passage of time,* sounds so much more acceptable than a conclusion that the witness is a liar. (See similarly, *when the evidence given by the plaintiff conflicted with that given by the defendant, I preferred the evidence of the former, having had the advantage of hearing and seeing them in the witness box*.) For a judge to begin his judgment with a statement that he *has every sympathy for the defendant* is fatal to the prospects of that party winning the case.

It is not only the feelings of litigants and witnesses that are spared. Judges and barristers depend on each other for satisfactory working conditions. So, when a barrister hears a judge say in his judgment that *the plaintiff's counsel presented an argument of the utmost ingenuity*, or that he *made powerful and helpful submissions*, or, worst of all, *said everything that could be said on behalf of his client*, he knows that his client has lost the case. Part of the beauty of A. P. Herbert's *Misleading Cases* is that the judges ignore these conventions. Only in fiction could Lord Merrymind, President of the Probate, Divorce and Admiralty Division of the High Court, refer in his judgment to 'the many errors in Sir Robin's laborious and, if he will forgive me, rather laughable argument'.[55]

Judges do not state or accept the obvious: for example, that Paris is the capital of France or that Monday is the day after Sunday. They *take judicial notice* of such facts. It does sometimes seem as if the Lord Chancellor organizes an annual competition with a prize for the judge who takes notice of the most obvious fact. A likely winner in any year would be Mr Justice Woolf's 1980 reference to 'the programme, principles and policy of the Labour Party which for the purposes of this judgment I will accept are inconsistent with the programme, principles and policy of the Conservative Party'.[56]

There are a number of handy euphemisms employed by judges to describe their reasoning in deciding a case. The *doctrine of precedent* applies 'a maxim among these lawyers, that whatever has been done before may legally be done again: and therefore they take special care to record all the decisions formerly made against common justice and the general reason of mankind'.[57] This raises a problem for judges. What parts of a previous decision are binding in this way? Lawyers have invented the concepts of *ratio decidendi* to indicate the central, binding element of a previous decision and *obiter dictum* to represent the peripheral part of the previous opinion which was not essential to the judgment and so is not binding on later judges. But how do we distinguish one from the other? The spurious scholarship of legal philosophers is blown away by the explanation reported by Lord Justice Asquith: 'The rule is quite simple: if you agree with the other bloke, you say it's part of the *ratio*; if you don't, you say it's *obiter dictum* with the implication that he is a congenital idiot.'[58]

When the essence of a previous decision with which a judge disagrees cannot so easily be dismissed as *obiter dictum*, the judge may, as a desperate last resort, categorize the previous decision as *per incuriam* (an acceptable legal euphemism for a judgment which was obviously wrong). It may be that the reasoning of the earlier decision is so dismissed because *the court did not have the benefit of hearing full argument upon the point*—that is, neither the barristers nor the judge saw the crucial issue. As Lord Hailsham said in the House of Lords in a 1972 case, 'I am driven to the conclusion that when the Court of Appeal described [an earlier House of Lords decision] as decided "per incuriam" or "unworkable" they really only meant that they did not agree with it'.[59]

Appellate judges are especially adept in the use of euphemisms when explaining why an appeal fails. *Whereas this court would not necessarily have exercised its discretion in the same way as the trial judge* means that the court does not agree with the trial judge but does not propose to do anything about his decision. Similarly, as soon as one hears an appeal court refer to the *special knowledge and experience of the lay members of the industrial tribunal* or to the fact that *it is only in the very rarest of cases that this court will interfere with a finding of fact by a trial judge*, one knows that an appeal has failed. The equivalent euphemism in the Judicial Committee of the Privy Council hearing appeals from the courts of Commonwealth countries is the reference to *the expert knowledge of local circumstances and conditions possessed by the trial judge.*

The Criminal Division of the Court of Appeal is sometimes heard to refer to *the trenchant summing-up of the trial judge*. In other words, he directed the jury to convict. This is to be distinguished from what the Criminal Division of the Court of Appeal call *a careful but trenchant summing-up*— that is, a direction to the jury to convict, but with a passing reference to the burden and standard of proof on the prosecution. That Court may decide *to apply the proviso*, a reference to section 2(1) of the Criminal Appeal Act 1968 which requires the Court to allow an appeal against conviction if the trial judge made an error of law, 'provided that the Court may, notwithstanding that they are of opinion that the point raised in the appeal might be decided in favour of the appellant, dismiss the appeal if they consider that no miscarriage of justice has actually occurred'. In other words, if the Court of Appeal think that the appellant committed the crime and they are disinclined to let him get away with it.

Stating his view in robust terms, Lord Justice Griffiths said in a 1984 judgment that 'no doubt one of the parties is often very fed up when an Industrial Tribunal has found the facts against him, but that is just too bad; there is nothing he can do about it'.[60] More frequently, judges express themselves in more measured terms. So, Lord Justice May explained in the Court of Appeal in 1986, a factual finding of an industrial tribunal should not be disturbed by a higher tribunal unless one could say, 'My goodness, that was certainly wrong'.[61] The artificial politeness that characterizes the English judicial style is so far removed from the realities of everyday speech that it threatens to make lawyers look ridiculous. The traditional test of whether a term should be implied into a contract is whether, if he had been asked by an *officious bystander* to agree to the term at the time the contract was made, the contracting party would have said 'of course'. As Lord Justice Roskill held in a 1972 case, 'I think he might well have been forgiven if he had replied ... in more vigorous and less restrained language'.[62]

Lawyers who disobey the rules of politeness may find themselves in difficulty. It is a contempt of court for a barrister, in his address to a jury in a criminal trial, intentionally to insult the foreman of the jury ('I thank God that there is more than one juryman to determine whether the prisoner stole the property, for if there were only one, and that one the foreman ... there is no doubt what the result would be').[63] For a barrister to use 'language so outrageous and provocative as to be likely to lead to a brawl in court' would also be in contempt of court.[64]

When reaching conclusions that lack common sense, judges like to refer to *the balance of convenience* (irrespective of the inconvenience caused by the judgment). In judicial language, *clearly* signifies a logical fallacy or a factual statement of doubtful accuracy.

The work of the Parliamentary draftsman often leaves the courts with the task of making sense of the incomprehensible. A judge rarely says that a statute is gibberish. (He may, if provoked, refer to *an anomaly*.) He may even complain, if his patience become exhausted, that *the language of the draftsman is not easy to comprehend*.

If judges are not averse to making law, they state that they are merely exercising the discretion given to them by *the doctrines of equity*, for example the doctrine that the court will not assist someone unless he comes to court *with clean hands*. Or they may assert that they are only applying *the common law*. This is a valuable judicial euphemism, suggesting a body of principles, indexed and labelled, known and belonging to everyone. In fact, as Jeremy Bentham taught, the common law is 'dog-law' made by the judges:

Do you know how they make it? Just as a man makes law for his dog. When your dog does anything you want to break him of, you wait till he does it, and then beat him for it. This is the way you make laws for your dog: and this is the way the judges make law for you and me.[65]

If, on the other hand, judges are reluctant to extend the frontiers of the law, they will refer to the dangers of applying *palm-tree justice* (not to be confused with poetic justice) or of measuring the law by *the length of the Chancellor's foot*.

Claims are heard, applications are disposed of, and appeals are determined. Barristers do not leave the court without a farewell. But they never wave the judge a cheery goodbye. Rather they depart with a misleading *I'm obliged, my Lord* or, if they have dismally failed to obtain what they were seeking from the judge, *I'm much obliged*. On occasions, the case does not require a decision from the judge. In the European Commission of Human Rights, a *friendly settlement* represents a Government climb-down, often in circumstances of continuing acrimony. In English courts what had seemed an unacceptable offer from the other side on the first morning of the trial will, after one's witnesses have *failed to come up to proof* (in other words, they told a pack of lies to their lawyers before the trial), be grabbed as *a good settlement* or, if that is too implausible, be accepted as *a moral victory*.

V

The substance of the law mirrors the practice of the law in its fondness for euphemisms. Here again one can see the reluctance of the law to call a spade a spade. Language, and the euphemisms it employs, evolve with the times. The Usury Laws, repealed in 1854, returned as the Money-lenders Acts 1900 and 1927. The relevant legal provisions are now contained in the Consumer Credit Act 1974 which talks of an 'extortionate credit bargain'. The Mental Health Act 1959 repealed the Lunacy and Mental Treatment Acts 1890 to 1930 and the Mental Deficiency Acts 1913 to 1938.

Sex is treated euphemistically in the law, as elsewhere. Until 1857, a cuckolded husband could sue the other man for *criminal conversation* with his wife. Only judges refer to couples partaking in *marital relations*, having *carnal knowledge*, or agreeing to 'enjoy conjugal felicity'.[66] A *common-law marriage* is not a legal marriage at all. It is not to be confused with a *marriage of convenience*, which is a marriage entered into to gain some legal advantage, for example under the immigration laws (though few people marry when it is inconvenient to do so, unless there is a *shotgun wedding*). Rape used to be known as a *criminal assault*. A *criminal operation* was a euphemism for an abortion. Sexual intercourse with a minor is a *statutory rape*. To *interfere with* someone is sexually to assault them.

In this oppressive climate of sexual innuendo, Mr Justice Ashworth was a brave man to comment in the Divisional Court in 1972 on the 'Victorian gentility which prevented people calling a penis a penis'. He was considering section 4 of the Vagrancy Act 1824 which made it an offence for someone to indulge in 'wilfully, openly, lewdly and obscenely exposing his person . . . with intent to insult any female'. Mr Justice Ashworth had no doubt that 'at any rate today, and indeed by 1824, the word "person" in connection with sexual matters had acquired a meaning of its own; a meaning which made it a synonym for "penis"'.[67] Judicial confusion in this context is understandable given the wide variety of factors which need to be considered. In 1985 the Family Division of the High Court considered a claim for an affiliation order (requiring a father to pay for the maintenance of his child). The issue was whether there was an irrebuttable presumption of law that a boy under the age of 14 (who had admitted being the father of the child) was incapable of sexual intercourse. The judge noted that he had 'been referred, surprisingly, to the Perpetuities and Accumulations Act 1964'.[68]

When a judge is unsure whether to use a euphemism in the sexual context (perhaps because none is readily available), he may compromise and refer, for example, to 'a so-called "sex-change operation"' involving 'a so-called "artificial vagina" '.[69] On occasions, the judge may mix euphemisms with direct language for no apparent reason. In a 1976 decision, Lord Denning explained that Mr Hook, a market trader, 'had an urgent call of nature'. All the 'lavatories or "toilets" as they are now called' were closed. So Mr Hook 'went into a side street near the market and there made water, or "urinated" as it is now said'. On being reprimanded by a security officer, 'Mr Hook made an appropriate reply. Again we are not told the actual words, but it is not difficult to guess. I expect it was an emphatic version of "You be off".'[70] How very different from the law reports of an earlier age: in 1663 Sir Charles Sidley was fined 'for shewing himself naked in a balcony, and throwing down bottles (pist in) . . . among the people in Convent (*sic*) Garden . . .'.[71] Modern judges are not so ready to repeat the language of those whose misbehaviour leads them to court.

In upholding a conviction for assault in 1976, Lord Russell explained that 'when the police arrived, [the defendant] called them adjectival pigs'.[72]

Commercial matters also provide fertile ground for the breeding of judicial euphemisms. The plain speaking of Lord Macnaghten, 'income tax, if I may be pardoned for saying so, is a tax on income',[73] is misleading in this respect. The world of bond washing and reverse annuities is quite prepared to tolerate euphemisms if it means tax liabilities can more easily be avoided (not *evaded*, as tax practitioners will emphasize). *Tax planning* is a very acceptable term for what is not always a laudable pursuit. It suggests constructive activities where usually what one finds is 'another circular game in which the taxpayer and a few hired performers act out a play; nothing happens save that the Houdini taxpayer appears to escape from the manacles of tax'.[74] Adjudication of whether such schemes have achieved their objective of defeating the Inland Revenue often becomes divorced from policy, principle, or common sense. In March 1981 five Law Lords spent three days deciding whether an appellant was liable to pay nearly £$\frac{1}{4}$ million income tax in respect of the year of assessment 1968–9 by asking themselves what Parliament had meant by the word 'whereby'.[75]

An *agreement subject to contract* is not a legal agreement at all. It is closely related to the *gentleman's agreement*, reported to have been defined by Mr Justice Vaisey as 'an agreement which is not an agreement, made between two persons, neither of whom is a gentleman, whereby each expects the other to be strictly bound without himself being bound at all'.[76] One knows when judges have identified a binding agreement because they will refer to the parties having reached a *meeting of minds* and having given *consideration* for each other's promise, which involves neither concern for the other party nor the provision of fair value for the promise given by that other party.

The hopes of many litigants have been destroyed by judges comparing their conduct unfavourably with that attributed to *the reasonable man*, also known as *the man on the top of the Clapham omnibus*. He is so remote from the imperfection that characterizes those who come to court that his appearances in the law reports suggest that he is 'devoid ... of any human weakness, with not one single saving vice'.[77]

In June 1985 a barrister objected to the use of the word 'blackmail' in the charge against his black client in an Old Bailey trial. The barrister complained to Judge Lipfriend that the use of the word was a 'derogatory stigma' against black people. In the best traditions of the Bar, he refused to be fobbed off with the excuse that section 21 of the Theft Act 1968 uses the offensive word. He preferred the term 'demanding money with menaces'. Judge Lipfriend was not persuaded by his submission.[78]

More often, Parliament does not confine judicial discretion as to the language to be used in court. Even where it appears to do so, there is much to be said for the liberating approach taken by Lord Russell in a 1980 House of Lords decision which turned on a matter of statutory interpretation. Applying the phrase used by another judge in 1891, Lord Russell confessed 'This beats me'. He decided to 'jettison the words in dispute as making no contribution to the manifest intention of Parliament'.[79] If this is unacceptable, perhaps judges could sometimes soften the blow by emulating the Seychelles judge 'who, having once been a lyric-writer ... tended to offer his judgments in verse'.[80] Certainly there is no excuse for judges complaining when Parliament attempts to make itself understood by non-lawyers. In 1924 Lord Justice MacKinnon noted that in

legislation protecting tenants 'the language used . . .
resembles that of popular journalism rather than the terms
of the art of conveyancing'.[81] Popular journalism has its
faults. But it is comprehensible.

VI

The layman has taken some revenge for the inaccessibility
and absurdity of legal language by using the law as source
material for euphemisms of his own. *The Solicitor General* is,
according to the experts,[82] a euphemism for the penis. To be
in Chancery is a pugilistic term meaning to have one's head
under an opponent's arm while he hits you with the fist of
his stronger arm.[83] Furthermore, *legal fiction* 'is used col-
loquially as a facetious euphemism for an untruth'.[84]

Each generation of laymen has mocked the lawyer in this
respect because it has well understood that in the language
of the law 'care has been taken that each particle of sense
shall be drowned in a deluge of words'.[85] There could be no
other explanation for section 72 of the Housing Act 1980,
described by Lord Roskill, a distinguished Law Lord, as 'the
worst piece of Parliamentary drafting for 1980'.[86] Section
72(1) provides that 'rent tribunals . . . are hereby abolished'.
Section 72(2) adds that 'the functions [previously] . . .
conferred on rent tribunals shall be carried out by rent
assessment committees'. So far so good. But section 72(3)
takes us back where we started by announcing that a 'rent
assessment committee shall . . . be known as a rent tribunal'.
As Chief Justice Holt pointed out in 1701, 'an Act of
Parliament can do no wrong, though it may do several
things that look pretty odd'.[87] To prove that Parliament is
not solely responsible for the excesses and absurdities in the
language of the law, and that the judiciary fully plays its
part, one need only look to the headnote of a case decided

167

by three judges in the High Court in 1916. The court needed to hear and consider legal argument before deciding that 'ice-cream is not "meat" within section 3 of the Sunday Observance Act 1677'.[88] So baffling is the language and procedure of the law that academics have begun to study non-verbal judicial behaviour in the hope of understanding what is going on in court.[89]

The retention by the judiciary of fancy dress and fancy language is to the detriment of the legal system. As Bentham explained,

seated in a chair in the character of a justice of the peace with common language in his mouth, a common coat upon his back and no hair upon his head but his own, Solomon himself would not gain the praise of wisdom. Seated on a woolsack, Bartholon would pass muster while talking about entering appearances or filing common bail, clothed in purple and fine linen, artificial hair and ermine.[90]

If the courts do not improve their performance in these respects, someone will have to *read them the Riot Act*.

CHAPTER 7

Publicity

I

ENGLISH law is committed to open justice. The courts conduct their proceedings in public. Only in wholly exceptional circumstances, where the presence of the public or public knowledge of the proceedings is likely to lead to a denial of justice or to some other detriment to the public interest, are courts justified in hearing cases in private.[1] Magistrates may not adopt a general policy of seeking to keep their identities secret from the press and the public.[2]

The principle of publicity is designed 'to discipline the judiciary—to keep the judges themselves up to the mark'.[3] It is, therefore, a matter of some regret and concern that, in many respects, judges continue to shun and avoid publicity, both in and out of court.

II

The English judge is not a public figure. He acts on the principle adopted by Lord Widgery, Lord Chief Justice 1971–80, that 'the best judge [is] the man who [is] least known to the readers of the *Daily Mail*'. Therefore, Lord Widgery advised, 'judges should not court publicity and certainly should not do their work in such a way as to "catch the eye of the newsman"'.[4]

169

Certain sacrifices have apparently been required of judges to preserve this immunity from fame or notoriety. It is said that 'traditionally judges do not go into hotels or restaurants (except to a function in a private room) in the county in which they are sitting'.[5] It is also 'the general rule . . . that judges must not visit brothels'.[6] Judges habitually resign from active participation in all bodies of a vaguely controversial nature on their appointment to the bench.[7] Some judges even avoid voting in general elections so that their impartiality shall be beyond reproach.[8] Mr Justice Harlan, who sat on the US Supreme Court 1955–71, adopted a similar practice with regard to Presidential elections and, for the same reason, 'never applauded at the President's State of the Union address'.[9] Occasionally, a judge takes this seclusion to extremes of which even Lord Widgery might have disapproved. Lord Atkinson (a Law Lord from 1905 to 1928) 'appears to have written nothing outside his judicial speeches. He spoke little in the House [of Lords]. He had no children or friends. It is said that, on his death, the Lord Chancellor's Office had difficulty tracing his wife in order to pay her his pension.'[10]

There is a lamentable absence of contributions by members of the English judiciary to the advance of jurisprudence. Henry de Bracton's *De Legibus* (dated about 1250, when the author was a judge of the King's Bench), Blackstone's *Commentaries* (published just before he was elevated to the bench in 1770), and Sir James Stephen's *History of the Criminal Law in England* (published in 1883, four years after he became a judge) are the main oases in a substantial desert.[11] The distinguished American judges, Holmes, Cardozo, Learned Hand, Frank, and Frankfurter, have, in this sense, no modern equals on the English side of the Atlantic Ocean.

It may be, as Mr Justice Roche told Harold Laski in 1927,

that most English judges are 'vaccinated against the dangers of speculation by their careers at the Bar'.[12] Or perhaps they work too long hours. Certainly, very few of them show any interest in publicly discussing their views of law and adjudication. In many cases, no doubt, this is not a great loss to legal philosophy. Oliver Wendell Holmes[13] recalled that a Vermont justice had rejected a claim 'brought by one farmer against another for breaking a churn . . . the justice said that he had looked through the statutes and could find nothing about churns'.[14]

Some judges have defied convention and written about the law. While he was Lord Chief Justice from 1922 to 1940, Hewart wrote controversial newspaper articles for the *News of the World* on topics such as 'Should a man be hanged?' and 'Licensing law reform' (but then he had, as a young barrister, supplemented his income by freelance work for the *Manchester Guardian*). In 1929 he published a tirade against modern government, *The New Despotism*.[15]

More frequently, judicial writings do not rise above the level of dull autobiography consisting of platitudes about the legal system, cosy recollections of lawyers and other judges, details of the strategies adopted in one's youth to win what seemed hopeless cases, and lengthy accounts of the otherwise forgotten disputes decided by the judge before his retirement. When anything controversial threatens to intrude into these accounts, judicial discretion is applied. Typical in this respect was the autobiography of Dame Elizabeth Lane.[16] She had 'a happy childhood'. She was 'very happy' at school. She enjoyed a 'happy life' as a barrister. Looking back after her retirement as a judge in 1979 she was grateful, not surprisingly, for the 'deep happiness' she had known. She told her readers that she was against 'modern promiscuousness', mugging of old people, violence on television, and members of the Campaign for Nuclear Disarmament who 'consider themselves wiser than their governments in the matter of national defence'. She believed our police force to be 'the best in the world'. She recalled that there were 'two judges who made it painfully obvious that a woman's appearance before them was unwelcome. They are both dead now: there is no need to mention their names.' She added that 'there were three judges whom I strongly disliked, one of whom I thoroughly despised. Although they are all dead, it seems unnecessary to refer to them by name.' Or to tell us whether they incurred her wrath for personal or for professional reasons and, if the latter, on what grounds. Judges are too often eager to protect the mysteries of their job. Such reticence ensures that their autobiographies cannot do justice to the important matters with which they have been concerned.

When a judge writes about judging in a more informative manner, he risks unpopularity for giving away trade secrets or for criticizing his colleagues.[17] Even the anodyne published observations of Lord Denning—in the six books he wrote between 1979 and 1984—on the issues of law he had determined were too much for traditionalists. A leading article in *The Times* questioned whether it was 'in the public interest, and in the interests of the reputation of justice, that he should, alongside the judgments he delivers in court, also be furnishing commentary and opinion both on his own work and on areas of the law of which he has less experience'. There was, according to the article, a need for judges to beware that 'in neither the tone nor the substance of their personal comments do they weaken confidence in themselves as judges or in the judicial process generally'.[18]

Applying such cautionary principles, the English judge rarely gives interviews to the press, radio, or television about himself or his work. Lord Hailsham (Lord Chancellor 1970–4 and since 1979) discouraged judges from courting such publicity. He believed that 'the judges are right in wanting to stay off [the television] and treating the [lack of television appearances] not as a restriction on their activities but as a protection against importunity'.[19]

Judges are provided with such 'protection' irrespective of whether they want it or need it. In January 1986 Lord Hailsham advised a number of judges not to appear on a BBC radio programme about barristers. This was a topic on which judges might be expected to have had a valuable contribution to make. Since the subject was not politically controversial or likely to prejudice the judicial determination of disputes coming to court, the case for judicial silence could not easily be made. According to Lord Hailsham, however, the 'independence of the judiciary' might be threatened by judicial participation in such a programme. What judges needed protection from—other than the pressure applied by the Lord Chancellor's Department—was unclear. Two judges demonstrated a commendable degree of independence by ignoring the Lord Chancellor and appearing on the programme.[20]

Lord Hailsham explained that he was merely 'representing the collective view of the judges on keeping the rules in place'.[21] The rules are the 'Kilmuir rules', formulated by Lord Chancellor Kilmuir in December 1955. They prohibit judicial participation on radio and television. The rules are contained in a letter dated 12 December 1955 from Lord Kilmuir to Lieutenant-General Sir Ian Jacob, the Director-General of the BBC. The letter was a response to a request by the BBC for a number of judges to be granted permission to participate in a series of radio lectures about great judges of the past, to be broadcast on the Third Programme.

Lord Kilmuir stated that he had

given a great deal of thought to this matter. The Lord Chief Justice, the Master of the Rolls and the President of the Probate, Divorce and Admiralty Division have been good enough to give me the benefit of their considered views, and what I write hereafter has united approval.

He acknowledged that there were advantages to the public in having a broadcast discussion of an important topic by qualified authorities. But, he pronounced, the overriding consideration was 'the importance of keeping the Judiciary in this country insulated from the controversies of the day'. Recognizing, perhaps, the distance between the proposed subject of the talks and popular controversy, and displaying an extreme lack of confidence in the ability of the judge to earn respect, Lord Kilmuir indicated that his real concern was anything that might be said by the judge out of court. He suggested that

so long as a Judge keeps silent his reputation for wisdom and impartiality remains unassailable: but every utterance which he makes in public, except in the course of the actual performance of his judicial duties, must necessarily bring him within the focus of criticism.

And he noted, somewhat sanctimoniously, that it would, in any event, 'be inappropriate for the Judiciary to be associated with any series of talks or anything which could be fairly interpreted as entertainment'. So, he concluded, 'as a general rule it is undesirable for members of the Judiciary to broadcast on the wireless or to appear on television'. He added that the Lord Chancellor had 'no sort of disciplinary jurisdiction over Her Majesty's Judges', but that, if asked to broadcast, the judge concerned ought to consult the Lord Chancellor 'who would always be ready to express his opinion'.

174

One judge has publicly stated that the Lord Chancellor is too ready 'to express his opinion' on this matter in forcible terms which implicitly threaten disciplinary sanctions. Judge James Pickles believed that he had been threatened with dismissal by the Lord Chancellor if he did not refrain from writing newspaper articles on topics such as the weakness of the prison system.[22] Judge Pickles defied the Lord Chancellor's Department by participating in two BBC radio programmes in 1986. In the first he interviewed a prostitute ('Judge's chat with a vice girl', exclaimed the headline in the *Star*)[23] and discussed the merits (as he saw them) of popular newspapers publishing pictures of partially clothed women. In the second he gave his views on crime and the sentencing of offenders.[24]

Even if the majority of today's judges are shrinking violets who would prefer not to appear on radio or television, it remains unclear why a member of an independent judiciary should be required to remain silent out of court. Judicial independence is compromised not by public explanation of the judge's views but by attempts to restrain him and threats to dismiss him if he does not conform to conventions which have no legal force and are contrary to the public interest. A judge should be fully entitled to speak out on matters of public concern so long as he does not give people cause for suspecting bias or partiality in the cases to be heard in his court and so long as he refrains from comment on matters of political controversy. The ban on judges appearing on radio or television (or writing newspaper articles) has no justification whatsoever.

The judge may have something of value to say, particularly on matters relating to the legal system. (In fact, the *contents* of Judge Pickles's statements in the media were of no interest whatsoever, being distinguished only by their numbing platitudes.) The extra-judicial writings of Lord

Scarman[25] made important contributions to public debates on central issues but did not threaten his independence as a Law Lord. The Lord Chancellor is an active party politician and a member of the Cabinet. Yet he sits, as does Lord Hailsham, with complete judicial independence on the Appellate Committee of the House of Lords. If the Lord Chancellor can wear the two hats of politician and judge, there is no good reason why other judges should be required to remain silent on non-party political matters. Judicial independence will not thereby be enhanced. And the public will lose the opportunity to learn about the procedures and substance of the law. Whatever one's view of the literary merits of Lord Denning's books, his writings did serve the valuable purpose of explaining to thousands of laymen the hitherto incomprehensible workings of their legal system. It is difficult to see how confidence in the law could be weakened by such writings.

Broadcasting is no different in principle to a written publication by the judge. It cannot seriously be suggested that a judge, who has had a lengthy and successful career as an advocate, is likely to be confused or intimidated by the pressures of speaking into a microphone. In any event, it is desirable for the public to have the opportunity to learn about the identity of those who sit in judgment over them. Judicial views inevitably influence judicial decisions,[26] so we are entitled to know more about the men (and the few women) who interpret and apply the law.

An enforced silence has farcical results. In 1986 a distinguished judge gave a public lecture on a legal topic of importance. Because of the Kilmuir rules, he felt obliged to decline to give a radio interview on the same subject to the BBC legal affairs programme, *Law in Action*, to be broadcast in the week of the lecture.

The folly of the Kilmuir rules is further indicated by the

fact that there are already many ways in which judges do express their views out of court. Judges frequently chair or conduct commissions and inquiries on a range of issues, some of them politically controversial. These have covered, amongst other sensitive topics, the Brixton riots (considered by Lord Scarman in 1981), miners' pay (Lord Wilberforce in 1972), and various aspects of disorder in Northern Ireland (for example, Lord Widgery's inquiry in 1972 into the events of 'Bloody Sunday' in which civilians were killed, and Lord Diplock's report in the same year on the legal procedures to deal with terrorist activities in the province). As Chairman of the Security Commission, Lord Bridge, a Law Lord, inquired into and reported on the politically controversial subject of telephone tapping in 1985. All the evidence was heard in secret and only the judge's conclusions were made public.[27]

Judges who are peers of the realm (such as the Law Lords and the Lord Chief Justice) contribute to legislative debates in the House of Lords. Although they usually confine themselves to anodyne questions of law reform, they have occasionally addressed controversial topics such as capital punishment.[28] Judges often give lectures on legal issues. Sometimes a judge will comment publicly on matters of social policy. In May 1983, during the General Election campaign, Lord Chief Justice Lane addressed the annual meeting of the National Association of Prison Visitors. He told his audience, 'We must start trying to get back a little way towards what your critics call Victorian morality. If we don't it will go on getting worse.'[29]

So concerned was Lord Hailsham about the dangers of judges opening their mouths out of court that he 'discourage[d] people on the Bench from seeking to defend themselves' when criticized.[30] Judges usually take this advice. But there have been exceptions, showing that it was incorrect

177

for Lord Denning to say that 'from the nature of our office, we cannot reply to their criticisms'.[31] Indeed, in 1972 Lord Denning himself made a statement in open court explaining how an application had come before the Court of Appeal in the case of three dockers committed to prison by the National Industrial Relations Court for contempt of court.[32] In 1973 Sir John Donaldson, then President of the NIRC, made a speech to the Institute of Chartered Accountants' Dinner in which he explained the decision of the NIRC to sequester trade union funds. 'As some members of that union and some members of the public appear to have misunderstood what occurred,' he said, 'may I take this opportunity of setting the record straight.'[33] In June 1986 Mr Justice Alliott called reporters to his chambers to explain his decision in a case brought by the Forestry Commission to compel a hippy convoy to leave the New Forest. The judge was concerned to emphasize that he had not, contrary to some press reports, allowed the convoy to remain on the land for a further seven days.[34]

Occasionally, one judge replies to criticism of another. In a Divisional Court judgment in 1983, Lord Justice Kerr commented that the Court of Appeal and House of Lords judgments in the GLC fares case in 1982 were

widely misunderstood and, in many cases, obviously misrepresented. Some of the public comments gave the misleading impression that ... the judgments ... were designed to thwart the wishes of the majority on the GLC for political motives. Such reactions, whether based on ignorance or whatever, can only be described as total rubbish.[35]

Law Lords have published letters in *The Times* in response to criticism of their judgments: Lord Davey in 1904, Lord Maugham in 1941,[36] and Viscount Dilhorne in 1975 took this step.[37] In 1975 Mr Justice Bridge adopted what he called 'the wholly exceptional course' of writing to *The Times* to respond to criticism of one of his decisions.[38]

Despite these indications that the English judge can contribute to public life outside his courtroom, he remains noted for his low profile. The giants of the modern bench were Lord Reid, Lord Diplock, and Lord Wilberforce. By their judgments in the 1960s and 1970s they all played a major role in developing judicial review of administrative action. Yet the characters and performance of these distinguished public servants remained substantially undiscussed by or for non-lawyers, despite the fact that they carried out their duties in public. 'The Law Lords have not attracted the attentions of biographers.'[39]

The one modern judge who was known to laymen was Lord Denning. As he realized, 'my appearances on television have been so frequent that taxi-drivers and passers-by recognize me'.[40] He was 'the proud possessor of T-shirts from universities all the world over. On them is reproduced a photograph of me in my full-bottomed wig—or a cartoon.'[41] In this, as in so many other respects, Lord Denning was unique among the members of the English judiciary. His idiosyncrasies were based on the strength of character and the commitment to open justice (though he by no means applied it consistently in all the cases he decided) of a remarkable man.[42] Most other judges, although equally committed to justice being administered in open court, regrettably prefer or tolerate seclusion from the public gaze in many respects.

The fault lies with the media as well as with the judiciary. The press and the electronic media devote far less attention to the meaning and implications of court decisions than they do to the posturings and pronouncements of politicians. The BBC appointed its first legal affairs correspondent, Joshua

Rozenberg, as recently as 1985. Judicial appointments, even at the level of a Law Lord, attract far less press attention than a promotion to a minor political office. By contrast, in the USA the nomination and appointment of a Supreme Court Justice cause intense press and public attention to be given to the views and background of the nominee. Since Law Lords, like Supreme Court Justices, make decisions which have a vital impact on society, it matters what prospective judges think about political and moral issues, such as trade union reform, the power of local authorities, or the prescription of contraceptives to girls under the age of 16. The English public, unlike the American public, does not find out what its judges believe before the cases are decided.

The reluctance of judges to speak out of court and the inadequate manner in which legal issues are reported results in 'popular opinion about judges and judging [being] a sad affair of empty slogans'.[43] To aid understanding of the judicial branch of government, judges should be more prepared to take off their wigs and explain their decisions to the public. In a 1980 lecture an Australian High Court judge, Sir Ninian Stephen, suggested that when a court issues an important judgment it could at the same time publish 'a detailed press release which does explain, in layman's language, what were the issues, who won and why'.[44] The need to translate legalisms into English might even concentrate the minds of the judges on producing a principled decision. The European Court of Human Rights in Strasbourg and the European Court of Justice in Luxembourg produce such press releases to assist non-specialists to understand what the judges have decided. The Court of Appeal and the House of Lords could usefully do the same.[45]

Two objections are raised to the suggestion of increased

visibility for the judiciary. First, that what the judge says out of court might cloud or contradict what he has said in his judgment. This poses no problem. The law is stated in the court judgment. What is said out of court is of importance in providing information for the public, but it does not constitute a source of law. Secondly, that increased prominence for judges out of court threatens their independence. We all know that judges, as intelligent human beings, have political, social, and moral views. The independence of the judiciary is not under greater threat because those views are more frequently the subject of public discussion. Judicial independence relies not on a man's silence out of court but on ensuring that he decides cases fairly according to law, by reference to the evidence and argument he hears in court, and irrespective of political pressure. Of course, judges need to avoid pre-judging, or giving the impression of pre-judging, issues which may come before their courts on future occasions. Judicial comment on cases the judges have already decided, and more general observations on the nature of the judicial function and on the strengths and weaknesses of our system of administering justice, cannot harm judicial independence.

Allowing judges to speak out of court is unlikely to lead to a dramatic change in the demeanour and personality of the English judge. There is certainly no danger of his emulating the example of a New York Supreme Court judge who appeared as a contestant on an American television quiz show in August 1980 and 'called the game to order' with the words 'Hear ye, hear ye!'[46] The removal of the restraints on the English judge would not change his character. But it would make him more willing to speak publicly about his job. Slowly but surely, public understanding of the legal system would be improved.

III

Jonathan Swift suggested that our judges are 'picked out from the most dextrous lawyers who are grown old or lazy'.[47] In fact, we have on the Bench civil servants who are greatly experienced in, and knowledgeable about, the workings of the legal system. They are often well able to appreciate the respects in which the procedure and the substance of the law need reform.[48] As Gerald Gardiner (Lord Chancellor 1964–70) observed in 1953, judges 'see the injustices and anomalies as they arise in practice to a greater degree than anyone else.'[49] The views of members of the judiciary on such matters would be more representative, more powerfully expressed, more widely read and considered, and more likely to be acted upon if our judges could be persuaded to meet in a regular conference. They could there discuss relevant matters to the benefit of themselves and the public, the latter being able to read of their concerns and conclusions in a published report. The Judicial Conference is an institution well known to American judges, in State and Federal jurisdictions.

The English judiciary was more gregarious in previous centuries. In 1617 Lord Chancellor Bacon addressed the judges prior to their departure on circuit. He reminded them that it was one of their duties 'upon your return, to present to the King the distastes and griefs of the people'. After completing their judicial tasks on circuit, the judges met in Serjeants' Inn and prepared a report for James I.[50] In 1715 Lord Chancellor Somers revived this practice, telling the judges that on their return from circuit the King expected them to 'inform him of all such things as you shall observe and may be for his service to know'.[51] Judges also acted 'as messengers from the Lords to the Commons', a custom that continued until as late as 1871.[52]

Until recently the machinery existed to encourage the judiciary to meet and report on a regular basis. In 1873 Parliament required a Council of the judges of the Supreme Court (that is the High Court and the Court of Appeal) to meet at least once a year, on a date fixed by the Lord Chancellor with the agreement of the Lord Chief Justice. All the judges had to be given notice of the meeting, which was to be held for the purpose of 'enquiring and examining into any defects which may appear to exist in the system of procedure or the administration of the law'. The Council was required to produce an annual report to the Secretary of State on the amendments, if any, to the law which the judges thought desirable 'for the better administration of justice'.[53] The legal obligation to call such meetings was removed in 1981,[54] possibly because successive Lord Chancellors had not complied with its terms.[55] The Council 'met only intermittently'[56] and did not produce an annual report.

Meetings of judges have occasionally occurred for particular purposes. In 1936 Lord Chief Justice Hewart 'called a meeting of the King's Bench judges and asked them to encourage rather than discourage the use of juries in civil actions'.[57] On the creation of the Restrictive Practices Court in 1956, Lord Chancellor Kilmuir invited all the judges to a meeting to reassure them about the merits of the new jurisdiction.[58] When the United Kingdom entered the European Community in 1973, the judges met to have the legal implications explained to them by a Law Lord.

Judicial meetings have resulted in important changes to law and practice. The M'Naghten Rules form the basis of the law on insanity as a defence to a criminal charge. In 1843 M'Naghten was acquitted (on the ground of insanity) of murdering the secretary to the Prime Minister, Sir Robert Peel. The Rules derive from the answers given by all the judges, with the exception of Mr Justice Maule, to abstract questions of law thereafter put by the House of Lords. Maule J expressed concern that the judges should be asked hypothetical questions of law, the answers to which 'may embarrass the administration of justice when they are cited in criminal trials'.[59] In thanking the judges for their answers, Lord Brougham noted the reservations of Mr Justice Maule, but insisted that 'there can be no doubt of your Lordships' right to put, in this way, abstract questions of law to the Judges, the answer to which might be necessary to your Lordships in your legislative capacity'.[60] The Judges' Rules (which governed the admissibility as evidence at a criminal trial of answers and statements made by an accused person) were originally formulated by the judges of the King's Bench Division in 1912 and 1918. A revised version was announced by the Lord Chief Justice in 1964 after being approved by a meeting of the Queen's Bench Division judges.[61] In 1986 a meeting of judges led to the change in practice which gave solicitors a right of audience in the High Court in formal or unopposed proceedings.[62]

On occasions, senior judges have been consulted by civil servants, in private, on matters of legal policy. At the end of 1983 it was revealed that the Master of the Rolls, Sir John Donaldson, had been asked to advise how the judiciary could play a more constructive role in industrial relations. Defending this episode against complaints that it harmed the independence of the judiciary, Lord Chancellor Hailsham said that it was 'a perfectly innocent conversation between a . . . civil servant . . . and the Master of the Rolls in which, following the practice which I think has been the practice of successive Governments, he sought to inform himself of matters which were within the Master of the Rolls' own experience and which the Master of the Rolls himself had largely dealt with in the course of a public lecture'.[63] The use of judicial experience is very sensible.

The only basis for criticizing such consultation is that it involved private, rather than public, expressions of judicial views to the Government of the day. There is a real danger of 'the diminution of public confidence in the courts if it is believed that the judges are in secret communication with another branch of the government'.[64]

It is difficult to reconcile Lord Hailsham's approach to that episode with his hostile reaction to judicial comments made in court in 1985 on another topic of public interest. The Government announced their intention to remove the right of appeal to the Court of Appeal against the refusal of a Divisional Court judge to grant leave to bring proceedings for judicial review of the decision of a public authority. A Bill before Parliament sought to achieve this objective. In granting leave in such an appeal in January 1985, Lord Justice Ackner said that the Court of Appeal was 'troubled' by the terms of the Bill. He added that the case before the court 'demonstrates ... very strongly the merits of the present rules which allow unrestricted access to the Court of Appeal in this field, where so much of the litigation is directed to preventing alleged abuses of power'.[65] Later the same week, Lord Justice Purchas, for the Court of Appeal, reiterated that concern.[66]

During the Committee Stage of the Bill in the House of Lords a few days later, Lord Hailsham delivered an astonishing rebuke to the critical judges. He told the House of Lords that he had received

letters of apology from the two members of the Court of Appeal. ... They should never have said what they said from the Bench, and they have both apologised to me. Let me say that what they said was improper. ... It is perfectly legitimate for the Judiciary to criticize the state of the law as it is and to draw the attention of Parliament [to it] in order that it may be improved. ... It is utterly improper in my judgment for a Court of Appeal judge or any other judge speaking on the Bench to criticize matters passing through Parliament.[67]

The Government's proposal to remove the right of appeal in such judicial review cases was eventually abandoned.

The idea that judges should be obliged to remain silent in court in the face of a proposal which, in the light of their knowledge and experience, they consider to be damaging to the administration of justice, is quite absurd. Coming from the Lord Chancellor, especially one who saw the protection of the independence of the judiciary as one of his main responsibilities, it is breathtaking. Judges should not be treated like children in Victorian times, required to remain silent unless spoken to. They are entitled, indeed they have a public duty, to speak out on matters concerning the administration of justice. The Lord Chancellor was the Minister responsible for the progress of the Bill in the House of Lords. That he should accept and should repeat an 'apology' from members of an independent judiciary for criticizing the Government's legislative proposal is far more damaging to the separation of powers than the entirely proper actions of Lords Justices Ackner and Purchas could possibly be.

This shabby episode demonstrates the continuing restraints which are placed on judges who wish to express their views on legal matters of public interest on which they are especially qualified to speak. It is far from clear why judges should be entitled to criticize a law enacted by Parliament but not to point to the same defect in a Bill before Parliament and so help to prevent bad law being created. How very different from the government of Henry V who, according to Shakespeare, told his Chief Justice that 'My voice shall sound as you do prompt mine ear, / And I will stoop and humble my intents / To your well-practis'd wise direction'.[68]

There are limits on the extent to which judicial expertise should be used by the other branches of government. Judges need to avoid being associated with any particular political party, lest their independence be impugned. It would no longer be acceptable for the Chief Justice to be a member of the Cabinet, as was Lord Mansfield from 1757 to 1765[69] and Lord Ellenborough in 1806.[70] Another precedent unlikely to be followed today is that for two months in 1918–19 Lord Cave was a Lord of Appeal and Home Secretary.[71] Nor would it be desirable for an English judge to imitate the practice of some US Supreme Court Justices, for example Felix Frankfurter, of habitually advising the President on politically controversial matters.[72]

So long as judges avoid associating themselves with political parties, and so long as they refrain from commenting on the legality of specific issues which may later come before their court, there is much to be said for the other branches of government taking advantage of the expertise of the judiciary in formulating public policy on matters concerned with the administration of justice. At present, the views of the judiciary on such matters are unlikely to be heard and considered unless the judge is privately approached by civil servants, or expresses himself in court, or defies the conventions by speaking up out of court. The attitude of Lord Eldon, Lord Chancellor in the early years of the nineteeth century, that 'it is better the law should be certain than that every judge should speculate upon improvements in it',[73] retains few adherents and deserves even fewer. We 'ought to use the knowledge and experience of the judges more fully than we do' since this constitutes 'a latent fund of suggestion of very high value'.[74] Lord Eldon would have disapproved of the idea of a judicial conference. Those who welcome judicial contributions to the making of policy on the administration of justice will recognize that the taking of private soundings is no substitute for the proper discussion and presentation of judicial views.

It is a big step in the right direction that Sir John Donaldson, the Master of the Rolls, makes an annual report on the work of the Court of Appeal. In his October 1986 report he sensibly suggested that the senior judges of the Divisions of the High Court might issue such an annual statement. This would 'provide Parliament and a wider public with an additional and authoritative source of information on the administration of justice in England and Wales and, in particular, on what defects exist and how they might be remedied'.[75]

Dr Johnson believed that no judge 'can give his whole attention to his office; and it is very proper that he should employ what time he has to himself, for his own advantage, in the most profitable manner . . . No man would be a judge, upon the condition of being obliged to be totally a judge.'[76] When Boswell 'argued warmly against the judges trading, and mentioned Hale as an instance of a perfect judge, who devoted himself entirely to his office', Johnson replied that Hale 'attended to other things besides law: he left a great estate'.[77] The suggestion that judges should devote more of their time out of court to making themselves and their views known to the public requires as a corollary that the judicial burden in court be lightened. At present, judges 'already, in the discharge of their proper function, have more than enough to do'.[78]

This was not always the case. During the reign of Henry VI in the fifteenth century, 'the judges never sat more than three hours a day, from eight in the morning till eleven, employing the rest of their time in refection [eating and drinking], reading and contemplation'.[79] By the beginning of the nineteenth century judicial duties had become burdensome. Robert Louis Stevenson's Lord Justice-Clerk, Lord

Hermiston, had no time to talk to his young son. Every evening he 'would take the decanter and the glass, and be off to the back chamber looking on the meadows, where he toiled on his cases till the hours were small'.[80] By contrast with his American counterpart, the English judge usually sits in court for five days a week during termtime, hearing and deciding cases. Court business is organized to ensure, misguidedly, that at no time during the day is the judge without a case before him in court. He has few, if any, days set aside for reading, reflecting, and writing judgments. The work of the judge needs to be reorganized in the manner suggested by John Copley, the Attorney-General (who later became Lord Chancellor Lyndhurst) in the 1820s: he was

anxious not to overload the judges with business so as to make them, as they actually were in too many instances, slaves to the technical part of the profession. He would give them the opportunity of cultivating general literature, he would allow them leisure to return to the pleasant pursuits of early days. . . . When an individual was raised to the bench he should have the opportunity of directing his mind beyond the mere technical duties of his office; he should be able to turn his attention to what was passing in the world.[81]

Judges need a few days a month out of court, and a sabbatical term every few years,[82] to give them the time to keep up to date with legal and extra-legal developments and the opportunity to make a contribution out of court to issues relating to the administration of justice.

IV

English courts do not welcome the presence of the electronic media. In this respect, twentieth-century Lord Chancellors apply principles similar to those of their seventeenth-century predecessor Francis Bacon: 'a popular judge is a deformed thing'.[83]

Section 41 of the Criminal Justice Act 1925 makes it a criminal offence to take, or attempt to take, a photograph, or (with a view to publication) to make a sketch or portrait of a juror, witness, litigant, or judge, in the courtroom, the court building, or the precincts, or to publish any such prohibited image. In the 1890s the *Law Times* suggested that Mr Justice Denman 'went much too far in saying he would have sketching barristers turned out of court'.[84] In July 1986 a woman was fined £100 for contempt of court, and had her film exposed, after photographing a judge at Wolverhampton Crown Court. Originally the judge had fined her £500. But a week after imposing the sentence he reduced the fine 'in the light of your apology and the embarrassment the case has caused your husband'. The guilty party, Mrs Joan Maynard, afterwards explained that she 'only took the photograph because it was the first time [she] had seen a judge dressed up'.[85]

Under section 9 of the Contempt of Court Act 1981 it is a contempt to tape record court proceedings, unless the court gives permission (which may be subject to such conditions as the court thinks fit as to the use to be made of any recording).[86] Even when the court gives permission for the making of a recording, under section 9(1)(b) it is a contempt of court to broadcast or otherwise publish a recording of legal proceedings.[87] The television camera does not receive any warmer welcome in our courts than the tape recorder.[88]

American courts have achieved a more satisfactory synthesis between the integrity of legal proceedings and the interests of the viewing and listening public. In 1981 the US Supreme Court unanimously held in *Chandler* v. *Florida* that a State may provide for radio, television, and still photographic coverage of a criminal trial despite the objection of the man or woman on trial.[89] The accused in a criminal trial has no general constitutional right to keep the broadcaster out of the courtroom. Similar principles would apply to a civil trial.

Most American States have allowed the television cameras into court, under a variety of conditions and in specified circumstances. The evidence produced by the camera has not been wholly flattering to the American system of justice. Inarticulate advocates, bigoted jurymen, careerist prosecutors, and incompetent judges have been seen to inhabit a legal system that leaves much to be desired by way of efficiency and fairness. Before English lawyers collapse into the easy chair of complacency and congratulate themselves on the superiority of their legal system, they need to consider why the cameras are not allowed to permeate the English court and what detriments this ban imposes on the English public.

The English legal system retains the essential defect identified by Henry Brougham in his epic six-hour speech to the House of Commons on law reform in 1828: the legal system is 'a sealed book' rather than 'a living letter'.[90] An important part of the governmental process is still isolated from and incomprehensible to the majority of citizens. If lawyers are concerned, as they should be, to educate and interest laymen in the workings of the legal system, it is absurd to ignore the most popular medium of mass communication.

The arguments against the introduction of cameras in court concentrate on five adverse consequences which it is claimed would result. The American experience demonstrates that none of these has substance.

First, it is said, the mechanical equipment would cause disruption. American courts introduced bans on photographers in court (and later extended the ban to the electronic media) after the farcical scenes at the 1935 trial of Bruno Richard Hauptmann, who was charged with the kidnapping and murder of the Lindbergh child. The photographers in court were partly responsible for the circus-like atmosphere that helped to prevent a fair trial. By contrast, technical equipment is nowadays extremely sophisticated. Cameras make no noise, need no special lighting, and take up little space, especially if confined to fixed positions in court. Judges possess ample powers to commit for contempt of court anyone who disturbs the proceedings. The granting of permission to broadcasters to film or record court business would not remove their obligation generally to conduct themselves in a manner which did not disrupt the court.

Secondly, it is objected that the presence of the camera or tape recorder would influence the conduct of the participants in the trial, civil or criminal. This assertion has neither evidence nor logic to support it. The lawyer who imagines himself to be Perry Mason and performs for the camera rather than for the court will soon find himself the victim of the unemployment endemic to the acting profession. It is very doubtful whether those who are appointed to the Bench are going to be adversely influenced by the fact that their performance may be broadcast to a wider audience.[91] If they are, their qualifications for serving as judges are doubtful.

There may be a danger that the presence of the camera could lead a jury to forget its responsibilities. After one televised trial in Florida in 1979, the defendants announced that they were considering an appeal against the $1.6 million judgment given against them. A ground of appeal was that the jury members were so excited by being on television that they were 'improperly motivated to return a sufficiently spectacular and newsworthy verdict in the hope and expectation that they would receive further television coverage'.[92] If juries are fickle enough to be influenced in this way, then it is jury trial, not television coverage, that ought to be called into question. In appropriate cases, juries are already prohibited until the end of the trial from reading newspaper accounts of the court proceedings because of concern that such accounts might unfairly influence their verdict. Judges have similar powers in relation to television coverage of what happened inside the courtroom.

Courts also have powers to deal with a witness who perjures himself, for whatever reason. So there is no need to banish the camera for fear that a witness might change his evidence. More worrying is the danger that a witness might be overawed by the presence of the television camera and so be unable to give evidence effectively. This argument ignores the fact that the theatrical and artificial atmosphere of the courtroom already inhibits the natural presentation of evidence to a considerable degree. The presence of the camera could do little extra damage in this respect especially if, as would be the case, the camera had a fixed, unobtrusive position in the courtroom.[93]

Whatever the merits of this argument about the impact of broadcasting on the jury and witnesses, it has no force in the many High Court cases, in almost every Court of Appeal case, and in every case in the House of Lords, where there are no witnesses and no jury.

Thirdly, those who oppose allowing the camera into court claim that certain witnesses and parties should be protected from publicity. In those American States which permit the broadcasting of court proceedings, the legislation or other governing rules invariably exclude the camera from defined types of trial (for example child custody, juvenile, matrimonial, or rape cases) in which privacy deserves protection, or when certain types of witness (such as police informers) are giving evidence. This poses no difficulty of principle. In appropriate circumstances, the law already allows the exclusion of the public or empowers the judge to prohibit the publication of relevant details. The broadcaster would be subject to the same types of restrictions as other journalists (although the potential ability of television to identify witnesses and litigants might justify the imposition of special restrictions on what the camera can record in particular cases).

Fourthly, it is said that it is unfair to a defendant in a criminal case, or to the parties in a civil case, that their legal proceedings should be broadcast to a large audience outside the courtroom. Such an argument entirely fails to convince. The existing prohibition on cameras in court applies whatever the wishes of the parties to the case. That many litigants are willing to allow their legal proceedings to be broadcast was demonstrated by the Yorkshire television programme *Case on Camera*, which began in 1984, adopting an idea developed on American television. The producers coaxed Judge Alan King-Hamilton out of retirement to hear evidence and arbitrate civil disputes which would otherwise have been decided in the County Court but which the parties had agreed to submit to trial on television. There was no shortage of litigants willing to appear on television.

Even if a defendant in a criminal case or a litigant in a civil case objects to his trial being broadcast, he has no right of veto in this respect. He cannot complain if the press decides to report his case, perhaps in embarrassing and sensational detail. A trial is a public event. It takes place in a public forum and involves no general rights to privacy. Again, even if this argument were to justify the exclusion of the electronic media from a trial court, it is difficult to give it any weight when one is considering appellate proceedings before the Court of Appeal or the House of Lords where issues of law, often of considerable public importance, are decided.

The fifth and final argument presented by way of resistance to the camera is that the broadcasting of court proceedings will, by the likely nature of the reports, trivialize, sensationalize, or degrade the true nature of the judicial function. In 1965, this argument persuaded a number of judges of the US Supreme Court.

In *Estes* v. *Texas*, Chief Justice Warren and two other Justices of the US Supreme Court concurred in the Court's decision (by 5 votes to 4) that the televising of a criminal trial against the wishes of the defendant was a violation of the defendant's constitutional right to due process of law. The three Justices were concerned that such broadcasting 'would cause the public to equate the trial process with the forms of entertainment regularly seen on television and with the commercial objectives of the television industry'. The judges noted that in the case before them, 'commercials for soft drinks, soups, eye-drops and seatcovers were inserted when there was a pause in the proceedings' and a repeat of the programme had replaced the late-night movie. The judges were anxious that

if trials were televised there would be a natural tendency on the part of broadcasters to develop the personalities of the trial participants, so as to give the proceedings more of an element of drama. . . . The television industry might also decide that the bare-boned trial itself does not contain sufficient drama to sustain an audience. It might provide expert commentary on the proceedings and hire persons with legal backgrounds to anticipate possible trial strategy, as the football expert anticipates plays for his audience.

Chief Justice Warren and his two brethren added that if television companies and trial judges were allowed to become 'partners in the staging of criminal proceedings' then the next step 'might be to schedule the trial for a time that would permit the maximum number of viewers to watch and to schedule recesses to coincide with the need for station breaks'. The television industry's obsession with ratings might, the judges suggested, lead to further steps being taken 'to heighten the dramatic appeal of televised trials'.[94]

In the same case, Justice Harlan, concurring in the decision that the presence of the cameras breached constitutional rights, noted that

the day may come when television will have become so commonplace an affair in the daily life of the average person as to dissipate all reasonable likelihood that its use in courtrooms may disparage the judicial process. If and when that day arrives the constitutional judgment called for now would of course be subject to re-examination.[95]

That day came in 1981 when *Chandler* was decided by the US Supreme Court. The Court recognized that the concerns expressed by Chief Justice Warren and others in the earlier case of *Estes* did not justify 'a constitutional rule barring still photographic, radio and television coverage in all cases and under all circumstances'. Television is, the Court recognized, 'an evolving technology which, in terms of modes of mass communication, was in its relative infancy in 1964, and is, even now, in a state of continuing change'.[96]

Other American courts have dismissed the argument based on the alleged integrity of legal proceedings. In 1979 the Supreme Court of Florida assessed the results of an experiment allowing the electronic media to cover proceedings in State courts. Wisely, the Court was not alarmed by

the spectre of a three-minute segment coverage of the local trial sandwiched between a dog food commercial on the one end and a pantyhose commercial on the other. That may be. However, nothing prohibits the print media from juxtaposing just such advertisements against its news story covering the same trial.

The Court decided that 'there [was] more to be gained than lost by permitting electronic media coverage of judicial proceedings subject to standards for such coverage'.[97]

Anyone who follows the reporting of English legal proceedings will appreciate that our legal system is already, by necessity, sufficiently strong to withstand sensational, trivial, distorted, and erroneous reporting. Preserving the dignity of the court is not a compelling reason for preventing the broadcasting of legal proceedings. Courts are well able to survive their representation by the media.

Even if broadcasting were to pose a threat to the integrity of our courts, still the presence of the camera would bring advantages which would outweigh the detriments. To encourage confidence in, and ensure wider and deeper understanding of, the legal system, it is essential now to allow the most popular medium direct access to our major courts. Newsworthy cases will continue to be reported from outside the courtroom. Such reports, whatever the skill of the relevant journalist, cannot convey an accurate image of legal proceedings.

There is no proper cause for objection to the broadcasting, at the very least, of appeal cases in the Court of Appeal and the House of Lords. The absence of witnesses and jurors, and the concentration on points of law, often of considerable public importance, deprive the camera's opponents of their most compelling arguments. On special occasions, the broadcaster would present the court hearing as a news item, to be given comparable treatment to the statements of Ministers. More routine proceedings might be filmed for documentary purposes, including the education of children and students. Members of the public who are unable to spend time in court would be able to see and hear, through the most popular and most direct medium, what is being done on their behalf. The European Court of Justice and the European Court of Human Rights, in both of which English lawyers appear, have (on occasions) opened their doors to the cameras without this leading to the vices of which the opponents of the electronic media are so afraid.

The English legal system is on the whole blessed with learned lawyers, judicious judges, and courts which offer an efficient service to the consumer. There is little for the courts to fear from the gaze of the television camera. But although justice is done in the English court, it is, in an important sense, not seen to be done. The Scottish judge, Lord Eskgrove, abused an eighteenth-century law reporter foolish enough to try to record the precise terms of a judgment delivered in court: 'The fellow takes down my very words!'[98] In 200 years' time, when the camera is as common a sight in the court as the law reporter's notebook is now, the general reluctance of today's judge to make himself known to the public out of court and his plaintive cry in court—'He wants to record my every word and action!'—will seem as absurd as the behaviour of Lord Eskgrove.

CHAPTER 8

Conclusion

I

THE qualities desired of a judge can be simply stated: 'that he be a good one and that he be thought to be so'.[1] Such credentials are not easily acquired. The judge needs to have 'the strength to put an end to injustice'[2] and 'the faculties that are demanded of the historian and the philosopher and the prophet'.[3]

The judge is expected to display such physical and mental tricks while watching an unpredictable daily drama with an ever-changing cast of characters. All human life is on display in the courtroom. The most inquisitive of spectators will find satisfaction in the presentation throughout the season of the personal conduct, thoughts, and motives of all manner of people who are unfortunate enough to find themselves involved with the law.

The drama which demands such close judicial attention will have suspense: as Mr Justice Megarry said in a 1968 judgment, 'the path of the law is strewn with examples of open and shut cases which, somehow, were not; of unanswerable charges which, in the event, were completely answered; of inexplicable conduct which was fully explained . . .'.[4] There is the cathartic tragedy of villains receiving their just deserts. There is rich comedy and there is the farce of litigants and lawyers chasing each other through a series of connecting rooms, trying to avoid the banana skins liberally placed under them by Parliament, the appeal courts, and fate.

Three distinct questions compete for the attention of the judge: what are the facts, what does the law require or permit, and is the law fair? The factual questions are important but often uninteresting. The moral questions are interesting but rarely of practical importance for judges whose job it is to apply the law (though Earl Warren, Chief Justice of the US Supreme Court 1953–69, would ask counsel acting for the State who cited supporting precedent, 'Yes, yes—but were you fair?').[5] Questions about the content of the law are frequently both interesting and important. On their answer may depend people's livelihood, reputation, or future well-being.

How judges should decide hard cases in which the law is unclear has troubled philosophers since biblical times. In Exodus we are told that the ordinary judges decided the easy cases, 'but the hard cases they brought unto Moses'.[6] Since then a variety of theories have been advanced, some more sensible than others, to explain where the limits of the law lie. Natural lawyers argue that the law is to be defined by reference to moral criteria. The Realist school asserts that the law depends on what the judge had for breakfast. One of the proponents of the new, but influential, school of economic lawyers, Richard Posner, is a judge of the US Court of Appeals. In 1986 Judge Posner, for the majority of his court, held that in deciding whether to grant an interlocutory (or preliminary) injunction pending the trial of a civil action, a court should use

the help of a simple formula: grant the preliminary injunction if but only if $P \times Hp > (1 - P) \times Hd$, or, in words, only if the harm to the plaintiff if the injunction is denied, multiplied by the probability that the denial would be an error (that the plaintiff, in other words, will win at trial), exceeds the harm to the defendant if the injunction is granted, multiplied by the probability that granting the injunction would be an error . . .

Judge Swygert, dissenting, urged that 'judges asked to issue a preliminary injunction must, in large part, rely on their own judgment, not on mathematical quanta'.[7]

Few English judges carry a slide-rule. Such a tool would not help them to ascend to the heights of classical allusion[8] or to decide cases which descend to the depths of degradation and despair. A computer would be immune from accusations of political bias and would avoid creating unnecessary aphorisms.[9] It could not produce the style that makes some judgments works of literature that are read and enjoyed long after the subject-matter of the litigation has ceased to be of importance. Nor could it possess the human quality of empathy which characterizes the decision of the great judge.

The slide-rule approach fails to understand that non-mathematical judgment is central to adjudication. If judging cases merely involved the application of settled rules to established facts 'there would be little of intellectual interest about it. The man who had the best card index of the cases would also be the wisest judge.'[10] Because it concerns the unique and unpredictable circumstances of other people's lives, adjudication cannot depend upon mathematical certainties and probabilities. The judge is expected to make sense of acts and omissions which may defy logical or emotional explanation. 'No court can make time stand still',[11] but every judge is expected regularly to perform other miracles of analysis. A man complaining about his expulsion from a trade union did not attend the hearing of the disciplinary tribunal, 'giving as his reason that he had made a previous engagement to be the judge at a "mock trial" sponsored by a girls' group. That seems a poor excuse.'[12] Even when the facts are credible, the law is not necessarily so. The judge is required to interpret and apply laws which may be devoid of any rational basis: a 'rule is none the less capable of being a rule of law, though no reason can be given for it'.[13]

No computer would be tolerated if it were responsible for those judgments which are so obviously erroneous or otherwise defective that they are immediately discarded.[14] No judge can be expected always to reach the right answer. To err is human and judges are not divine (though on the retirement of Lord Justice Lawton in December 1986, Lord Lane paid him the extraordinary tribute that 'if Fred has ever made a mistake, I have yet to come across it').[15] Since judges are capable of misinterpreting the law after hearing and considering detailed argument, the rest of us—lawyers as well as laymen—can be excused for our own errors of analysis. The unpredictable nature of litigation should be more widely understood. Partly because there is no guarantee that the judge will decide the law correctly, the best legal advice is that given in the Sermon on the Mount: 'If someone sues you, come to terms with him promptly while you are both on your way to court . . .'[16] Judge Learned Hand was the wisest of judges in confessing that he would, as a litigant, 'dread a lawsuit beyond almost anything else short of sickness and of death'.[17] Since judicial error is inevitable so long as cases are decided by men rather than machines, we need to consider who pays for these judicial mistakes. When, by reason of a judicial error, a party to legal proceedings incurs additional costs—for example in having to bring or defend an appeal—the Lord Chancellor ought to have power to meet the expense out of central funds.[18]

The law is an art, not a precise science in which empirically verifiable results can be produced. No lawyer can be sure what the result will be if he presents certain witnesses and certain precedents before a court of law. As Jeremy Bentham advised (and allowing for inflation), if one wants to know the content of the law, too often 'as well-grounded a guess might be had of an astrologer for five shillings as of a counsel for twice or thrice as many guineas'.[19] It is not in the interests of the lawyer to advertise that fact. As the advocate in Kafka's *The Trial* tells K, 'progress had always been made, but the nature of the progress could never be divulged'.[20] A judge who 'made a bet' on the result of certain litigation 'would be disqualified' from sitting on the Bench to hear the case.[21] No sensible litigant would indulge in such a wager.

II

Subjection to the daily pressures of judging other people's lives is bound to make some judges behave in strange ways. The seventeenth-century Sir John Maynard had so devoted a passion for the law that 'he left a will purposely worded so as to cause litigation, in order that sundry questions, which had been "moot points" in his lifetime, might be settled for the benefit of posterity'.[22] Mr Justice Byles, who sat on the Bench in the second half of the nineteenth century, is reported to have said that he always found 'difficulty in appreciating the arguments of counsel whose legs are encased in light-coloured trousers'.[23] Lord Justice Scrutton 'was possibly the only Englishman of his time [1856–1934] who never shaved in his life'.[24]

Those who sit in judgment over their fellow citizens have an extremely difficult task to perform. They will best be assisted if we appreciate their limitations. To mystify the judiciary is unfairly to create expectations which judges cannot possibly satisfy.

Judges

The way in which some judges and many laymen see the judicial role is illustrated by an anecdote told by Judge Alan King-Hamilton.[25] On an evening in 1976, a group of teenagers ran after the then 71-year-old judge as he was returning home. They jostled him and ran off with his bowler hat. 'With its disappearance my dignity had gone', the judge thought. He chased the youths, who were apprehended by a passer-by. The judge demanded the return of his hat. When a member of the public threatened the youths that he would 'fetch the Law', King-Hamilton announced, 'You needn't bother; the Law is here already. I am a judge.' His hat was promptly returned to him. This story of the judge and the 'would-be muggers' indicates the continuing majesty of the law. It illustrates the sometimes frightening but often farcical nature of clashes between the law and the lawless. It emphasizes the extent to which, for the vast majority of citizens, men like King-Hamilton are indeed the Law. Such men are decent and dignified, if occasionally wrongheaded, individuals who strive to thwart what they see as the bully and the cheat but who sometimes forget the words of Lord Herschell on being invited by Gladstone in 1886 to become Lord Chancellor: 'one thing at any rate I am resolved, and this is, I will not become a pompous bloke.'[26]

The judiciary is not the 'least dangerous branch' of government.[27] Judges are not mere 'lions under the throne'.[28] They send people to prison and decide the scope and application of all manner of rights and duties with important consequences for individuals and for society. Because the judiciary has such a central role in the government of society, we should (in the words of Justice Oliver Wendell Holmes) 'wash ... with cynical acid'[29] this aspect of public life. Unless and until we treat judges as fallible human beings whose official conduct is subject to the same critical analysis as that of other organs of government, judges will remain members of a priesthood who have great powers over the rest of the community, but who are otherwise isolated from them and misunderstood by them, to their mutual disadvantage.

Some politicians, and a few jurists, urge that it is unwise or even dangerous to tell the truth about the judiciary. Judge Jerome Frank of the US Court of Appeals sensibly explained that he had

little patience with, or respect for, that suggestion. I am unable to conceive ... that, in a democracy, it can ever be unwise to acquaint the public with the truth about the workings of any branch of government. It is wholly undemocratic to treat the public as children who are unable to accept the inescapable shortcomings of man-made institutions ... The best way to bring about the elimination of those shortcomings of our judicial system which are capable of being eliminated is to have all our citizens informed as to how that system now functions. It is a mistake, therefore, to try to establish and maintain, through ignorance, public esteem for our courts.[30]

English judges have every reason to be proud of the quality of their performance and no reason to fear more extensive public knowledge and assessment of their work. Nevertheless, there are aspects of judicial administration— appointment, training, discipline, criticism, mysticism, and publicity—which hinder, or detract from, their ability to serve society. We need judges who are not appointed by the unassisted efforts of the Lord Chancellor and solely from the ranks of middle-aged barristers. We need judges who are trained for the job, whose conduct can be freely criticized and is subject to investigation by a Judicial Performance Commission; judges who abandon wigs, gowns, and unnecessary linguistic legalisms; judges who welcome rather than shun publicity for their activities.

It is unlikely that men and women will ever cease to wound, cheat, and damage each other. There will always be a need for judges to resolve their disputes in an orderly manner. As people grow ever less willing to accept unreservedly the demands of authority, the judiciary, like other public institutions, will be subjected to a growing amount of critical analysis. The way in which 'Judge & Co.'[31] is run is a matter of public interest and will increasingly become a matter of public debate.

NOTES

Abbreviations

A	Atlantic Reporter (USA)
ABAJ	American Bar Association Journal
AC	Law Reports: Appeal Cases (UK)
AIR SC	All India Reports: Supreme Court
ALJR	Australian Law Journal Reports
All ER	All England Law Reports
B & S	Best and Smith's Reports (UK)
Bing (NC)	Bingham's New Cases (UK)
Cal Rptr	California Reporter
Ch	Law Reports: Chancery Division (UK)
Ch D	Law Reports: Chancery Division (UK)
Cl and F	Clark and Finnelly's Reports (UK)
CLJ	Cambridge Law Journal (UK)
CLR	Commonwealth Law Reports (Australia)
CMLR	Common Market Law Reports
Cmnd	Command Papers (UK)
Crim App Reports	Criminal Appeal Reports (UK)
Crim LR	Criminal Law Review (UK)
DLR	Dominion Law Reports (Canada)
ECR	European Court Reports
ER	English Reports
F/F 2d	Federal Reporter (USA)
FEP Cases	Fair Employment Practice Cases (USA)
F Supp	Federal Supplement (USA)
HC	House of Commons (UK)
HL	House of Lords (UK)
HL Cases	House of Lords Cases (UK)
HLR	Harvard Law Review (USA)

ICR	Industrial Cases Reports (UK)
IRLR	Industrial Relations Law Reports (UK)
JP	Justice of the Peace (UK)
KB	Law Reports: King's Bench Division (UK)
LJ	Law Journal (UK)
LJCP	Law Journal: Common Pleas (UK)
LJQB	Law Journal: Queen's Bench (UK)
LQR	Law Quarterly Review (UK)
LR App Cas	Law Reports: Appeal Cases (UK)
LR PC	Law Reports: Privy Council Appeals
LR QB	Law Reports: Queen's Bench (UK)
LT	Law Times (UK)
MLR	Modern Law Review (UK)
NE	North Eastern Reporter (USA)
NI	Northern Ireland Reports
NLJ	New Law Journal (UK)
NSWLR	New South Wales Law Reports (Australia)
NSWR	New South Wales Reports (Australia)
NW	North Western Reporter (USA)
P	Law Reports: Probate, Divorce and Admiralty Division (UK)
PL	Public Law (UK)
QB	Law Reports: Queen's Bench Division (UK)
QBD	Law Reports: Queen's Bench Division (UK)
SALR	South African Law Reports
SC	Session Cases (Scotland)
S Ct	Supreme Court Reporter (USA)
SE	South Eastern Reporter (USA)
SLT	Scots Law Times
So	Southern Reporter (USA)
Sol J	Solicitors' Journal (UK)
SW	South Western Reporter (USA)
Sw & Tr	Swabey and Tristram's Probate Reports (UK)
TLR	Times Law Reports (UK)
US	United States Reports
Ves	Vesey's Chancery Reports (UK)
VLR	Victoria Law Reports (Australia)

WLR	Weekly Law Reports (UK)
WR	Weekly Reporter (UK)
WWR	Western Weekly Reports (Canada)
YLJ	Yale Law Journal (USA)

Preface

1. Franz Kafka, *The Trial* (1925) (Penguin Modern Classics, 1974), p. 134.

1. Introduction

1. *Gargantua and Pantagruel*, transl. J.M. Cohen (Penguin Classics, 1955), Bk. 3, chs. 39–43.
2. *R v. Deputy Industrial Injuries Commissioner ex parte Moore* [1965] 1 QB 456, 488 (Lord Justice Diplock). See also ch. 8, n. 21.
3. 69 *ABAJ* 730 (1983). See also *The Times* 3 Feb. 1982.
4. Archibald Cox, *The Warren Court* (1968), p. 49.
5. Lord Denning, *The Discipline of Law* (1979), p. 289. See *Cassidy* v. *Minister of Health* [1951] 2 KB 343, 363 where Lord Justice Denning said it was 'unfortunate that the principle which I have enunciated was not drawn to the attention of the court in [an earlier case], but that was my fault, because I was counsel in the case'.
6. Louis Blom-Cooper QC and Gavin Drewry, *Final Appeal: A Study of the House of Lords in its Judicial Capacity* (1972), p. 146.
7. *Salisbury* v. *Gilmore* [1942] 2 KB 38, 51 (Lord Justice MacKinnon).
8. See, for example, *R* v. *Shivpuri* [1986] 2 WLR 988 where the Law Lords concluded that a decision they had made a year earlier on the law of criminal attempts was wrong in law and so would be overruled. See also *R* v. *Hancock* [1986] AC 455, 472–3 where the Law Lords said that guidelines on directing juries in murder trials laid down by the House of Lords in a case a year earlier were 'unsafe and misleading'. For good measure, the Law Lords added that a 1961 House of Lords judgment was 'unhappy'. And see *Mandla* v. *Dowell Lee* [1983] 2 AC 548, 568, where Lord Templeman erroneously stated that 'the fields of activity in which discrimination is made a *criminal* [my emphasis] offence are

employment, education and the provision of goods, facilities, services and premises'.

9. *The Times* 20 Aug. 1981.
10. Edward Foss, *Biographia Juridica: A Biographical Dictionary of the Judges of England 1066–1870* (1870), p. 399.
11. The case was *Dred Scott* v. *Sandford* 19 Howard 393 (1857). See, for example, Henry J. Abraham, *The Judicial Process* (5th edn., 1986), p. 227. See also Charles Warren, *The Supreme Court in United States History* (rev. edn., 1937), vol. 2, p. 357: 'It may fairly be said that Chief Justice Taney elected Abraham Lincoln to the Presidency.'
12. See ch. 3, p. 65.
13. See Robert Stevens, *Law and Politics: The House of Lords as a Judicial Body 1800–1976* (1979), p. 95, on how the Law Lords' decision in *Taff Vale Railway Co.* v. *Amalgamated Society of Railway Servants* [1901] AC 426 'drove the unions to political action—specifically to the support of the Labour party—and produced concrete results in the 1906 general election in the form of a massive Liberal landslide, with many of the MPs in the category of "Lib-Labs"'.
14. *Gillick* v. *West Norfolk and Wisbech Area Health Authority* [1986] AC 112, 201 (Lord Templeman).
15. *Tutton* v. *A. D. Walter Ltd.* [1985] 3 WLR 797, 807 (Denis Henry QC sitting as a Deputy High Court judge).
16. Francis Bacon 'Of Judicature' in *Essays* (1625) (Everyman edn., 1973), p. 162.
17. Lord Reid, 'The Judge as Law Maker' 12 *Journal of the Society of Public Teachers of Law* 22 (1972).
18. A. P. Herbert, *Uncommon Law* (1977 edn.), p. 156.
19. Cited in R. F. V. Heuston, *Lives of the Lord Chancellors 1885–1940* (1964), p. 581.
20. *Rondel* v. *Worsley* [1969] 1 AC 191, 257–8 (Lord Pearce). In the same case, Mr Justice Lawton, in the High Court, said that the plaintiff seemed to think that the term 'fraudulent' was 'some kind of legal lubricant which made the words of his statement of claim read better': [1967] 1 QB 443, 453.
21. William O. Douglas, *The Court Years 1939–75* (1980), p. 217.
22. *O'Hair* v. *Paine* 312 F Supp 434 (1969). The District Court judge added, at p. 438, that 'with regard to the scheduling of the Apollo 8 flight during the Christmas season, it is approaching the absurd to say that this is a violation of the [Constitution] because of the religious significance of that date'.

23. *Osei* v. *Old Time Gospel Hour* 35 FEP Cases 1504 (US District Court: 1984).
24. *Clark* v. *Florida* 106 S Ct 1784, 1786 (1986).
25. This was Lord Atkin's description of work in the Court of Appeal: Geoffrey Lewis, *Lord Atkin* (1983), p. 93. See similarly H. Montgomery Hyde, *Norman Birkett* (1964), p. 546, for the same opinion by Birkett (who sat in the Court of Appeal from 1950–6).
26. See ch. 3, p. 53.
27. Interview with Joshua Rozenberg broadcast on BBC Radio 4, 25 Nov. 1985. See also *Attorney-General's Reference (No. 1 of 1985)* [1986] QB 491, 506, where Lord Lane wisely observed (on behalf of the Court of Appeal) that 'there are topics of conversation more popular in public houses than the finer points of the equitable doctrine of the constructive trust'.
28. Section 10(4) Supreme Court Act 1981 read with section 4 Promissory Oaths Act 1868.
29. William Blackstone, *Commentaries on the Laws of England* (1765), vol. 1, p. 69.
30. L.N. Tolstoy, *Resurrection* (1899) (transl. Rosemary Edmunds, Penguin Classics, 1966), pp. 41 and 47.
31. Above, n. 10 at pp. 315–16.
32. *The Times* 20 Nov. 1981.
33. Above, n. 10 at p. 762. See ch. 5, p. 139, on the Treason Act 1351 and for examples of assaults on judges.
34. *The Times* 28 Sept. 1984.
35. Section 16(4) Courts Act 1971.
36. Lord Chancellor's Department *Judicial Appointments: The Lord Chancellor's Policies and Procedures* (1986), p. 4. The Report of a Justice Sub-Committee on *The Judiciary* (1972), para. 126, suggested that 'there is a need for regular medical examination[s] for judges if satisfactory tests can be devised'.
37. 415 HL 1218–19 (18 Dec. 1980: Second Reading of the Supreme Court Bill). In September 1986 judges at the Central Criminal Court in London were asked to work overtime to help reduce the backlog of pending cases. Normal court hours of 10.30 a.m. to 4 p.m., with an hour for lunch, were increased so that the court day began at 10 a.m. and ended at 5 p.m. See *The Times* 20 Sept. 1986. A Committee appointed by the Lord Chancellor's Department has recommended that judges should work longer hours in court and should have shorter holidays: ibid. 12 Mar. 1987. Sir John

Donaldson, Master of the Rolls, has pointed out that judges already work long hours out of court: ibid. 21 Mar. 1987.

38. *Coldunell Ltd* v. *Gallon* [1986] QB 1184, 1211. In Tel Aviv, Israel, six judges have claimed compensation from the State National Insurance fund for physical disabilities and illnesses which they claim are the consequence of the 'tension-filled atmosphere' in which they work: *Jewish Chronicle* 3 and 10 Oct. 1986. Jamaican courts operate under particular difficulties, due to a shortage of money. Subscriptions to the law reports ceased in 1980 and telephone services had been disconnected since July 1985 because the bill had not been paid: *Observer* 4 Jan. 1987.

39. Section 53 Administration of Justice Act 1985.

40. 120 *NLJ* 746–7 (1970).

41. Shimon Shetreet, *Judges on Trial* (1976), p. 374, and *Code of Conduct for the Bar of England and Wales* (3rd edn. incorporating amendments up to 31 Dec. 1984), Annex 8, para. (3).

42. 312 HL 1314 (19 Nov. 1970: Second Reading of the Courts Bill).

43. Sir Alfred Denning, *The Road to Justice* (1955), p. 17.

44. Learned Hand, 'Mr Justice Cardozo' (1939) in *The Spirit of Liberty: Papers and Addresses of Learned Hand* (collected by Irving Dilliard, 1977 edn.), p. 131.

45. Judge Alan King-Hamilton QC, *And Nothing But the Truth* (1982), p. 180.

46. John Lord Campbell, *The Lives of the Chief Justices of England* (3rd edn., 1874), vol. 3, p. 265.

47. Exodus 18: 21–2.

48. *The Federalist Papers* (1788), No. 78.

49. H. Montgomery Hyde, above, n. 25 at p. 486.

50. John Mortimer, *The Trials of Rumpole* (1979), p. 100.

51. *Guardian* 5 Nov. 1985 and 72 *ABAJ* 18 (Feb. 1986).

52. Lord Hailsham, *Speech to the Common Law Bar Association* (3 July 1985).

53. C. P. Harvey, *The Advocate's Devil* (1958), pp. 149 and 151–2.

54. Above, n. 10 at p. 63.

55. Above, n. 52.

56. Learned Hand, 'The Preservation of Personality' (1929), above, n. 44 at p. 43.

57. Lord Hailsham in an Interview with Joseph Yahuda 148 *JP* 739, 757 (1984).

58. Iain Adamson, *The Old Fox* (1963)—a biography of Gilbert Beyfus QC—pp. 144–5.
59. 525 HC 1062–3 (23 Mar. 1954: Second Reading of the Judges' Remuneration Bill). See also Lord Justice Bowen in *Leeson* v. *General Council of Medical Education and Registration* 43 Ch D 366, 385 (1889): 'Judges, like Caesar's wife, should be above suspicion ...'
60. Above, n. 18 at p. 140.
61. 474 HC 1748 (3 May 1950: Second Reading of the High Court and County Court Judges Bill).
62. Geoffrey Lewis, above, n. 25 at pp. v–vi.
63. H. Montgomery Hyde, above, n. 25 at pp. 360–1.
64. *The Times* 10 Feb. 1981 and 13 Feb. 1981.
65. Ibid. 18 Dec. 1979.
66. *International Herald Tribune* 17 Aug. 1983.
67. 65 *ABAJ* 1461 (1979).
68. *Guardian* 20 Feb. 1981. In 1986 the judge at the trial in Grenada of those accused of murdering Maurice Bishop, the former Prime Minister, walked out of the courtroom and refused to return until he was paid his overdue salary: *Independent* 16 Oct. 1986.
69. 71 *ABAJ* 25 (June 1985). See also *Atkins* v. *US* 556 F 2d 1028 (1977) where the US Court of Claims considered and rejected the contention of 140 US Federal judges that they had a constitutional right to pay increases in line with inflation. The Supreme Court declined to overrule that decision: 434 US 1009 (1978).
70. 71 *ABAJ* 21 (1985).
71. *Time Magazine* 20 Aug. 1979.
72. Heuston, above, n. 19 at p. 513.
73. Lord Denning 467 HL 88 (29 July 1985: Debate on the Lord Chancellor's Salary Order).
74. Ibid.
75. Above, nn. 42 and 57.
76. *The Works of Jeremy Bentham* (ed. Bowring: 1843), vol. 7, p. 270 n.
77. *Guardian* 22 July 1986.
78. James Morris, *Pax Britannica* (1979), p. 194.
79. 'The Lion and the Unicorn' in *The Collected Essays, Journalism and Letters of George Orwell* (ed. Sonia Orwell and Ian Angus, 1970), vol. 2, pp. 81–3.
80. Benjamin Cardozo, 'Law and Literature' in *Selected Writings of Benjamin Nathan Cardozo* (ed. Margaret E. Hall, 1947), p. 427.

81. *Dictionary of National Biography* (ed. Sir Leslie Stephen and Sir Sidney Lee, reprinted 1921–2), vol. xv, p. 226.
82. Above, n. 10 at p. 124.
83. Ibid. p. 415.
84. J. B. Atlay, *The Victorian Chancellors* (1906), vol. 1, p. 41.
85. John Lord Campbell, *Lives of the Lord Chancellors* (5th edn., 1868), vol. 4, pp. 287–8.
86. Above, n. 10 at p. 150.
87. F. D. MacKinnon, 'The Origin of the Commercial Court' 60 *LQR* 324 (1944). See also *Dictionary of National Biography 1931–40* (ed. L. G. Wickham Legg, 1949), p. 799 (biography of Lord Justice Scrutton).
88. B. J. MacKinnon 34 *Canadian Bar Review* 115, 117 (1956).
89. Matthew 7: 1.
90. *Weir of Hermiston* (1896), ch. 1.
91. *The Times* 18 Aug. 1981.
92. Above, n. 71.
93. *In the Matter of Willard L. Mikesell* 243 NW 2d 86, 101 (1976).
94. *Daily Telegraph* 25 July 1985.
95. *The Times* 5 and 8 Sept. 1984.
96. *People* v. *Arno* 153 Cal Rptr 624, 628 n 2 (1979).
97. *United Steelworkers of America* v. *Weber* 443 US 193, 222 (1979) (dissenting opinion in the US Supreme Court by Justice Rehnquist, joined by Chief Justice Burger). See also *Florida* v. *Royer* 460 US 491, 519–20 (1983) (another dissenting opinion of Justice Rehnquist, joined by Chief Justice Burger and Justice O'Connor): 'The plurality's meandering opinion contains in it a little something for everyone. . . . Indeed, in both manner and tone, the opinion brings to mind the old nursery rhyme: "The King of France / With forty thousand men / Marched up the hill / And then marched back again". The opinion none the less, in my view, betrays a mind-set more useful to those who officiate at shuffleboard games, primarily concerned with which particular square the disc has landed on, than to those who are seeking to administer a system of justice . . .'
98. Above, n. 6 at pp. 86–7.
99. Above, n. 14 at p. 841 (Lord Fraser).
100. *R* v. *Immigration Appeal Tribunal ex parte Enwia* [1984] 1 WLR 117, 130 (Court of Appeal).
101. *Government of the USA* v. *McCaffery* [1984] 1 WLR 867, 872–3.

102. *British Steel Corporation* v. *Granada Television Ltd.* [1981] AC 1096, 1195 (Lord Salmon). Sometimes it is the majority of the court which expresses its regret at disagreeing with the minority judgment. See, for example, *Sagnata Investments Ltd.* v. *Norwich Corporation* [1971] 2 QB 614, 631 (Edmund Davies LJ: 'I have the misfortune to differ from [Lord Denning] regarding the outcome of this appeal') and 637 (Phillimore LJ: 'it is my misfortune to disagree with the judgment of Lord Denning MR').
103. *Mallalieu* v. *Drummond* [1983] 2 AC 861, 868 (Lord Elwyn-Jones).
104. *Forensic Fables* (1961), pp. 275–6. On the language of the law see ch. 6, pp. 147–68.
105. *Liversidge* v. *Anderson* [1942] AC 206, 232, 244–5.
106. *R* v. *IRC ex parte Rossminster Ltd.* [1980] AC 952, 1011.
107. R. F. V. Heuston, 'Liversidge v. Anderson in Retrospect' 86 LQR 33, 43 (1970).
108. Ibid., p. 48.
109. Geoffrey Lewis, above, n. 25 at p. 143.
110. Robert Stevens, above, n. 13 at p. 287.
111. *Place* v. *Searle* 48 TLR 428, 429–30 (1932).
112. George Pollock, *Mr Justice McCardie* (1934), pp. 212–16.
113. *Magor and St Mellons Rural District Council* v. *Newport Corporation* [1952] AC 189, 191.
114. *Cassell & Co. Ltd.* v. *Broome* [1972] AC 1027, 1054 (Lord Hailsham).
115. Robert Jackson, *The Chief* (1959), p. 197.
116. *Dictionary of National Biography 1951–60* (ed. E. T. Williams and Helen M. Palmer, 1971), p. 40.
117. Above, n. 85, vol. 1, pp. 340–1.
118. C. H. S. Fifoot, *Lord Mansfield* (1936), p. 47.
119. Above, n. 10 at p. 776.
120. Lord Cockburn, *Memorials of his Time* (ed. W. Forbes Gray, 1945), p. 80.
121. Henry J. Abraham, above, n. 11 at pp. 206–7, and Henry J. Abraham, *Justices and Presidents* (2nd edn., 1985), p. 176.
122. John R. Schmidhauser, *Judges and Justices* (1979), p. 119.
123. William O. Douglas, above, n. 21 at p. 33.
124. Bernard Schwartz, *Super Chief: Earl Warren and his Supreme Court* (1983), p. 54.
125. Robert G. McCloskey, *The Modern Supreme Court* (1972), p. 54.
126. Above, n. 124 at p. 254.

127. *65 ABAJ* 1154, 1155 (1979). In November 1986 Rose Bird was voted out of her office of Chief Justice of the California Supreme Court. She was the first Chief Justice to suffer that fate since the introduction in 1934 of confirmatory ballots for Supreme Court Justices in the State. See *The Times* 6 Nov. 1986.
128. *In Re J. P. Linahan* 138 F 2d 650, 652–3 (1943) (Jerome Frank J).
129. Richard Kluger, *Simple Justice* (1977), p. 656.
130. Above, n. 19 at p. 531.
131. Above, n. 124 at pp. 99, 260, 692.
132. Henry J. Abraham, above, n. 11 at p. 77.
133. Henry J. Abraham, *Justices and Presidents*, above n. 121 at p. 184.
134. *Holmes–Laski Letters* (ed. Mark DeWolfe Howe, 1953), p. 845.

2. Expertise and Bias

1. Charles Dickens, *Bleak House* (1853), ch. 5.
2. *Donoghue* v. *Stevenson* [1932] AC 562.
3. *The Times* 31 Jan. 1986.
4. *R* v. *Horseferry Road Justices ex parte IBA* [1986] 3 WLR 132.
5. *65 ABAJ* 1786 (1979).
6. F. D. MacKinnon 62 *LQR* 34 (1946).
7. Sections 4(1) and 6(1) Supreme Court of Judicature (Consolidation) Act 1925.
8. The statistics come from the Lord Chancellor's Department: *The Professional Judiciary in England and Wales* (Fact Sheet No. 4: May 1986).
9. An Interview with Joseph Yahuda 148 *JP* 739, 755 (1984).
10. 116 *NLJ* 1389 (1966). See also Harman J (son of Harman LJ) in *Cornhill Insurance PLC* v. *Improvement Services Ltd* [1986] 1 WLR 114, 116: 'the telexes were . . ., like [so much modern paraphernalia, far less efficient than the old-fashioned] written message delivered by hand.'
11. Tony Palmer, *The Trials of Oz* (1971), pp. 65, 165, 177.
12. David Hooper, *Public Scandal, Odium and Contempt* (1984), p. 113. Cf. Eric Grimshaw and Glyn Jones, *Lord Goddard: His Career and Cases* (1958), p. 17: Goddard 'is not one of those irritating judges who ask "Who IS Marilyn Monroe?" or "What is a TV jingle?"'.
13. *Guardian* 29 Nov. 1979.
14. *The Times* 4 July 1985.

15. A.P. Herbert, *Uncommon Law* (1977 edn.), p. 82. See also ch. 1, n. 60.
16. *Thaarup* v. *Hulton Press Ltd.* 169 LT 309, 310 (1943).
17. *The Times* 6 January 1982. Lord Chancellor Hailsham wrote to an MP confirming that 'contributory negligence does not, of course, constitute any defence to rape, nor in my view in the absence of actual sexual provocation should imprudence on the part of a victim operate as a factor of mitigation in the reduction of a sentence': *The Times* 12 Jan. 1982.
18. Ibid. 11 Dec. 1982.
19. Ibid. 20 Dec. 1983. For a similar lack of judicial reticence in America see Ibid. 8 Feb. 1986: a Philadelphia Judge asked not to be assigned any more rape cases after he had described the victim of an alleged rape as 'the ugliest girl I have ever seen' and so refused to convict the defendant of the offence.
20. See ch. 1, p. 22.
21. *Mason* v. *Mason* 11 Family Law 143, 144 (1980).
22. John Mortimer, *Clinging to the Wreckage* (1983), pp. 240–1. The case was *DPP* v. *Jordan* [1977] AC 699.
23. *Bushell's Case* 124 ER 1006, 1012 (1670).
24. *Jacobellis* v. *Ohio* 378 US 184, 197 (1964) (Stewart J in the US Supreme Court).
25. *Tolley* v. *J. S. Fry and Sons Ltd.* [1930] 1 KB 467, 475 (Scrutton LJ in the Court of Appeal).
26. *The Times* 7 Jan. 1978.
27. *Cooke* v. *New River Co.* 38 Ch D 56, 71 (1888).
28. *Sutherland* v. *Stopes* [1925] AC 47, 68.
29. *Roberts* v. *Hopwood* [1925] AC 578, 591–4.
30. *Wheeler* v. *Leicester City Council* [1985] AC 1054, 1080 (Lord Templeman).
31. *Ministry of Defence* v. *Jeremiah* [1980] ICR 13, 22 (Lord Denning).
32. *Dictionary of National Biography 1931–40* (ed. L. G. Wickham Legg, 1949), p. 558.
33. *Forensic Fables* (1961), pp. 97–8. For further examples of irrelevant judicial utterances see ch. 4, pp. 79–83.
34. *Hipperson* v. *Newbury District Electoral Registration Officer* [1985] QB 1060, 1069.
35. John Lord Campbell, *Lives of the Lord Chancellors* (5th edn., 1868), vol. 9, p. 363.
36. Ibid., vol. 10, p. 238.

37. John Lord Campbell, *The Lives of the Chief Justices of England* (3rd edn., 1874), vol. 3, pp. 128–9.
38. Ibid., vol. 4, p. 40.
39. J. B. Atlay, *The Victorian Chancellors* (1908), vol. 2, p. 67.
40. *Craig v. Harney* 331 US 367, 391 (1947) (Mr Justice Frankfurter).
41. Above, n. 37, vol. 1, p. 287.
42. *Manchester, Sheffield & Lincolnshire Railway Co.* v. *Brown* (1883) LR 8 AC 703, 716.
43. *R* v. *Taylor* [1977] 1 WLR 612, 615 (Lawton LJ). See also *Charles Roberts & Co. Ltd* v. *British Railways Board* [1965] 1 WLR 396, 400 (Ungoed-Thomas J): 'Economics and trade form no part of a judge's qualifications. In general judges are not qualified to decide questions of economic policy, and such questions by their nature are not justiciable.' (The final nine words have become less true in the last twenty years.)
44. William Hazlitt, *The Spirit of the Age* (1825) (Oxford University Press, 1970 edn.), p. 242.
45. *Holmes–Laski Letters* (ed. Mark DeWolfe Howe, 1953), p. 1412.
46. Robert Louis Stevenson, *Weir of Hermiston* (1896), ch. 3.
47. Above, n. 35, vol. 8, p. 55 n.
48. Above, n. 37, vol. 3, pp. 419–21.
49. *Dimes* v. *Grand Junction Canal* (1852) 3 HL Cases 759.
50. *Johnson* v. *Darr* 272 SW 1098 (1925). Cf *Atkins* v. *US* 556 F 2d 1028 (1977), discussed in ch. 1 at n. 69. In that case, concerning judicial salaries, the US Court of Claims said that although the judges had a direct pecuniary interest in the result, they would hear the case under the doctrine of necessity—that is, a judge is not disqualified from trying a case because of personal interest in the matter at issue if there is no other judge available.
51. Henry J. Abraham, *Justices and Presidents* (2nd edn., 1985), p. 245.
52. *Code of Conduct for the Bar of England and Wales* (3rd edn., incorporating amendments up to 31 Dec. 1984), Annex 8, para. (10).
53. *Rothermere* v. *Times Newspapers Ltd.* [1973] 1 All ER 1013, 1017 (Lord Denning).
54. *Public Utilities Commission* v. *Pollak* 343 US 451, 466–7 (1952).
55. *Ex parte Church of Scientology of California, The Times* 21 Feb. 1978.
56. *The Times* 16 Nov. 1984. See also *Livesey* v. *The New South Wales Bar Association* (1983) 57 ALJR 420 (High Court of Australia).
57. *Moss* v. *McLachlan* [1985] IRLR 76.

58. *Blank* v. *Sullivan & Cromwell* 418 F Supp 1, 4 (1975).
59. *In Re S* [1981] QB 683, 689–92.
60. *R* v. *Thomas Castro: Skipworth and Castro's Case* (1873) LR 9 QB 219, 230–1, 237–8.
61. Above, n. 15 at p. 374.
62. *Bromley LBC* v. *GLC* [1983] 1 AC 768, 771–2.
63. Above, n. 45.
64. Felix Frankfurter, 'The Judicial Process and the Supreme Court' in *Of Law and Men* (ed. Philip Elman, 1956), p. 40.
65. *Tyrer* v. *United Kingdom*, Judgment of 25 April 1978, Separate Opinion at para. 12.
66. Aristotle, *The 'Art' of Rhetoric* (transl. John Henry Freese, Loeb Classical Library, 1925). I.1. 7.
67. Benjamin Cardozo, 'The Nature of the Judicial Process' in *Selected Writings of Benjamin Nathan Cardozo* (ed. Margaret E. Hall, 1947), p. 178.
68. *In Re J. P. Linahan* 138 F 2d 650, 651 (1943) (Frank J). After Eichmann was captured in Argentina in 1960, he was taken to Israel and charged with war crimes, crimes against the Jewish people, and associated offences. He was convicted by the District Court. His appeal to the Supreme Court failed. In 1962 he was hanged. The Supreme Court rejected the complaint that 'the Judges of the District Court, being Jews and feeling a sense of affinity with the victims of the plan of extermination and Nazi persecution were psychologically incapable of giving the Appellant an objective trial'. The District Court had dealt with this issue as follows: 'The judge, when dispensing justice in a Court of Law, does not cease to be a human being, with human passions and human emotions. Yet he is enjoined by the Law to restrain and control such passions and emotions, else there will never be a judge qualified to try a criminal case which evokes deep feelings and revulsion, such as a case of treason or murder or any other grave crime. It is true that the memory of the Catastrophe shocks every Jew to the depths of his being, but once this case has been brought before us it becomes our duty to control even these emotions when we sit in judgment. We shall abide by this duty.' See J. E. S. Fawcett, 'The Eichmann Case' 38 *British Year Book of International Law* 181, 183 (1962).
69. 26 HC 1022 (30 May 1911).
70. 'The Work of the Commercial Courts' 1 *CLJ* 6, 8 (1923).
71. J. A. G. Griffith, *The Politics of the Judiciary* (3rd edn., 1985), p. 199.

72. *Ex parte Wilder* 66 JP 761 (1902).
73. *In Re J. P. Linahan*, above, n. 68 at p. 652.

3. Appointment and Training

1. A. W. Brian Simpson, *Cannibalism and the Common Law* (1984), p. ix.
2. Ibid., pp. 69, 71, 93.
3. Ibid., p. 94.
4. *R* v. *Dudley and Stephens* 14 QBD 273, 287 (1884).
5. Above, n. 1 at p. 252.
6. *Harrison* v. *Michelin Tyre Co. Ltd.* [1985] ICR 696, 698 (Comyn J).
7. *The Mirror of Justices* (ed. William Whittaker for the Selden Society, 1895), Book 2, ch. 2, p. 44.
8. R. F. V. Heuston, *Lives of the Lord Chancellors 1885–1940* (1964), p. 269.
9. Section 10(3) Supreme Court Act 1981.
10. Section 6 Appellate Jurisdiction Act 1876.
11. See ch. 2, p. 31.
12. Ibid.
13. Section 16(3) Courts Act 1971 as amended by section 12 Administration of Justice Act 1977.
14. Section 21(2) Courts Act 1971.
15. 417 HL 1221 (2 March 1981: Committee Stage of the Supreme Court Bill)—Lord Chancellor Hailsham. By July 1985 there were forty-one solicitor Recorders and thirty-one solicitor Circuit Judges: Lord Hailsham's speech to the Common Law Bar Association on 3 July 1985.
16. See ch. 2, p. 31.
17. *Of Law and Life and Other Things that Matter* (ed. Philip B. Kurland, 1965), p. 75.
18. Louis Blom-Cooper, 'The Judiciary in an Era of Law Reform' 37 *Political Quarterly* 378, 382 (1966). See also John Lord Campbell, *The Lives of the Chief Justices of England* (3rd edn., 1874), vol. 2, pp. 401–2 for a similar explanation of why 'the anticipation of high judicial qualities has often been disappointed'.
19. Robert Jackson, *The Chief* (1959), p. 157 (and similarly at p. 338).
20. John Lord Campbell, *Lives of the Lord Chancellors* (5th edn., 1868), vol. 8, p. 218.

21. Virginia Woolf, *Three Guineas* (1938), ch. 2.
22. Lord Macmillan 50 *LQR* 275, 276 (1934), cited in R. E. Megarry, *Miscellany-at-Law* (1955), pp. 49–50.
23. Plato, *The Republic* (transl. H. D. P. Lee, Penguin Classics, 1955), p. 151.
24. For details of the backgrounds of judges see Tony Gifford, *Where's the Justice?* (1986), p. 25.
25. Section 11(2) Supreme Court Act 1981 and section 2(1) Judicial Pensions Act 1959.
26. Section 17 Courts Act 1971, which gives the Lord Chancellor the power, if he 'considers it desirable in the public interest', to allow the Circuit judge to remain in office until the age of 75.
27. R. E. Megarry, *Lawyer and Litigant in England* (1962), pp. 123–4.
28. See ch. 6, p. 150.
29. Above, n. 15 at col. 1223. Sir John Donaldson, Master of the Rolls, has suggested that solicitors should be eligible for appointment to the High Court Bench: *The Times* 30 July 1986.
30. Above, n. 15 at col. 1220.
31. John Mortimer, *Regina v. Rumpole* (1981), p. 38.
32. Above, n. 8 at pp. 523–4.
33. Above, n. 27 at pp. 120–2.
34. *The Judiciary* (Report of a Justice Sub-Committee, 1972), p. 25.
35. Henry J. Abraham, *The Judicial Process* (5th edn., 1986), p. 83.
36. Bob Woodward and Scott Armstrong, *The Brethren* (1979), p. 87.
37. Shimon Shetreet, *Judges on Trial* (1976), pp. 62 and 65.
38. Henry Cecil, *The English Judge* (1970), p. 109. On the lifestyle expected of English judges see also ch. 1, p. 11.
39. John Mortimer, *The Trials of Rumpole* (1979), p. 148.
40. See ch. 4, pp. 102–3, on disciplining judges for their conduct out of court.
41. Candidates for judicial office must 'not [be] disqualified by any personal unsuitability': Lord Chancellor's Department *Judicial Appointments: The Lord Chancellor's Policies and Procedures* (1986), p. iv. See p. 66 on secrecy in this context.
42. *The Times* and the *Washington Post* 28 Aug. 1981.
43. Henry J. Abraham, *Justices and Presidents* (2nd edn., 1985), p. 329. See also above, n. 35 at p. 31. In England and Wales, by contrast, at the end of 1986 there were only three female High Court judges and sixteen female Circuit judges: *The Times* 30 Dec. 1986.
44. Above, n. 36 at p. 47.

45. Sir Neville Faulks, *A Law Unto Myself* (1978), p. 114.
46. For other exceptions see Shetreet, above, n. 37 at p. 79.
47. See above, p. 53.
48. Edward Foss, *Biographia Juridica: A Biographical Dictionary of the Judges of England 1066–1870* (1870), p. 415.
49. David M. Walker, *The Oxford Companion to Law* (1980), p. 106, suggests—very credibly—that 'latterly he was out of touch with legal developments'.
50. Above, n. 8 at pp. 77–8. The case was *Continental Tyre and Rubber Co. v. Daimler Co.* [1916] 2 AC 307.
51. Section 11(10) Supreme Court Act 1981.
52. Above, n. 38 at p. 88.
53. 'Law in Science and Science in Law' (1899) in *Collected Legal Papers* (1920), p. 230.
54. Aristotle, *The Politics*, translated by T. A. Sinclair, revised and re-presented by Trevor J. Saunders, (Penguin Classics, 1981) Book II, ch. 9, p. 146.
55. Above, n. 23 at pp. 151–2.
56. 1 Kings 12: 12–14.
57. C. H. S. Fifoot, *Lord Mansfield* (1936), p. 48.
58. See ch. 4, pp. 76 and 89.
59. Campbell, above, n. 18, vol. 1, p. 86.
60. 1 Kings 3: 7, 16–28.
61. David Daube, *Civil Disobedience in Antiquity* (1972), p. 52.
62. Sir Thomas Skyrme, *The Changing Image of the Magistracy* (1979), pp. 143–4.
63. Above, n. 20, vol. 4, p. 291.
64. Anthony Trollope, *The Three Clerks* (1858), ch. 40.
65. Above, n. 20, vol. 7, p. 128.
66. Above, n. 41 at p. iii. Little has changed since 1786 when James Boswell recognized the settled principle of English jurisprudence that 'there are a great many places in the gift of the Lord Chancellor': *Boswell: The English Experiment 1785–1789* (ed. Irma S. Lustig and Frederick A. Pottle, 1987), p. 23.
67. Above, n. 20, vol. 2, p. 381. See similarly vol. 4, p. 132.
68. Above, n. 41 at p. iii.
69. Lord Hailsham, *The Door Wherein I Went* (1978), p. 254.
70. Section 16(1) Courts Act 1971 provides the power in relation to Circuit judges. Section 10(1) and (2) of the Supreme Court Act 1981 and section 6 of the Appellate Jurisdiction Act 1876 state the

Queen's powers concerning more senior judges. The roles of the Lord Chancellor and the Prime Minister in relation to senior judges are based on convention.

71. Cited above, n. 8 at pp. 149–50.
72. Above, n. 20, vol. 5, pp. 251–2.
73. Above n. 20, vol. 4, pp. 321–3 and 422, and Campbell, above n. 18, vol. 2, pp. 352 and 358–62.
74. Above, n. 8 at p. 57.
75. See ch. 7, p. 180.
76. *Gill* v. *El Vino Co. Ltd.* [1983] QB 425, 431 (Lord Justice Griffiths).
77. Section 31(1) Data Protection Act 1984. However, the Lord Chancellor and his officials 'will always be ready to go as far as they possibly can to bring any problem out into the open with a candidate who wants to know his position': above n. 41 at p. 4.
78. Above, n. 43 at p. 39. See above, pp. 56–7 for one example: Judge Carswell.
79. Above, n. 31 at p. 100.
80. Above, n. 34 at pp. 29–30. See also Peter Scott QC 1 *Counsel* 48, 49 (1986).
81. Above, n. 8 at p. 52.
82. *Aubrey's Brief Lives* (ed. Oliver Lawson Dick, 1972), pp. 92–3.
83. Lord Hailsham, *Hamlyn Revisited: The British Legal System Today* (1983), p. 50.
84. Patrick Devlin, *The Judge* (1979), p. 38. See similarly F.D. Mac-Kinnon, *On Circuit* (1940), pp. 3–4: 'Lord Haldane, I presume, honoured me by his selection [of me as a judge] because he had listened with approval to arguments of mine in the House of Lords and the Privy Council. If he had bethought him that perhaps the most serious work of a King's Bench Judge is to try prisoners at the Assizes and at the Old Bailey, and had enquired how far experience qualified me for that task, I am sure he would never have appointed me at all. As a youth I was once fined for riding a bicycle without a light. I had for some years occasionally sat at Petty Sessions as a county magistrate, and sometimes attended Quarter Sessions under the chairmanship of Lord Parmoor. These were the only occasions on which I had ever been inside a criminal court.' On hearing his first criminal cases, MacKinnon 'sat with my finger in the index of Archbold [the leading textbook], and I hope my uneasiness was not too apparent'. Lord Parker, appointed as a High Court judge in 1950 (and Lord Chief Justice 1958–71), 'said that

the first summing-up in a criminal case that he heard was one he delivered himself': *Dictionary of National Biography 1971–80* (ed. Lord Blake and C. S. Nicholls, 1986), p. 656.

85. Above, n. 45 at pp. 126–7 and 137.
86. *Forensic Fables* (1961), pp. 355–7. On bachelor judges and women's clothes see ch. 1, p. 22–3.
87. William Shakespeare, *Measure for Measure*, I. i. 47.
88. 463 HL 851 (9 May 1985) and 149 JP 328 (25 May 1985).
89. Jerome Frank, *Courts On Trial* (1973 edn.), p. 251.
90. Above, n. 34 at p. 42.
91. Felix Frankfurter, 'The Supreme Court in the Mirror of Justices' 105 *University of Pennsylvania Law Review* 781, 794–5 (1957).
92. Learned Hand, *The Spirit of Liberty: Papers and Addresses of Learned Hand* (collected by Irving Dilliard, 1977 edn.), p. 81.
93. Above, n. 84 at pp. 22–9.
94. *Bwllfa and Merthyr Dare Steam Colleries (1891) Ltd.* v. *Pontypridd Waterworks Co.* [1903] AC 426, 431, cited with approval by Lord Roskill in *Secretary of State for Defence* v. *Guardian Newspapers Ltd.* [1985] AC 339, 367.
95. John Campbell, *F. E. Smith: First Earl of Birkenhead* (1983), p. 471.
96. Cited in *Jones* v. *NCB* [1957] 2 QB 55, 63 (Lord Denning).
97. *Miliangos* v. *George Frank Textiles Ltd.* [1976] AC 443, 481 (Lord Simon).

4. Performance and Discipline

1. *Sacher* v. *US* 343 US 1, 12 (1952).
2. Lord Hailsham, *The Door Wherein I Went* (1978), p. 255.
3. Boswell, *Life of Johnson* (ed. R. W. Chapman, corrected by J. D. Freeman, 1970), p. 619 (14 April 1775).
4. *Daniel and Susanna* in *The Apocrypha*.
5. John Lord Campbell, *Lives of the Lord Chancellors* (5th edn., 1868), vol. 4, p. 416.
6. Robert Stevens, *Law and Politics: The House of Lords as a Judicial Body 1800–1976* (1979), p. 279 n.
7. *Hawksley* v. *Fewtrell* [1954] 1 QB 228, 240.
8. Plato, *The Republic* (transl. H.D.P. Lee, Penguin Classics, 1955), p. 147: 'how far better it is to arrange one's life so that one has no need of a judge dozing on the bench'.

9. Edward Foss, *Biographia Juridica: A Biographical Dictionary of the Judges of England 1066–1870* (1870), p. 223.
10. Above, n. 5, vol. 6, pp. 121–2.
11. W. T. Shore (ed.), *The Baccarat Case* (Notable British Trials Series, 1932), p. xi, comment by Sir Edward Clarke, counsel for the Plaintiff. 'Lord Coleridge had appropriated half of the public gallery and had given tickets to his friends.' As W. T. Shore observed, at p. ii, 'the Court [was] turned by the consent of the judge into a theatre'.
12. C. H. Rolph, *As I Was Saying* (1985), p. 167.
13. Ibid, p. 202.
14. Gilchrist Alexander, *After Court Hours* (1950), p. 183, cited in Shimon Shetreet, *Judges On Trial* (1976), pp. 242–3.
15. *R.* v. *Langham* (1972) Crim. LR 457.
16. *R.* v. *Weston-super-Mare Justices ex parte Taylor* (1981) Crim. LR 179.
17. Above, n. 5, vol. 6, p. 194 n.
18. J. B. Atlay, *The Victorian Chancellors* (1906), vol. 1, p. 295, and (1908), vol. 2, pp. 19–20.
19. Robert Jackson, *The Chief* (1959), p. 277.
20. Lord Cockburn, *Memorials of his Time* (ed. W. Forbes Gray, 1945), p. 199.
21. *The Times* 24 Oct. 1986. As recently as 1970 a County Court judge hearing a divorce case criticized a woman for coming to court in a trouser-suit, saying that she should remember she was not at a fun-fair: *Guardian* 24 Feb. 1970, cited in *Borrie and Lowe's Law of Contempt* (2nd edn., 1983), p. 20. On judicial aphorisms see also ch. 2, pp. 32–8.
22. Judge Alan King-Hamilton QC, *And Nothing But the Truth* (1982), pp. 176–7.
23. *Guardian* 23 Feb. 1986.
24. *R* v. *Secretary of State for the Home Department ex parte Swati* [1986] 1 All ER 717, 719.
25. C. P. Harvey, *The Advocate's Devil* (1958), p. 33.
26. Above, n. 5, vol. 10, p. 290.
27. 160 HC (4th Series) 397 (6 July 1906).
28. (1749) Book VIII, ch. 11.
29. *The Letters of Evelyn Waugh* (ed. Mark Amory, 1982), pp. 485–6.
30. Edward Marjoribanks, *The Life of Sir Edward Marshall Hall* (1929), p. 315.

31. Above, n. 25 at p. 33. The case was *Hoystead* v. *Commissioner of Taxation* [1926] AC 155.
32. Above, n. 20 at p. 83.
33. Robert Louis Stevenson, *Weir of Hermiston* (1896), ch. 3.
34. W. Forbes Gray, *Some Old Scots Judges* (1914), p. 2.
35. *The Times* 21 Aug. 1981.
36. Brian McKenna, 'The Judge and the Common Man' 32 *MLR* 601, 605 (1969).
37. Lord Denning, *The Due Process of Law* (1980), p. 58.
38. *Jones* v. *National Coal Board* [1957] 2 QB 55. For further examples of similar proceedings arising out of the injudicious conduct of Hallett J see *Bunting* v. *Thorne RDC*, *The Times* 26 Mar. 1957 (Court of Appeal), and *R* v. *Clewer* 37 Cr. App. Reports 37 (1953) (Court of Criminal Appeal).
39. R. F. V. Heuston, *Lives of the Lord Chancellors 1885–1940* (1964), p. 481.
40. E. S. Turner, *May It Please Your Lordship* (1971), p. 222.
41. Lord Birkett, *Six Great Advocates* (1961), p. 44, quoting the opinion of Sir Edward Clarke KC.
42. John Lord Campbell, *The Lives of the Chief Justices of England* (3rd edn., 1874), vol. 2, p. 329.
43. H. M. Hyde, 'Diary of a Judge', cited in Brian Abel-Smith and Robert Stevens, *Lawyers and the Courts: A Sociological Study of the English Legal System 1750–1965* (1967), p. 289 n.
44. F. D. MacKinnon 60 *LQR* 324 (1944).
45. Above, n. 25 at p. 32. See also above, ch. 3, p. 51. Rumpole describes such a judge as 'suffering from a bad case of premature adjudication': John Mortimer, *Rumpole's Last Case* (1987), p. 65.
46. Above, n. 18, vol. 2, p. 344.
47. Ibid, vol. 2, p. 201.
48. R. E. Megarry, *Miscellany-at-Law* (1955), p. 10.
49. *Dictionary of National Biography 1931–40* (ed. L. .G. Wickham Legg, 1949), p. 800.
50. Above, n. 41 at p. 20.
51. See A. M. Sullivan, *The Last Serjeant* (1952), pp. 307–8. The case was *Hobbs* v. *Nottingham Journal Limited* [1929] 2 KB 1.
52. *Brassington* v. *Brassington* [1962] P 276, 281.
53. *R.* v. *Hircock* [1970] 1 QB 67.
54. *R.v. McKenna* [1960] 1 QB 411.
55. R. E. Megarry, *A Second Miscellany-at-Law* (1973), p. 5.

56. *Radnor* v. *Shafto* 32 ER 1160, 1162 (1805).
57. *Lord Eldon's Anecdote Book* (ed. Anthony Lincoln and Robert McEwen, 1960), p. 131.
58. William Hazlitt, *The Spirit of the Age* (1825) (Oxford University Press, 1970 edn.), p. 238.
59. Sir Rupert Cross, 'The Making of the English Criminal Law: Sir James Fitzjames Stephen' (1978) *Crim. LR* 652, 655–6. See also 90 *LT* 293 (February 1891): 'Early in the week it was stated that Mr Justice Stephen had tendered his resignation. This was contradicted on Wednesday, and he was stated to be well. Such a contradiction is much to be regretted. The truth is that his Lordship is not well, and that his resignation, if not actually sent in, is impending. Professional opinion is that it ought not to be delayed.'
60. A. A. Paterson, 'The Infirm Judge' 1 *British Journal of Law and Society* 83, 84 (1974); Alec Samuels, 'Judicial Misconduct in the Criminal Trial' (1982) *Crim. LR* 221, 224–5; and Hugo Young, 'Playing Ball When the Lord Chief Justice Lost his Marbles' *Guardian* 2 July 1984.
61. Shetreet, above, n. 14 at pp. 112–13.
62. Ibid., p. 167.
63. Cited in Campbell, above, n. 5, vol. 5, p. 89.
64. *The Judiciary* (1972), paras. 77 and 80.
65. *The Mirror of Justices* (ed. William Whittaker for the Selden Society, 1895), Book 5, ch. 1, p. 166.
66. Above, n. 5, vol. 1, p. 244.
67. Above, n. 42, vol. 1, p. 112.
68. Above, n. 5, vol. 4, pp. 407–8.
69. Above, n. 9 at p. 83.
70. Ibid, pp. 275 and 510.
71. Above, n. 42, vol. 3, p. 75.
72. Sir William Holdsworth, *A History of English Law* (7th edn., 1956), vol. 2, pp. 294–5.
73. Above, n. 42, vol. 1, p. 107.
74. For these and other cases, see Shetreet, above, n. 14 at pp. 126–8.
75. Section 11(3) Supreme Court Act 1981.
76. Section 6 Appellate Jurisdiction Act 1876.
77. *McCawley* v. *R* 26 CLR 9, 59 (1918) (Isaacs and Rich JJ in the High Court of Australia).
78. Shetreet, above, n. 14 at pp. 143–51.
79. Above, pp. 83–4.

80. Above, n. 37 at p. 62.
81. Above, n. 39 at pp. 303–4.
82. John Campbell, *F. E. Smith: First Earl of Birkenhead* (1983), p. 480.
83. Above, n. 19 at p. 144.
84. Section 17(4) Courts Act 1971. In December 1983 a Circuit judge was dismissed after admitting smuggling offences.
85. Section 6(1) Justice of the Peace Act 1979, as amended by section 65 Administration of Justice Act 1982.
86. *The Times* 25 Sept. 1985.
87. *Ex parte Ramshay* 18 QB 173, 189–90, 196 (1852).
88. The identity of the concurring judge is specified in section 11: for example, in the event of a High Court judge becoming infirm, the Lord Chancellor needs the agreement of the senior judge of the relevant division of the High Court.
89. Section 12 Administration of Justice Act 1973.
90. Paterson, above, n. 60 at pp. 84–5. See above, p. 87, on ill judges.
91. See ch. 3, p. 53.
92. Above, n. 18, vol. 2, p. 281.
93. *The Times* 5 Jan. 1984. For another example of Lord Chancellor Hailsham rebuking an errant judge see ch. 2 at n. 17.
94. Above, n. 2 at p. 257.
95. 120 *NLJ* 649 (1970).
96. Shetreet, above, n. 14 at p. 181.
97. Above, n. 53 at p. 72.
98. Ibid., p. 68.
99. Above, n. 20 at p. 83. On Braxfield see above, p. 83.
100. *Sirros* v. *Moore* [1975] QB 118, 132. Nor is the State liable for the wrongful acts of a judge: section 2(5) of the Crown Proceedings Act 1947 provides that the Crown cannot be sued for the tortious conduct of any person 'while discharging or purporting to discharge any responsibilities of a judicial nature vested in him'.
101. *Re McC (A Minor)* [1985] AC 528, 550. See also *R* v. *Waltham Forest Justices ex parte Solanke* [1986] 3 WLR 315 where the Court of Appeal applied section 52 of the Justices of the Peace Act 1979 and so restricted to one penny the damages which magistrates would have to pay the applicant for sending him to prison for six weeks when they had no power to do so. The Master of the Rolls, Sir John Donaldson, noted at p. 317 that 'the applicant himself put the claim at £1½ million. I am bound to say that I find it rather

high ...', but the statute avoided the need to assess the actual damages.

102. *67 ABAJ* 1248 (1981) and *72 ABAJ* 28 (June 1986).
103. Paragraph 6 of Schedule 3 to the Act.
104. *New York Times* 9 Aug. 1980. In 1984 a US District Court judge, Harry Claiborne, was convicted of income-tax evasion and sentenced to two years' imprisonment. He refused to resign, so the Senate voted in 1986 to impeach him: *The Times* 10 Oct. 1986.
105. Ibid. 5 Apr. 1986.
106. *In the Matter of the Complaint against the Honourable Christ T. Seraphim* 294 NW 2d 485 (1980). See also *In Re Judge Edward A. Haggerty Jr.* 241 So 2d 469 (1970) where the Supreme Court of Louisiana upheld the recommendation of the Judiciary Commission of Louisiana that a Criminal District Court judge be removed from office. The court concluded, at pp. 478–80, that 'to consort with public gamblers and criminal characters, engage in heavy, habitual drinking in public, promote and be a part of a scandalous and sordid party in the company of prostitutes such as that held at the motel, resist arrest and engage in fisticuffs with arresting officers, are hardly things to put the judicial branch in good repute. ... An effort was made to excuse the assemblage as a traditional bachelor's party of intimate friends in advance of the wedding of Kenneth Reeves. This does not appear to have been entirely factually supported ...'
107. For a detailed discussion of the origins of US practice see *Judicature* (November 1979). See also Walter Gellhorn, 'The Swedish Justitieombudsman' 75 *YLJ* 1 (1965), and Mauro Cappelletti, 'Who Watches the Watchman?' 31 *American Journal of Comparative Law* 1 (1983) for comparative surveys.
108. Above, n. 5, vol. 5, p. 294.
109. Above, n. 3. See also *Terrell* v. *Secretary of State for the Colonies* [1953] 2 QB 482 where Lord Goddard CJ held that a colonial judge held office during the pleasure of the Crown and so could be dismissed. He said, at p. 495, 'so accustomed are we in this country nowadays to the exceptional position occupied by the judges of the supreme court that we are apt perhaps to forget that their independence is comparatively modern in the long history of our law'.
110. *Fray* v. *Blackburn* 3 B & S 576, 578 (1863).

111. Above, n. 100 at p. 132.
112. Above, n. 101 at p. 541.
113. Margaret Brazier, 'Judicial Immunity and the Independence of the Judiciary' (1976) *PL* 397, 408–9.
114. Other observers have similarly concluded that there is a need for an independent complaints tribunal. See, for example, the Justice Sub-Committee Report, above, n. 64 at para. 104, and see 123 *NLJ* 482–3 (1973). However, the Committee responsible for a more recent Justice Report, *The Administration of the Courts* (1986), was 'divided on the need for any change in the existing arrangements for dealing with complaints against the judiciary' (p. 25).
115. See ch. 5.
116. See ch. 2 at n. 17.
117. Sir Thomas Skyrme, *The Changing Image of the Magistracy* (1979), pp. 137–8.
118. Above, n. 3 at p. 612 (6 April 1775).
119. Henry Cecil, *The English Judge* (1970), p. 109.
120. Henry Cecil, *Sober as a Judge* (1958), ch. 11.
121. Above, n. 117 at p. 146.
122. Ibid., p. 147.
123. See ch. 3, pp. 57–8, on appointment to the bench.
124. *The Times* 30 May 1986. On the power of the Lord Chancellor to dismiss Circuit judges see above, n. 84. In September 1986 opposition from the judiciary caused the Government of New South Wales, Australia, to abandon a plan to give a judicial commission the power to dismiss errant judges. The Chief Justice and thirty other judges had issued a statement expressing their concern that judges might be dismissed without reference to Parliament. See *The Times* 18 Sept. 1986 and the *Guardian* 19 Sept. 1986.
125. Such a Commission would have been valuable in satisfying Mr Manus Nunan that, contrary to his public complaint in 1986, the decision of Lord Hailsham not to renew his appointment as a Recorder in 1984 was based on relevant factors. See *Guardian* 13, 14, and 16 June 1986.
126. Above, p. 89.
127. Francis Bacon, 'Of Judicature' in *Essays* (1625) (Everyman edn., 1973), p. 164.

5. Criticism

1. John Lord Campbell, *Lives of the Lord Chancellors* (5th edn., 1868), vol. 1, p. 405.
2. *Lord Eldon's Anecdote Book* (ed. Anthony Lincoln and Robert McEwen, 1960), pp. 42–3.
3. John Mortimer, *Rumpole of the Bailey* (1978), pp. 147–8.
4. John Mortimer, *Regina* v. *Rumpole* (1981), *passim* and all the other collections of Rumpole stories.
5. *Nathaniel Redding's Case*, Sir Thomas Raymond's Reports 376 n. (1680). Later that term the court remitted the fine and the sentence of imprisonment.
6. *In the Matter of Thomas James Wallace* (1866) LR 1 PC 283, 286, 294.
7. *Mr Lechmere Charlton's Case* 40 ER 661, 664, 670–1 (1837). Not every discourtesy to the court is a contempt: *Weston* v. *Central Criminal Court Courts Administrator* [1977] QB 32 (Court of Appeal). See also *Lewis* v. *Ogden* 58 ALJR 342 (1984) where the High Court of Australia held that it was not a contempt for a barrister, during his address to the jury during a criminal trial, to suggest that the judge had not been even-handed in his conduct of the trial. The court concluded (at p. 346) that 'the appellant's conduct was extremely discourteous, perhaps offensive, and deserving of rebuke by his Honour', but it was not a contempt. Cf. ch. 6, p. 161 on a barrister's rudeness in court. Note also that 'if counsel felt . . . a grievance, it should form the basis of an appeal or an application for judicial review, not an offensive attack on both clerk and justices in open court': *R* v. *Feltham Justices ex parte Nye, The Times* 15 Feb. 1985.
8. Brian Abel-Smith and Robert Stevens, *Lawyers and the Courts: A Sociological Study of the English Legal System 1750–1965* (1967), p. 33, and J.B. Atlay, *The Victorian Chancellors* (1906), vol. 1, p. 285.
9. Above, n. 1, vol. 10, pp. 276–7.
10. Shimon Shetreet, *Judges on Trial* (1976), p. 239, Fenton Bresler, *Lord Goddard* (1977), p. 233, and Eric Grimshaw and Glyn Jones, *Lord Goddard: His Career and Cases* (1958), pp. 126–7.
11. William Hazlitt *The Spirit of the Age* (1825) (Oxford University Press, 1970 edn.), pp. 235–6.
12. Above, n. 1, vol. 10, pp. 64–5.

13. 865 HC 1092 (4 December 1973).
14. 996 HC 538–540 (18 Dec. 1980). It is out of order for a Member of Parliament to say, as a criticism of a particular judge, that 'he thinks that an observation of that particular judge was an impertinence . . .': 474 HC 1751 (3 May 1950: Second Reading of the High Court and County Court Judges Bill)—Reginald Manningham-Buller (later Attorney-General and Lord Chancellor) in a statement approved by the Deputy Speaker.
15. *R v. Gray* [1900] 2 QB 36, 40 (Lord Russell of Killowen CJ).
16. *R v. Almon* 97 ER 94, 100 (1765).
17. *R v. Watson* 2 Term Reports (Durnford and East) 199, 205 (1788).
18. *McLeod v. St Aubyn* [1899] AC 549, 561.
19. Above, n. 15 at p. 37.
20. 82 LT Reports 534 (1900).
21. *Dictionary of National Biography 1931–40* (ed. L. G. Wickham Legg, 1949), p. 211. See also ch. 4 at p. 81.
22. Above, n. 15 at pp. 39–42.
23. *R v. Vidal*, The Times 14 Oct. 1922.
24. *R v. Freeman*, The Times 18 Nov. 1925.
25. *R v. Editor of the New Statesman ex parte DPP* 44 TLR 301 (1928).
26. *R v. Wilkinson*, The Times 16 July 1930.
27. *R v. Colsey*, The Times 9 May 1931. On whether it is a defence to the charge of scandalizing the judiciary that an allegation of judicial bias is true, see n. 37 below. See ch. 2, pp. 39–46, on judicial bias.
28. *Ambard v. Attorney-General for Trinidad and Tobago* [1936] AC 322, 335.
29. *R v. Commissioner of Police of the Metropolis ex parte Blackburn (No. 2)* [1968] 2 QB 150, 155.
30. *Badry v. DPP* [1983] 2 AC 297, 304 (Lord Hailsham for the Privy Council in an appeal from Mauritius). In *Secretary of State for Defence v. Guardian Newspapers Limited* [1985] AC 339, 347, Lord Diplock said that contempt by scandalizing the judiciary 'is virtually obsolescent in England'.
31. Above, n. 28.
32. *R v. Dunabin ex parte Williams* 53 CLR 434 (1935).
33. *R v. Murphy* 4 DLR 3d 289 (1969).
34. *Namboodiripad v. Nambiar* AIR 1970 SC 2015.
35. *R v. Brett* (1950) VLR 226.
36. *S v. Van Niekerk* (1970) 3 SALR 655.

37. *Gallagher* v. *Durack* 57 ALJR 191 (1983). See also the similar case of *Attorney-General for New South Wales* v. *Mundey* (1972) 2 NSWLR 887 in the Supreme Court of New South Wales, Australia. It may well be a defence to a charge of contempt that the allegation of bias is true. In *R* v. *Nicholls* 12 CLR 280 (1911), the High Court of Australia held that it was not a contempt for a newspaper to describe a judge as 'a political judge, that is, he was appointed because he had well served a political party'. The court said that it was unclear whether the words used were calculated to obstruct or interfere with the course of justice. Griffiths CJ added, at p. 286, that even if the words had suggested a lack of impartiality, 'I am not prepared to accede to the proposition that an imputation of want of impartiality to a Judge is necessarily a contempt of court. On the contrary, I think that if any Judge of this Court or of any other Court were to make a public utterance of such character as to be likely to impair the confidence of the public, or of suitors or any class of suitors in the impartiality of the Court in any matter likely to be brought before it, any public comment on such an utterance, if it were a fair comment, would, so far from being a contempt of court, be for the public benefit, and would be entitled to similar protection to that which comment upon matters of public interest is entitled under the law of libel.'
38. Above, n. 1, vol. 2, p. 378.
39. See, for example, *Morris* v. *Crown Office* [1970] 2 QB 114 where the Court of Appeal allowed an appeal against sentences of imprisonment imposed on Welsh students who had disrupted court proceedings. Davies L. J. said (at p. 127): 'On occasions one has the misfortune to encounter someone who makes a disturbance in court. Usually when that happens it is a case of a disappointed litigant who, from a sense of rage or disappointment at the result of his case, loses control of himself and gives vent to his feelings by an outburst either by word of mouth or physically.'
40. *R* v. *William Stone* 6 Term Reports (Durnford and East) 527, 530 (1796).
41. *R* v. *Jordan* 36 WR 797 (1888).
42. *Fox* v. *Wheatley* (1893) cited in *Oswald's Contempt of Court* (3rd edn. by George Stuart Robertson, 1910), p. 53.
43. *Gohoho* v. *Lintas Export Advertising Services, The Times* 21 January 1964 cited in Anthony Arlidge and David Eady, *The Law of Contempt* (1982), p. 180.

44. *R* v. *Logan* (1974) *Crim. LR.* 609.
45. 62 LJ 131 (1926).
46. *Royle* v. *Gray* 1973 SLT 31.
47. *Ex parte Tuckerman* (1970) 3 NSWR 23.
48. *Guardian* 4 July 1981.
49. A. P. Herbert, *Uncommon Law* (1977 edn.), p. 109. In 1986, at Croydon Crown Court, a juror apologized to a woman judge who had warned him about contempt after he had sent a note about her to defence counsel. The note said, 'How would you like that as a mother-in-law?': *Sun* 8 November 1986.
50. *Ex parte Fernandez* 30 LJCP 321, 322 (1861).
51. Abel-Smith and Stevens, above, n. 8 at pp. 125–6. See also ch. 4 at p. 87 for comments on Mr Justice Stephen in the 1890s.
52. C. P. Harvey, *The Advocate's Devil* (1958), p. 162.
53. Fenton Bresler, above, n. 10 at pp. 77–8 citing the recollection of Pritchard J.
54. Ibid., p. 327.
55. *The Times* 8 June 1971.
56. Ibid., 10 June 1971.
57. Dame Elizabeth Lane, *Hear the Other Side* (1985), p. 161.
58. Patrick Devlin, *Easing the Passing* (1985), pp. 39, 92, 122.
59. *Sunday Telegraph* 3 Nov. 1985.
60. *Times Literary Supplement* 13 Dec. 1985.
61. Interview with Joshua Rozenberg broadcast on BBC Radio 4, 25 November 1985. See also Patrick Devlin, *Easing the Passing* (1986 edn., with postscript), pp. 219–22.
62. Above, n. 57 at p. 156.
63. See ch. 7 on publicity.
64. *The Judiciary* (1972).
65. 121 NLJ 943 (1971) and *The Times* 25 Oct. 1971.
66. Above, n. 64 at p. v.
67. *Holmes–Laski Letters* (ed. Mark DeWolfe Howe, 1953), p. 1398.
68. *Anderton* v. *Ryan* [1985] AC 560.
69. Glanville Williams, 'The Lords and Impossible Attempts, or Quis Custodiet Ipsos Custodies?' 45 *CLJ* 33 (1986).
70. *R* v. *Shivpuri* [1986] 2 WLR 988, 1002.
71. *Guardian* 6 Aug. 1979.
72. Above, n. 29.
73. See ch. 2, n. 17, and ch. 4, p. 93.
74. *The Times* 26 June 1975.

75. Lord Hailsham, *Hamlyn Revisited: The British Legal System Today* (1983), pp. 54–5.
76. *The Times* 25 July 1984. Lord Hailsham made a similar speech in 1987: ibid. 16 Apr. 1987.
77. *Baugh* v. *Delta Water Fittings Ltd.* [1971] 1 WLR 1295, 1300.
78. *Lane* v. *Willis* [1972] 1 WLR 326, 332. Sachs LJ, at p. 333, and Roskill LJ, at pp. 335–6, agreed with this rebuke.
79. Cmnd. 4078 (1969), p. 15.
80. Cmnd. 5794 (1974), para. 162.
81. See ch. 2, pp. 42–3.
82. *Skipworth and Castro's Case* LR 9 QB 230, 237 (1873).
83. For examples of judicial responses to criticism see ch. 7, pp. 177–9.
84. Above, n. 29 at p. 155.
85. *Doyle* v. *Economist Newspaper Ltd.* [1980] NI 171. The case was thereafter settled at the door of the Northern Ireland Court of Appeal.
86. Edward Foss, *Biographia Juridica: A Biographical Dictionary of the Judges of England 1066–1870* (1870), p. 149.
87. *Harrison's Case* 79 ER 1034 (1638).
88. *Hutton* v. *Harrison* 123 ER 1151 (1638).
89. *Aston* v. *Blagrave* 1 Strange's Reports 617 (1725).
90. *Kent* v. *Pocock* 2 Strange's Reports 1168 (1742).
91. Ecclesiasticus 8: 14.
92. Above, n. 29 at p. 155.
93. *Bridges* v. *California* 314 US 252, 270–1 (1941).
94. *Craig* v. *Harney* 331 US 367, 376 (1947) (Douglas J for the US Supreme Court).
95. Above, n. 93 at p. 263.
96. *Wood* v. *Georgia* 370 US 375, 389 (1962) (Chief Justice Warren for the US Supreme Court).
97. *Balogh* v. *St Albans Crown Court* [1975] QB 73, 82. The young man was released by order of the Court of Appeal: his conduct was not a contempt as he had not disrupted court proceedings, his plan having been foiled by the police.
98. *R* v. *Wilkes* 98 ER 327, 347 (1770).
99. *Attorney-General* v. *BBC* [1981] AC 303, 315–16. Eveleigh LJ agreed at p. 317.
100. Ibid., p. 343. See similarly his evidence to the Phillimore Committee on Contempt of Court, above, n. 80 at p. 98. See also *Attorney-General* v. *Times Newspapers Limited* [1974] AC 273, 301 (Lord

Reid). See similarly *Toledo Newspaper Company* v. *US* 247 US 402, 424 (1918) (Holmes J, dissenting): 'a judge of the United States is expected to be a man of ordinary firmness of character.'

101. *Attorney-General* v. *BBC*, above, n. 99 at p. 335.

102. See ch. 4, pp. 89–90.

103. 'In theoretical terms criticism of the judiciary should almost certainly be treated as a form of political speech, and therefore enjoy the highest degree of legal protection': Eric Barendt, *Freedom of Speech* (1985), p. 222.

104. *Tejendrasingh* v. *James Clarke & Co. Ltd.*, Court of Appeal Judgment of 20 Nov. 1985.

105. *Re Hawkins' Habeas Corpus Application* 53 WWR 406 (1965).

106. *US ex rel. Robson* v. *Malone* 412 F 2d 848 (1969). See also *In the Matter of Frederick J. Chase* 468 F 2d 128 (1972) where the US Court of Appeals held that the refusal of a defendant in a criminal trial to stand up when the judge entered the courtroom could amount to a contempt of court.

107. *Presidential Statement: Opening of Court* [1972] ICR 1, 6.

108. *Hipperson* v. *Newbury District Electoral Registration Officer* [1985] QB 1060, 1065.

109. E. S. Turner, *May It Please Your Lordship* (1971), p. 197.

110. R. E. Megarry, *Miscellany-at-Law* (1955), p. 8.

111. 10 QBD 1, 3 (1882).

112. Abel-Smith and Stevens, above, n. 8 at pp. 80–1.

113. Charles Dickens, *Bleak House* (1853), ch. 2.

114. R. M. Jackson, *The Machinery of Justice in England* (7th edn., 1977), p. 475. At the 1953 dinner for the judges, the Lord Mayor, Sir Rupert de la Bère, said that 'he believed that Her Majesty's judges had a greater understanding of human nature than any other body of men in the world': 216 *LT* 374 (1953) cited in Michael Kirby, *The Judges* (Boyer Lectures for the Australian Broadcasting Corporation, 1983).

115. On Hewart's misconduct in court see ch. 4, p. 84.

116. Patrick Devlin, *The Judge* (1979), p. 25.

117. *Hamlet*, III. i. 70–2.

118. Above, n. 113, ch. 1.

119. *In Re Dyce Sombre, a Lunatic* 41 ER 1207, 1209 (1849) (Lord Chancellor Cottenham). Despite the risks of contempt of court, at times judges 'suffer from being pestered by telephone and otherwise by persons who bear some grievance': *R* v. *Felixstowe*

Justices ex parte Leigh [1987] 2 WLR 380, 392 (Divisional Court).

120. *Martin's Case* 39 ER 551 (1747).
121. Henry Cecil, *The English Judge* (1970), p. 90.
122. *Anon* 2 Dyer's Reports 188b (1631). See also *Borrie and Lowe's Law of Contempt* (2nd edn., 1983), p. 12.
123. *Oswald's Law of Contempt*, above, n. 42 at p. 42.
124. John C. Fox, 'The Practice in Contempt of Court Cases' 38 *LQR* 185 (1922). He gave his own account of what happened: after the egg was thrown, 'the judge turned round and said, "What was that?". Mr Glasse QC replied, "An egg". The Vice-Chancellor: "Where did it come from?" Mr Glasse: "A hen, I presume".'
125. *R v. Astor and Others ex parte Isaacs* 30 TLR 10, 11 (1913) (Scrutton J).
126. Above, n. 97 at p. 84 and Eric Grimshaw and Glyn Jones, above, n. 10 at p. 34.
127. Borrie and Lowe, above, n. 122 at p. 51.
128. Brian McKenna, 'The Judge and the Common Man' 32 *MLR* 601, 603 (1969).
129. *Attorney-General v. Times Newspapers Ltd.*, above n. 100 at p. 321 (Lord Simon).
130. *Oswald's Law of Contempt*, above, n. 42 at p. 42.
131. *R v. Crowley, The Times* 2 March 1973 cited in Arlidge and Eady, above, n. 43 at pp. 179–80.
132. *The Times* 17 July 1982.
133. 73 *ABAJ* 31 (February 1987).
134. Treason Act 1351. See ch. 1, p. 6, on threats to kill judges.

6. Mysticism

1. *Ex parte Daisy Hopkins* 61 LJQB 240 (1891).
2. Ibid., p. 250 n.
3. *2 Henry VI*, IV. ii. 86–7.
4. *The Three Clerks* (1858), ch. 41.
5. *My Past and Thoughts: The Memoirs of Alexander Herzen* (1861–6) (transl. Constance Garnett, 1968 ed.), vol. 3, pp. 1095–6. See, similarly, the description by Kenneth Tynan of the obscenity trial of *Lady Chatterley's Lover* in 1960, with the judge, Mr Justice Byrne, 'resembling beneath the scarlet weight of his robes some relict of

feudal Japan': *The Law as Literature* (selected by Louis Blom-Cooper, 1961), p. 141.

6. *The Old Curiosity Shop* (1841), ch. 63.
7. *Courts on Trial* (1949) (1953 edn.), ch. 18.
8. Above, n. 6 at ch. 16.
9. Charles Dickens, *Bleak House* (1853), ch. 19.
10. *St Edmundsbury and Ipswich Diocesan Board of Finance* v. *Clark* [1973] 2 WLR 1042, 1048 (Mr Justice Megarry).
11. *Alice's Adventures in Wonderland* (1865), ch. 11.
12. 'The Judge and the Common Man' 32 *MLR* 601, 602 (1969).
13. [1972] ICR 1, 6.
14. Above, n. 10 at p. 1048. On Sir Lancelot Shadwell's exercise of judicial functions while bathing in the Thames see Edward Foss, *Biographia Juridica: A Biographical Dictionary of the Judges of England 1066–1870* (1870), p. 609.
15. Foss, above, n. 14 at p. 188.
16. 'Clippings from the Nineties' 234 *LT* 476, 477 (1963).
17. F. D. MacKinnon, *On Circuit* (1940), p. 237.
18. John Mortimer, *Rumpole of the Bailey* (1978), p. 196.
19. *Mallalieu* v. *Drummond* [1983] 2 AC 861, 869.
20. *Gulliver's Travels: A Voyage to the Houyhnhnms* (1726), ch. 5.
21. *The Works of Jeremy Bentham* (ed. John Bowring, 1843), vol. 7, p. 282.
22. Ibid., vol. 7, pp. 280–2. See also H. L. A. Hart, 'The Demystification of the Law' in *Essays on Bentham: Jurisprudence and Political Theory* (1982), pp. 29–30.
23. William Shakespeare, *The Merchant of Venice*, III. ii. 75–7.
24. Thomas More, *Utopia* (1516) (transl. Paul Turner, Penguin Classics 1965), p. 106.
25. Quoted in David Mellinkoff, *The Language of the Law* (1963), p. 37.
26. *Re Trepca Mines Ltd.* [1959] 3 All ER 798.
27. *Morris* v. *Crown Office* [1970] 2 QB 114, 128.
28. *Cowan* v. *Scargill* [1984] ICR 646, 648.
29. *Sydall* v. *Castings Ltd.* [1967] 1 QB 302, 313–14.
30. *London Engineering and Iron Shipbuilding Company (Ltd)* v. *Cowan* 16 LT Reports 573 (1867). See also 24 LJ 28 (1889): a solicitor at the Quarter Sessions told the Recorder that 'he was instructed to defend a prisoner, his instructions being expressly not to instruct counsel'. He was refused a right of audience.

31. *Doxford and Sons (Ltd)* v. *The Sea Shipping Company (Ltd)* 14 TLR 111 (1897).
32. *Practice Direction (Solicitors: Rights of Audience)* [1986] 1 WLR 545. This posed yet further difficult questions for the legal system. See 83 *The Law Society's Gazette* 1607 (1986): 'The Law Society has agreed with the Lord Chief Justice that solicitors exercising rights of audience in the Supreme Court should sit in junior counsel's row.'
33. *Abse* v. *Smith* [1986] QB 536 (Court of Appeal).
34. *In the Matter of the Serjeants at Law* 6 Bing (NC) 187, 239 (1840). Fusion of the professions remains a problem at lunchtimes. Solicitors have complained about the lack of refreshment facilities for them when attending House of Lords cases. 'The Yeoman Usher of the Black Rod has now agreed that solicitors will be accommodated for lunch in the small entrance hall of counsel's dining room': *The Law Society's Gazette*, p. 231 (28 Jan. 1987).
35. Luke 11: 52.
36. *A Night at the Opera.*
37. Franz Kafka, *The Trial* (1925) (Penguin Modern Classics, 1974), pp. 195–6.
38. *O'Brien* v. *Sim-Chem Ltd.* [1980] 1 WLR 734, 737.
39. Above, n. 20.
40. Ibid., *A Voyage to Brobdingnag*, ch. 7.
41. Above, n. 21, vol. 10, p. 429.
42. *US* v. *Palmer* 3 Wheaton's Reports 610, 636 (1818), cited by Jerome Frank, above, n. 7 at ch. 21.
43. A. P. Herbert, *More Uncommon Law* (1982 ed.), p. 279.
44. John Lord Campbell, *Lives of the Lord Chancellors* (5th ed., 1868), vol. 5, p. 223.
45. *The Times* 25 Nov. 1980.
46. A. P. Herbert, *Uncommon Law* (1977 ed.), p. 9.
47. *Tolley* v. *J. S. Fry and Sons Ltd.* [1930] 1 KB 467, 473. The case later went to the House of Lords: [1931] AC 333.
48. *Shaw* v. *Shaw* 2 Sw & Tr 517, 519 (1861).
49. *Moriarty* v. *Regent's Garage and Engineering Company Ltd.* [1921] 1 KB 423, 450. See also *Worringham* v. *Lloyds Bank Ltd.* [1979] IRLR 440, 442 where Lord Denning described an earlier opinion of an Advocate-General in the European Court of Justice as 'not very easy for English readers to follow'.
50. *R* v. *Cox* [1968] 1 WLR 88, 91, 93.

51. Henry J. Abraham, *The Judicial Process* (5th ed., 1986), pp. 130–1.
52. *Practice Direction (Judges: Mode of Address)* [1977] 1 WLR 1435.
53. *Bondina Ltd.* v. *Rollaway Shower Blinds Ltd.* [1986] 1 WLR 517, 521 (Sir George Waller agreeing with Lord Justice Dillon's judgment).
54. Bob Woodward and Scott Armstrong, *The Brethren* (1979).
55. Above, n. 43 at p. 253.
56. *Parkin* v. *ASTMS* [1980] ICR 662, 669.
57. Above, n. 20.
58. 'Some Aspects of the Work of the Court of Appeal' 1 *Journal of the Society of Public Teachers of Law* 350, 359 (1950).
59. *Broome* v. *Cassell & Co.* [1972] AC 1027, 1054.
60. *Gilham* v. *Kent County Council (No. 2)* [1985] ICR 233, 240.
61. *Neale* v. *Hereford and Worcester County Council* [1986] ICR 471, 483.
62. *Secretary of State for Employment* v. *ASLEF (No. 2)* [1972] ICR 19, 72. See also ch. 1, pp. 18–23, on forceful judicial language.
63. *Ex parte Pater* 5 B & S 299 (1864).
64. *Parashuram Detaram Shamdasani* v. *King-Emperor* [1945] AC 264, 269 (Lord Goddard for the Judicial Committee of the Privy Council). See also ch. 5, p. 107, on a barrister's rudeness to the judge.
65. Above, n. 21, vol. 5, p. 235.
66. *Paterson* v. *Paterson* (1938) SC 251, 259 cited in R. E. Megarry, *A Second Miscellany-at-Law* (1973), p. 161.
67. *Evans* v. *Ewels* [1972] 1 WLR 671, 674.
68. *L* v. *K* [1985] 3 WLR 202, 206.
69. *Corbett* v. *Corbett* [1971] P 83, 90.
70. *R* v. *Barnsley LBC ex parte Hook* [1976] 3 All ER 452, 454–5.
71. *R* v. *Sidley* 83 ER 1146 (1663). The story is told in *The Diary of Samuel Pepys* (ed. Robert Latham and William Matthews, 1971), vol. 4, pp. 209–10.
72. *DPP* v. *Majewski* [1977] AC 443, 498.
73. *LCC* v. *Attorney General* [1901] AC 26, 35.
74. *W. T. Ramsay Ltd.* v. *IRC* [1979] 1 WLR 974, 979 (Lord Justice Templeman).
75. *IRC* v. *Garvin* [1981] 1 WLR 793.
76. Megarry, above, n. 66 at p. 326.
77. Above, n. 46 at p. 4.
78. *The Times* 27 June 1985.
79. *O'Brien* v. *Sim-Chem Ltd.* [1980] 1 WLR 1011, 1017.
80. James Cameron, *Cameron in The Guardian 1974–84* (1985), p. 188.

81. *Salter* v. *Lask* [1925] 1 KB 584, 588.
82. Judith S. Neaman and Carole G. Silver, *A Dictionary of Euphemisms* (1983), p. 34.
83. See, for example, above, n. 44, vol. 10, p. 290 n.
84. J. E. S. Simon, 'English Idioms from the Law' 76 *LQR* 283, 304 (1960).
85. Above, n. 21, vol. 7, p. 281.
86. 125 *SJ* 232 (1981), cited in Francis Bennion, *Statute Law* (1983), p. 124.
87. *City of London* v. *Wood* 12 Modern Reports 669, 687–8 (1701).
88. *Slater* v. *Evans* [1916] 2 KB 403, cited in Glanville Williams, 'Language and the Law II' 61 *LQR* 179, 189 (1945).
89. Peter David Blanck, Robert Rosenthal, and LaDoris Hazzard Cordell, 'The Appearance of Justice: Judges' Verbal and Nonverbal Behaviour in Criminal Jury Trials' 38 *Stanford Law Review* 89 (1985).
90. Above, n. 21, vol. 7, p. 282.

7. Publicity

1. See *Scott* v. *Scott* [1913] AC 417 and *R* v. *Chief Registrar of Friendly Societies ex parte New Cross Building Society* [1984] QB 227, 235. It remains an indefensible anomaly that interlocutory (that is, preliminary) applications in the Queen's Bench Division (though not in the Chancery Division) of the High Court, for example when a party seeks an injunction, are heard in private. Such privacy is especially indefensible since it is usually not a contempt of court to publish information relating to the private hearing (provided one can discover what occurred): section 12 Administration of Justice Act 1960.
2. *R* v. *Felixstowe Justices ex parte Leigh* [1987] 2 WLR 380.
3. *Home Office* v. *Harman* [1983] 1 AC 280, 303 (Lord Diplock). Lord Scarman added in his dissenting judgment (joined by Lord Simon), at p. 316, that 'there is also another important public interest involved in justice done openly, namely that the evidence and argument should be publicly known, so that society may judge for itself the quality of justice administered in its name, and whether the law requires modification'. On the public interest in open

justice, see also *Scott* v. *Scott*, above, n.1 at p. 477 (Lord Shaw citing Jeremy Bentham): 'Publicity is the very soul of justice. It is the keenest spur to exertion and the surest of all guards against improbity. It keeps the judge himself while trying under trial.' And see *Attorney-General* v. *Leveller Magazine Limited* [1979] AC 440, 450 where Lord Diplock said that 'if the way that courts behave cannot be hidden from the public ear and eye, this provides a safeguard against judicial arbitrariness or idiosyncrasy and maintains the public confidence in the administration of justice'.

4. *The Times* 7 Aug. 1972. Lord Widgery was quoting an aphorism of Lord Justice MacKinnon in *On Circuit* (1940), p. 27: 'He is the best judge whose name is known to the fewest readers of *The Daily Mail*.'

5. Dame Elizabeth Lane, *Hear the Other Side* (1985), p. 146.

6. Shimon Shetreet, *Judges on Trial* (1976), p. 372.

7. Ibid., pp. 363–7. Shetreet suggests, at pp. 364–5, that 'a judge will be expected to refrain from participation' in sports which are 'objectionable to a significant segment of the public on moral or other grounds. . . . Under this general rule a judge may be chairman of tennis, cricket or rugby associations but is excluded from professional football (soccer), horse races, dog races, hare courses and the like. . . . A Law Lord who took it upon himself to help draft rules for animal races was asked by the Lord Chancellor to discontinue these activities.'

8. Ibid., p. 337.

9. Bob Woodward and Scott Armstrong, *The Brethren* (1979), p. 127 n, and William O. Douglas, *The Court Years 1939–75* (1980), p. 368.

10. Robert Stevens, *Law and Politics: The House of Lords as a Judicial Body 1800–1976* (1979), p. 259 n.

11. Also of note are important textbooks written, in part, by judges: see, for example, Lord Goff and Gareth Jones, *The Law of Restitution* (3rd edn., 1986), and Sir Robert Megarry and H. W. R. Wade, *The Law of Real Property* (5th edn., 1984).

12. *Holmes–Laski Letters* (ed. Mark De Wolfe Howe, 1953), p. 928.

13. See ch. 2, p. 39, for the dismissal of Holmes's theory of adjudication by Mr Justice Macnaghten.

14. Oliver Wendell Holmes, 'The Path of the Law' in *Collected Legal Papers* (1920), p. 196.

15. Robert Jackson, *The Chief* (1959), pp. 39, 213, 327–8.

16. Above, n. 5 at pp. 1, 21, 37, 65, 82, 85, 109, 121, 161, 174, 179. On Dame Elizabeth see ch. 3, p. 59.
17. See ch. 5, pp. 123–4, on the response to Lord Devlin's book about the Bodkin Adams trial.
18. *The Times* 24 May 1982.
19. Joseph Yahuda, 'An Interview with the Lord Chancellor' 148 *JP* 739, 757 (1 Dec. 1984).
20. Hugo Young, 'The Voices You Can't Hear Under the Woolsack' *Guardian* 23 Jan. 1986.
21. Letter from Lord Hailsham to the *Guardian* 27 Jan. 1986. Those 'rules' did not prevent Lord McCluskey, a Scottish judge, from delivering the 1986 Reith Lectures, 'Law, Justice and Democracy', on BBC radio.
22. *Guardian* 14 Feb. 1986. See also Judge James Pickles, *Straight from the Bench* (1987).
23. *Star* 6 May 1986.
24. *Listener* 8 May 1986.
25. See, for example, Sir Leslie Scarman, *English Law—The New Dimension* (1974).
26. See ch. 2, pp. 43–6.
27. For a full survey of the use of the judiciary to chair or conduct commissions and inquiries see J. A. G. Griffith, *The Politics of the Judiciary* (3rd edn., 1985), pp. 34–45.
28. See Louis Blom-Cooper and Gavin Drewry, *Final Appeal: A Study of the House of Lords in its Judicial Capacity* (1972), ch. 10.
29. *The Times* 19 May 1983.
30. Above, n. 19 at pp. 756–7.
31. *R v. Commissioner of Police of the Metropolis ex parte Blackburn (No. 2)* [1968] 2 QB 150, 155. See ch. 5 on criticism of the judiciary.
32. *Churchman v. Joint Shop Stewards' Committee* [1972] 1 WLR 1094, 1101.
33. 123 *NLJ* 1111 (1973).
34. *The Times* 7 June 1986. In March 1987 Judge Lymbery gave an interview to the Press Association to explain his decision to release on bail a man accused of murder who, while on bail, murdered a policeman.
35. *R v. London Transport Executive ex parte GLC* [1983] QB 484, 492.
36. See ch. 1, p. 21.
37. See Alan Paterson, *The Law Lords* (1982), pp. 218–19.
38. Above, n. 6 at p. 320.

39. Above, n. 28 at p. 154.
40. Lord Denning, *Landmarks in the Law* (1984), p. v.
41. Lord Denning, *The Closing Chapter* (1983), pp. 18–19.
42. See Sir Alfred Denning, *The Road to Justice* (1955), p. 64, for a statement of his belief in open justice.
43. Ronald Dworkin, *Law's Empire* (1986), p. 11.
44. *56 Australian Law Journal* 4 (1982).
45. In some cases of exceptional public importance and interest, the courts have taken steps to make their judgments more easily comprehensible to the layman. See, for example, the summary of his judgment given by Lord Wilberforce in *Heatons Transport (St Helens) Ltd* v. *TGWU* [1973] AC 15, 112–13 and see *R* v. *Boundary Commission for England ex parte Foot* [1983] QB 600, 615 where Sir John Donaldson MR noted that 'since a very large number of people are interested in this appeal and since it is most unlikely that our decision, whether for or against the applicants, will meet with universal approval, it is important that it should at least be understood'.
46. 'Tic Tac Dough' *ABC Television* (15 Aug. 1980).
47. *Gulliver's Travels: A Voyage to the Houyhnhnms* (1726), ch. 5.
48. But see ch. 2, pp. 37–8 on judicial limitations on many non-legal topics.
49. Gerald Gardiner, 'The Machinery of Law Reform in England' 69 *LQR* 46, 55 (1953).
50. Sir William Holdsworth, *A History of English Law* (7th edn., 1956), vol. 1, pp. 272–3.
51. John Lord Campbell, *Lives of the Lord Chancellors* (5th edn., 1868), vol. 5, pp. 303–4.
52. F. D. M.[acKinnon], 62 *LQR* 35 (1946). See generally E. C. S. Wade, 'Consultation of the Judiciary by the Executive' 46 *LQR* 169 (1930).
53. Section 75 Supreme Court of Judicature Act 1873 and section 210 Supreme Court of Judicature (Consolidation) Act 1925.
54. Schedule 7 of the Supreme Court Act 1981.
55. See, for example, 66 *Sol. J.* 278, 279–80 (1922).
56. Patrick Devlin, *The Judge* (1979), p. 53.
57. Above, n. 15 at p. 301.
58. Brian Abel-Smith and Robert Stevens, *Lawyers and the Courts: A Sociological Study of the English Legal System 1750–1965* (1967), p. 294.

59. *Daniel M'Naghten's Case* 10 Cl & F 200, 204 (1843).
60. Ibid., p. 212. See similarly Lord Lyndhurst, ibid., p. 214.
61. Practice Note: Judges' Rules [1964] 1 WLR 152.
62. See ch. 6, p. 150.
63. 446 HL 727–8 (21 Dec. 1983).
64. Louis L. Jaffe, 'Professors and Judges as Advisors to Government' 83 *HLR* 366, 373 (1969).
65. *R v. Commissioner for the Special Purposes of the Income Tax Acts ex parte Stipplechoice Ltd* [1985] 2 All ER 465, 467.
66. *R v. Beverley County Court ex parte Brown, The Times* 25 Jan. 1985.
67. 459 HL 944–5 (5 Feb. 1985: Committee Stage of the Administration of Justice Bill).
68. *2 Henry IV*, v. ii. 119–21.
69. C. H. S. Fifoot, *Lord Mansfield* (1936), p. 40.
70. Above, n. 51, vol. 9, pp. 2–4.
71. Above, n. 28 at p. 168.
72. See, for example, Bruce Allen Murphy, *The Brandeis/Frankfurter Connection* (1982).
73. *Sheddon v. Goodrich* 8 Ves 481, 497 (1803), cited in R. E. Megarry, *A Second Miscellany-at-Law* (1973), p. 135.
74. Harold Laski, 'Justice and the Law' in *Studies in Law and Politics* (1932), p. 292.
75. Sir John Donaldson, *Court of Appeal: Civil Division—Review of the Legal Year 1985–86* (8 Oct. 1986), pp. 2–3.
76. Boswell, *Life of Johnson* (1791) (ed. R. W. Chapman, Oxford University Press, 1970), p. 612 (6 Apr. 1775).
77. Ibid., p. 613 (6 Apr. 1775).
78. C. K. Allen, 'Administrative Consultation of the Judiciary' 47 *LQR* 43, 48 (1931).
79. Above, n. 51, vol. 1, p. 143 n.
80. Robert Louis Stevenson, *Weir of Hermiston* (1896), ch. 2.
81. J. B. Atlay, *The Victorian Chancellors* (1906), vol. 1, p. 37. On Copley later becoming a lazy judge see ch. 1, p. 16. See ch. 1, pp. 6–7, on the burdens imposed on the judge.
82. R. E. Megarry, *Lawyer and Litigant in England* (1962), p. 163, recommended sabbaticals for the judiciary.
83. Cited in Campbell, above, n. 51, vol. 3, p. 135.
84. 'Clippings from the Nineties' 234 *LT* 507 (1963).
85. *Guardian* 4 July 1986 and *Daily Telegraph* 15 July 1986.
86. A Practice Direction has been issued on the exercise of this

discretion to allow the tape-recording of proceedings: [1981] 3 All
ER 848.

87. The *Report of the Committee on Contempt of Court* (Cmnd. 5794–:
1974), at para. 43(*b*), was more liberal in this respect. It recommended that recordings 'should not themselves be broadcast or
otherwise made public without the leave of the appropriate court,
and then only for specified purposes [such as] educational purposes
(e.g. at a police college) or the broadcasting of a historical account
long after the trial'.

88. See *J. Barber & Sons* v. *Lloyd's Underwriters* [1986] 3 WLR 515, 517
(Evans J): 'video recording of evidence given in English courts is
not permitted'.

89. 449 US 560 (1981).

90. Cited in Robert Stevens, above, n. 10 at p. 24 n.

91. See ch. 5, p. 132.

92. *Judicature* (Apr. 1980), p. 425.

93. In *J. Barber & Sons*, above, n. 88, Evans J held that evidence for
the purposes of Californian proceedings to be given before an
examiner in England under the Evidence (Proceedings in Other
Jurisdictions) Act 1975 could be videotaped. He noted, at p. 517,
that he had 'heard strongly worded claims by the defendants that
the presence of a camera would oppress them and cause additional
stress. . . . Of course it is a stressful matter to give evidence. . . . In
the case of these four defendants I cannot accept that there will be
additional stress, certainly not enough to outweigh the value and
convenience of videotaping the proceedings.'

94. 381 US 532, 571–4 (1965).

95. Ibid., pp. 595–6.

96. Above, n. 89 at pp. 573–4.

97. In *Re Petition of Post-Newsweek Stations, Florida Inc.* 370 So. 2d 764,
776, 780 (1979).

98. Lord Cockburn, *Memorials of his Time* (ed. W. Forbes Gray, 1945),
pp. 102–3. A retired High Court judge has argued in favour of
allowing cameras into the courts: Sir Peter Bristow *Judge for
Yourself* (1986), p. 60.

8. Conclusion

1. Jeremy Bentham, 'Draft for the Organisation of Judicial Establishments' in *The Works of Jeremy Bentham* (ed. Bowring, 1843), vol. 4, p. 359.
2. Ecclesiasticus 7: 6.
3. Felix Frankfurter, 'The Judicial Process and the Supreme Court' in *Of Law and Men* (ed. Philip Elman, 1956), p. 39.
4. *John v. Rees* [1970] Ch. 345, 402.
5. Bernard Schwartz, *Super Chief: Earl Warren and his Supreme Court* (1983), p. 628.
6. Exodus 18: 26.
7. *American Hospital Supply Corporation v. Hospital Products Limited* 780 F 2d 589, 593, 609 (1986).
8. 'It would be a misuse of language to describe Diogenes as having occupied accommodation within the meaning of the [Housing (Homeless Persons)] Act [1977]': *R v. Hillingdon LBC ex parte Puhlhofer* [1986] A.C. 484, 517 (Lord Brightman).
9. 'The purchaser of a BL car sells his soul to the company store': *British Leyland Motor Corporation Limited v. Armstrong Patents Co. Limited* [1986] A.C. 577, 629 (Lord Templeman).
10. Benjamin Cardozo, *The Nature of the Judicial Process* (1921), p. 21.
11. *Scripps–Howard Radio Inc. v. Federal Communications Commission* 316 US 4, 9 (1942) (Frankfurter J).
12. *Annamunthodo v. Oilfields Workers' Trade Union* [1961] AC 945, 955.
13. *Aries Tanker Corporation v. Total Transport Limited* [1977] 1 WLR 185, 190 (Lord Wilberforce).
14. See, for example, *Garden Cottage Foods Limited v. Milk Marketing Board* [1984] AC 130, 138 where Lord Diplock for the House of Lords said that the terms of the injunction granted by the Court of Appeal were so unclear 'that counsel for the company has not attempted to defend them'. See ch. 1, p. 2 on errors by Law Lords.
15. 137 *NLJ* 96 (1987).
16. Matthew 5: 25.
17. Cited in Jerome Frank, *Courts on Trial* (1949) (1973 ed.), p. 40.
18. On a similar power consequent on the death or incapacity of a judge see ch. 1, p. 7.
19. *The Works of Jeremy Bentham*, above, n. 1, vol. 2, p. 396.

20. Franz Kafka, *The Trial* (1925) (Penguin Modern Classics, 1974), p. 138.
21. *R* v. *Farrant* 20 QBD 58, 62 (1887) (Stephen J). In *Foster* v. *Hawden* 83 ER 520 (1677) a verdict was set aside as 'the jury not agreeing [had] cast lots for their verdict'. The jury were ordered 'to attend here next term to be fined'. In *Langdell* v. *Sutton* 94 ER 791 (1737) the jury had determined their verdict 'by hustling half-pence in a hat'. They were ordered to 'attend to be publicly admonished, that the country may take warning'.
22. Edward Foss, *Biographia Juridica: A Biographical Dictionary of the Judges of England 1066–1870* (1870), p. 441.
23. C. P. Harvey, *The Advocate's Devil* (1958), p. 34.
24. *Dictionary of National Biography 1931–1940* (ed. L. G. Wickham Legg, 1949), p. 799.
25. Judge Alan King-Hamilton QC, *And Nothing But the Truth* (1982), pp. 225–6.
26. J. B. Atlay, *The Victorian Chancellors* (1908), vol. 2, p. 458.
27. *The Federalist Papers* (1788), No. 78.
28. Francis Bacon, 'Of Judicature' in *Essays* (1625) (Everyman edn., 1973), p. 165.
29. Oliver Wendell Holmes, 'The Path of the Law' in *Collected Legal Papers* (1920), p. 174.
30. Above, n. 17 at pp. 2–3.
31. Jeremy Bentham's term for the judiciary: *Works*, above, n. 1, vol. 5, p. 396.

INDEX

249

Index

Brightman, Lord, 147
broadcasting court hearings, *see* television and radio
Brougham, Lord: law reform, 107, 191; reading newspapers on the Bench, 79
Buller, Mr Justice: appointed at age of 32, 62; on criticizing judges, 110; partiality, 39
Burger, Chief Justice, 5
Byles, Mr Justice: inability to understand counsel wearing light-coloured trousers, 203; solicitors not to be heard, 150

Cabinet, judge as member of, 187
Caesar, Sir Julius: counsel playing jokes, 16; suing for libel, 130
Campbell, Lord: irritability of, 84–5; on unreliable witnesses, 4
cannibalism, judicial views on, 47–9
Cantley, Mr Justice, 32
Cardozo, Mr Justice: anguish in reaching judgment, 8; anti-semitism towards, 24
Carswell, Judge, 56–7
Cave, Lord, 187
Cave, Mr Justice, 78
Cecil, Henry, 102
Charlie, making the judge look a, 2
charm school for judges, 12
Churchill, Sir Winston: on judicial bias, 44; private life of judges, 11
civil war, precipitating a, 3
Claassen, Mr Justice, 117
Clark, Mr Justice, 40
Cockburn, Lord Chief Justice, and Tichborne Claimant, 42–3, 129
Coffin, Judge Frank, 13
Coke, Sir Edward: legal language, 149; never went to the theatre, 38
Coleridge, Lord Chief Justice: legal euphemisms, 141–2; murder under duress, 48–9; sleeping on the Bench, 77
colleagues, judicial: relations with, 18–27
comments by judges, *see* aphorisms
Commercial Court, origins of, 16
complaints against judges, *see* remedy for injudicious behaviour
conference of judges, 182–4
contempt of court: bribery of judges, 137–8; gestures in court, 119–20; language

of lawyers, 106–7; refusing to stand up in court, 133–6; scandalizing the judiciary, 109–18; shouting out in court, 118; taking clothes off in court, 118
Copley, John, *see* Lyndhurst, Lord
corporal punishment, 44
Cottenham, Lord Chancellor: bias, 40; contempt judgment, 107
Council of judges, 183
Cowper, Lord Chancellor, 65
Cranworth, Lord, 37
criticism of judges, 6, 105–39, 205
Crompton, Mr Justice, 98
Cumming-Bruce, Lord Justice, 151

dangers of judicial office, 6, 138–9
Darling, Mr Justice: criticism of, 111–13; judicial humour of, 81–3
Davey, Lord, 178
Davies, Lord Justice: defendants speaking Welsh, 149; judge expressing doubts about earlier decision, 128
Dedlock, Sir Leicester, 136–7
delay in deciding cases, 14, 86–7
Denning, Lord: books by, 172–3; criticism of judges, 115, 132; immunity against suit, 95, 98; impartiality, 41, 43; judges cannot respond to criticism, 177–8; judicial ambition, 8; public knowledge of, 179; response to criticism, 178; retirement, 61; usurpation of legislative role, 23
Devlin, Lord: admiration of judges, 137; appointment, 60; book on Bodkin Adams, 123–4; Dilhorne, Viscount, views on, 123–4; retirement, 5; training, 69, 71–2
Dilhorne, Viscount: Bodkin Adams trial, 123–4; response to criticism of Lord Goddard, 122; letter to *The Times*, 178–9
Diplock, Lord: criticism of, 109; legal language, 149; Northern Ireland inquiry, 177
disciplining judges, 88–104
divine inspiration, 8
divorced judges, 57
Doderidge, Mr Justice, 77

250

Index

Index

Index

cial need for leisure, 189; sat as seldom as possible, 16

McCardie, Mr Justice: aphorisms of, 36; dispute with Lord Justice Scrutton, 21–3; suicide of, 12; unable to understand the decision of another judge, 155
Macclesfield, Lord, 89
McKenna, Mr Justice: handbag flung at, 138; wigs and gowns, 145
McKinnon, Judge, 35
MacKinnon, Lord Justice, 166–7
Macnaghten, Mr Justice, 39
McReynolds, Mr Justice, 24
McWhirter, Norris, 30
Malins, Vice-Chancellor, 138
Manningham-Buller, Reginald, see Dilhorne, Viscount
Mansfield, Lord: asking counsel's view of judgment, 105–6; criticism of, 109; failure to consult other judges, 24; ignoring criticism, 132; impartiality of, 39–40; member of Cabinet, 187; on judicial qualities, 8
mathematical formula for deciding cases, 200–1
Maugham, Lord, 21, 178
Maule, Mr Justice, 183–4
May, Lord Justice, 160
Maynard, Sir John, 203
meetings of judges, 182–4, 187
Megarry, Mr Justice: unpredictability of litigation, 199; wigs, judges deciding cases without wearing, 145–6
mistakes, judicial, 2, 125–6
M'Naghten Rules, 183–4
Moses: qualities of the good judge, advice received, 8–9; deciding hard cases, 200
murder of judge, 6, 139

National Industrial Relations Court, 145
newspaper articles by judge, 171
Nixon, President Richard, appointment of judges, 56–7
Norbury, Lord, 87
North, Mr Justice, 85
number of judges, 31

oath, judicial, 5

obituaries of judges, 121
obscenity, judicial views on, 34
Ombudsman, 95–6, 101
Ormrod, Lord Justice, 34
Orwell, George, 15

Pakistan, 153
Parke, Baron, 15
Parker, Lord, 122
Parliamentary criticism, 108–9
Parry, Sir Edward, 139
pay, judicial, 12–14
Pengelly, Baron, 89
performance, judicial, 75–88
Phillimore Report on contempt, 128–9
photographing judges, 190
Pickles, Judge James, 175
Plato: on age of judges, 62; on judicial qualities, 53; on sleeping judges, 77
pleasures of judicial office, 9–10
politicians criticizing judges, 108–9, 126–7
pomp and ceremony, 9
Posner, Judge, 200–1
predicting judicial attitude, 27
press releases by courts, 180
priesthood, judicial office like, 8, 10, 14
private life of judges, 11, 57–8, 101–3
publicity: candidates for appointment, 66; judicial activities, 12, 169–98; judicial decisions, 11–12. See also television and radio
Purchas, Lord Justice: concern about proposal to limit appeal in judicial review, 185–6; strain of two-judge court, 7

qualifications, judicial, 8–9, 49–51
qualities, judicial, 199

Radcliffe, Lord, 60
rape, judicial comments on, 33–4, 100–1
rebuke to judge by Lord Chancellor, 93
refusal of judicial office, 9
relative, judge as barrister's, 40
remedy for injudicious behaviour, 88–103
resignation, 7–8, 90
retirement, 53
revolution, judge accelerating a, 3
revulsion at judicial duties, 9
Rich, Mr Justice, 116

Index